IN WHOSE RUINS

POWER, POSSESSION, AND THE LANDSCAPES OF AMERICAN EMPIRE

Alicia Puglionesi

SCRIBNER

New York   London   Toronto   Sydney   New Delhi

Scribner
An Imprint of Simon & Schuster, Inc.
1230 Avenue of the Americas
New York, NY 10020

First Scribner hardcover edition April 2022

SCRIBNER and design are registered trademarks of The Gale Group, Inc.,
used under license by Simon & Schuster, Inc., the publisher of this work.

For information about special discounts for bulk purchases,
please contact Simon & Schuster Special Sales at 1-866-506-1949
or business@simonandschuster.com.

The Simon & Schuster Speakers Bureau can bring authors to your live event.
For more information or to book an event, contact the Simon & Schuster Speakers
Bureau at 1-866-248-3049 or visit our website at www.simonspeakers.com.

Manufactured in the United States of America

1   3   5   7   9   10   8   6   4   2

Library of Congress Cataloging-in-Publication Data is available.

ISBN 978-1-9821-1675-0
ISBN 978-1-9821-1677-4 (ebook)

"... then the wide-spread ruins of our cloud-capp'd towers, of our solemn temples, and of our magnificent cities, will, like the works of which we have treated, become the subject of curious research and elaborate investigation."

DeWitt Clinton, "The Iroquois: Address Delivered before the New York Historical Society, Dec. 6, 1811"

CONTENTS

CONTENTS

PART 4:
TRACE ELEMENTS

MUTATIONS
OF THE COUNTRY

Where does power come from and where does it go? The United States has long been haunted by premonitions of decline, by memento mori of fallen empires real and imagined. Thinking that ancient Indigenous earthworks were the ruins of a lost white civilization akin to the America of his day, the poet William Cullen Bryant mused on that "disciplined and populous" race: "The gopher mines the ground / Where stood their swarming cities. All is gone; / All—save the piles of earth that hold their bones." Bryant's buoyant 1832 ode to US expansionism was tempered by these backward glances, notes of unease connected with the "restless murmurs" that many people sensed arising from the land itself. Was there a limit to empire? Was the promise of America as a "second creation"—a world born anew into the ingenious hands of its European discoverers—hiding something more sinister?

Much inspirational literature prepared young people to mine this second creation for profit, tracing an arc of history in which all of nature had ripened to fall into their grasp. "Millions of years before the earth was prepared for the habitation of man," wrote the author of *How to Achieve Success*, "nature's great laboratory was at work, for the accomplishment of a PURPOSE . . . to meet the demands of civilization." Intending that civilization to run on steam, oil, and electrical power, God formed "store-houses of inexhaustible wealth, only waiting for the necessities of man to unlock their doors and bear away the treasure." It's no coincidence that Charles H. Kent, the author of these stirring lines, was a land agent by profession. The first step to success was acquiring land, enclosing nature's storehouses under private title. The rest, according to Kent, was as simple as turning a key in a lock.

From these rhetorical heights of entitlement, there was still the ever-present possibility of a fall. "Yes, the world is advancing," thundered Kent; "we must keep pace with the advance, or be crushed beneath its ponderous wheels." While Bryant looked backward at the vanished mound-building civilization with confidence that the United States would inherit and exceed its accomplishments, Kent looked forward and saw that there would be no resting place. The only way to elude failure was to outrun it—thus the need for *How to Achieve Success* and countless similar titles cascading from the nineteenth century's lightning-fast steam-powered presses. In a somewhat circular manner, the sources of power opened up by American enterprise fueled perpetual anxiety about their exhaustion.

A century later, we might recognize Kent's sanctified quest for "inexhaustible wealth" and its shadow, the fear of losing power, at the core of many present-day political convulsions. White supremacy, neofascism, and climate change denial each in related ways assert that unlimited strength and resources are a birthright that loyal Americans must defend against creeping threats. Lodged deep under the callus of American exceptionalism are the complex, brutal mechanics of the "second creation," the human choices that, without the self-propelling cover of divine sanction, would appear to merit restitution. Rather than engaging with the problem of justice inherent in honest accountings of American history, the imperative to "keep pace with the advance" conjures a darkly fantasized future where the ruins of US civilization whisper in "restless murmurs" to some alien poet. There can be no question of how current Americans, caught between denial and fatalism, might decide to use power differently.

Perhaps this seems like a trite psychological diagnosis when the stakes are immediate and deathly real. But the anxiety of origins is a motive force, a gnawing worm whose trail guides the American imagination. If the nation's power came from someone else and will go to someone else, holding on to it requires not just a physical grip ("from my cold dead hands," cries patriot Charlton Heston) but a narrative grasp of what the nation is and where it came from.

Controlling the past and the story of origins is essential to controlling the future.

There's an alluring poetry about tracing powerful forces to their origins. Rivers were a special focus of nineteenth-century scientific expeditions seeking their remotest sources. Such mappings laid the groundwork for colonization in North and South America, Africa, and Asia, but they also sought a spiritual mastery of the terrain, contemplated the essence of power itself in the humble springs from which great rivers cascaded. British explorers raced to the headwaters of the Nile, so obsessed with finding its source that the victors persisted until ulcers ate through their feet. This part isn't poetic; neither is the fact that scores of African workers died hauling around "great men" such as Livingstone and Stanley. Yet the origin quest was celebrated in Europe as part of man's heroic struggle to wrest secret knowledge from nature and bring the light of Christianity to the places Europeans shaded "dark." Science and faith are not just ornaments for empires—they produce the belief that these empires are necessary and good.

Decades before the famous Livingstone expedition, the American Henry Rowe Schoolcraft set out to find the source of the mighty Mississippi River. It lay somewhere west of Lake Superior, a land that settlers regarded as wilderness. Schoolcraft had failed at various pursuits in his early life and, like so many others, sought redemption on the frontier. Rigid, self-promoting, and sometimes egomaniacal, he saw the work that lay ahead for American empire—taking Indigenous land and disciplining Indigenous people—and threw in his lot with this business.

First in 1820, and again in 1832, Schoolcraft got himself hired as a scientist on military expeditions in present-day Minnesota, promising to find the Mississippi's source and map it for the United States. The second time, becoming somewhat desperate, he split off from the main party with an Indian guide. Ozaawindib, or Yellow Head, identified in reports as the leader of a nearby Ojibwe village, agreed to bring Schoolcraft and his military escort to the requested place. The deceptively simple term *guiding* entailed drawing up maps, finding passable routes, and wrangling men laden with bulky supplies across difficult terrain. They slogged up a series of tributaries to a lake, where Schoolcraft planted an American flag and called it a day with his feet mercifully intact. Claiming the privilege of first discovery, he named the lake Itasca.

In Schoolcraft's reports we get one kind of origin quest: a white explorer locates and names the source of a river. Yet the real story of that event is how settlers, through narrative, attempted to remake the land and people for white consumption. In the years that followed, Schoolcraft kept changing his strategy, as though uncertain if the trick had worked. Ozaawindib told Schoolcraft the name of the lake was Omashkoozo-Zaaga'igan, or Elk Lake, widely used not only by Ojibwe who frequented the place, but by white traders and missionaries. Schoolcraft wanted a new name to fit the occasion, something more heroic that would appeal to readers back east. At first, it seemed that he had made up Itasca entirely from his imagination, splicing together the Latin words *veritas* and *caput* to mean "true source."

However, Schoolcraft also knew that his readers were intrigued by exotic depictions of Native people. Two decades after the expedition, he declared that the name's origin was Ojibwe. "Having previously got an inkling of some of their mythological and necromantic notions" during his years living among the Ojibwe, he spun a story that he attributed to Ozaawindib. According to the popular version, Itasca was the beautiful daughter of a powerful spirit. She caught the eye of the god of the underworld, who wanted to marry her and "bear her away to the gloomy regions of the dead." When she resisted, a violent storm wrecked her lodge and buried her under a hill of rock and sand. Beneath the hill she wept for her lost family until her tears formed the lake that bore her name.

White readers enjoyed the resemblance to the Greek myth of Persephone, abducted to the underworld by Hades; unfortunately, later investigations by the Minnesota Historical Society found no such story among Ojibwe residents of the area. Was it a pure fabrication? Or was it some stranger "mutation of the country," as Schoolcraft cryptically described it? Perhaps his wife Jane, a talented Ojibwe writer and the source of many Schoolcraft stories, had furnished it for the occasion. In ways that he refused to specify, he enlisted Indigenous words and ideas in his history of white discovery.

Part of his agenda in promoting this and other "Indian legends" was to make Indigenous culture fit European gender norms. In a sentimental poem, he described Itasca, a chaste Indian maiden, lying "within a beauteous basin, fair outspread," a passive sexual object. "Flitting shy," she "so long concealed" her location from aggressive men—it's hard not to see a projection of Schoolcraft's Victorian ideals of female modesty and male desire. These efforts paint a picture of masculine conquest over passive, feminine nature. Despite much confusion among local historians about exactly where Schoolcraft got "that name Itasca," they admitted that it "took" in the country's imagination.

Indigenous realities are obscured from this origin story on many levels. For instance, Ozaawindib did not appear in history simply to lead explorers to the Mississippi's source. Kai Minosh Pyle, a Two-Spirit Métis and Sault Ste. Marie Nishnaabe writer, realized that "there were two Ozaawindibs" in the historical record because scholars hadn't recognized that Schoolcraft's guide lived for much of her life as a woman within Ojibwe society. Schoolcraft frequently praised Ozaawindib's prowess and strength, which he touted as virtues of Indian masculinity. Pyle explains that Ozaawindib was an *agokwe*, someone deemed male at birth, but who often filled female roles and partnered with husbands. This was not always an easy position, yet it was largely respected among Ojibwe people, while white writers, when they dared to, described it with horror. For Pyle, recognizing Ozaawindib means recognizing how colonization erased gender-diverse figures and traditions, which many Two-Spirit, queer, trans, and gender-nonconforming Native people seek to understand today as part of their history. *Agokwe* could go to war and sometimes traveled in male dress, which is how Schoolcraft may have encountered Ozaawindib in 1832. Though they traveled together for weeks, perhaps Ozaawindib chose not to elaborate on her life; it's equally possible that Schoolcraft lacked insight or purposely censored this aspect of Ojibwe society.

European gender and sexual norms were widely used as a tool of colonial discipline, a blunt instrument to break and recast Indigenous relations. Ozaawindib faced disapproval from some—Pyle found that her father may have pressured her to live as a man—yet could play a powerful role in Ojibwe society. More broadly, Indigenous people across the continent organized their families and nations in many ways that did not fit the passive feminine and active masculine ideals of the Euro-American ruling class, which also did its best to stamp out unacceptable queerness among its own kind. Making a case study of "savages" helped to keep the white population in line, proud of the repressive structures they might otherwise have questioned. Schoolcraft's work of "discovering" Indian culture, as revealed by Native informants concerned for their own status and survival under colonial rule, was an effort at remaking it as straight, monogamous, and ripe for conversion to Christianity. Whatever eluded these boundaries was left off the map. On the way to Lake Itasca, the expedition party crossed a river that settlers later named after Schoolcraft; the Ojibwe named it for Ozaawindib.

Because of Schoolcraft's wild inconsistency and evasiveness, Itasca remains a mystery. Many of his peers found his stories farcical. "There is no such word nor even any remotely resembling it in the Ojibway language," wrote one missionary working in the region. Yet Schoolcraft's reversal after he claimed to have invented the name suggests that there's more to the story. Buried among his mountains of papers, a handwritten version of the Lake Itasca myth has a completely different plot from the published version, set in a more recognizable Ojibwe universe. Kai Pyle also notes that many Dakota speakers in the region today regard Itasca as a Dakota name. If nothing is certain, these flashes of recognition might be what matters. While Schoolcraft was known to make up fake Native sources, he was just as likely to erase real ones when it suited him, and his actual sources often took advantage of his credulity. The "mutations of the country" can twist in both directions, out of the hands of the would-be namers.

The Minnesota state legislature embraced Schoolcraft's "true source" and made it a park dedicated to the idea of the nation's most iconic river—the Mississippi, praised in story and song as a symbol of something like the American spirit. Yet, to the nonexpert, Lake Itasca was unimpressive. In the summer, its flow was barely a trickle. It failed to evoke the Mississippi's awesome "magnitude and power." In the 1930s, the chief ranger called his own park "swampy, muddy, and dirty." Officials became determined to remake Itasca into a more fitting shrine to American enterprise. They built a concrete dam across the lake's mouth, ensuring a steady stream of water, and raised the banks with trucked-in topsoil. The project superintendent described this as restoring the lake's "natural form," in which it had never previously existed. When tourists—the state estimates a half million per year—take pictures by the historical marker, they may not realize that the scene was elaborately constructed to look like the single, iconic source of the mighty Mississippi.

To designate a specific spring as the origin, someone has to decide at every juncture which is river and which is tributary, hundreds or thousands of choices in succession. Ozaawindib had this intricate knowledge of a region webbed with waterways, and Schoolcraft claimed the singular discovery. To tell a larger story about origins, we can ask, of all the tributaries that run together, which are remembered and which are obscured? Who named them and how did the naming itself do the work of conjuring power? Merely tracing the mutations of the country can't restore what has been taken or destroyed; time's river can't flow backward. Yet the past gives force to present demands. It can burst the channels of monuments and history books, as many streambeds swell with rain.

A desire for power isn't bad. Struggles for freedom are struggles for empowerment. Yet they're also struggles against a deep-seated power structure, racial, economic, and technological, built up over hundreds of years. That structure often seems immovable and inevitable. It has real material foundations, but just as real are the evolving narratives, philosophies, and justifications that twine through it, supporting and making possible each new articulation. Stories about the what and why of entrenched power are just as necessary as its armories, and it just as inexorably produces them. We need these stories in advance to even imagine what power might look like.

This is why seekers of power are tellers of stories. To begin with, someone must have faith in them. Schoolcraft constantly flexed his expertise, his mastery of Indian culture and "the Indian mind," and implied that this knowledge would win for the United States of America everything that had been Indian. Military force and settler violence took the land, but stories told by scientists, poets, and religious visionaries gave meaning and purpose to these actions. They were more than mere propaganda; they formed the moral and spiritual grid of the nation's power, which is not inevitable, but is remade in the minds of each generation and can be unmade.

Even the most literal sources of power—the materials that we burn in engines and pack into bombs—were not simply found in nature. People had to believe in the possibility of their value, and that very belief shaped their transformation into national icons. Oil was a medicinal substance that welled up from underground streams on the land of the Seneca Nation, encroached upon by western Pennsylvania and New York. The first oil wells were drilled there by speculators whose story of petroleum as a miraculous blessing created vast new markets for their product. Uranium, which Diné historians Esther Yazzie-Lewis and Jim Zion regard as "a monster" slumbering in the mountains of their homeland, became "our friend Mr. Atom" to mainstream Americans in the years after World War II, when they were promised safety and prosperity through nuclear development. As the story is told and retold, the harm that these uses of power cause becomes a necessary sacrifice. This book is about the process that fuses materials and narratives, that turns land into property, matter into energy, and desire into a desperate faith.

The four sections that follow linger on four sites where Americans extracted literal power from the landscape and symbolic power from history. They're not the most well-remembered places, having worn out their usefulness and lapsed into unruly states. In the arc of their exploitation, they show the subtle threads that pull together land, minerals, knowledge, and people in the service of an expanding empire. Each site represents a different resource and the set of stories and beliefs that made it such a tantalizing treasure.

To sooth the conscience of fortune-seekers who left a trail of fire, flood, and ghosts, their stories affirmed that this was indeed the destined course of history. Beneath such fantasy lies a haunted

A stock certificate from the Pennsylvania Rock Oil Company depicts
a Lady Liberty figure beckoning prospectors to the oil frontier,
the cornucopia at her feet overflowing with the land's bounty.

The "Atomic Frontier Days" festival in Richland, Washington,
celebrated the convergence of settler history—the covered wagon—
with the dawning nuclear age in the US west.

landscape; both victims and perpetrators can haunt, and they are often bound together by the forces that made them. Kent's "ponderous wheels" of progress that crushed so many were what Eve Tuck and C. Ree call "an engine for curses." Haunting—"the relentless remembering and reminding that will not be appeased"—is not just the work of ghosts, but of the living, and is the purpose of this history. Each site in this book harbors counternarratives, forces of resistance both human and nonhuman that defied exploitation and embodied alternatives.

Throughout, I use the term *American* in reference to the United States and its residents, not as a negation of the rest of North and South America, but as a shorthand for the myths and politics of US national identity with which the book is engaged. I will introduce Indigenous peoples and places in Indigenous languages and in English and alternate between these depending on context. I've adopted the terms and spellings that specific Indigenous nations use in their public communications, while acknowledging that these are not fixed, unanimous preferences, and they continue to change.

The term *Indian*, imposed by Europeans in reference to the Native people of North America, was ubiquitous until the 1960s and has been rejected and reappropriated since then by some of the diverse groups it claimed to define; today, the terms *Indigenous* or *Native* are more favored by these groups in the US, and I generally use them when speaking from a contemporary perspective, while using *Indian* in the context of historical sources. Grouping Indigenous nations together under any single term can reinforce racism and colonialism—each nation has its own name and history—yet it has also provided a self-definition for the varied Indigenous political identities and movements discussed in this book. I describe white US residents as settlers, white people, or Europeans so as not to leave whiteness an unspoken assumption. In revisiting histories of US power, my aim is not only to expose threads of destructive myth-making, but to foreground continuous Indigenous presence and knowledge in the poetry, scholarship, art, and science of Native thinkers whose work I encourage readers to seek out.

• • •

As an agent of Manifest Destiny, Henry Rowe Schoolcraft had few natural gifts—the source of his power was Bamewawagezhikaquay, or Jane Johnston, an Ojibwe woman who married him in 1823. Jane Johnston and her community took him in and shared their political influence and historical knowledge. In return, he made them the raw material for his theories of white superiority. Building a career as an Indian expert, he extended his reach into archaeology, a field consumed by debates over whether ancient North America had once been inhabited by a lost white race. In the same way that Schoolcraft tried to speak for and claim the knowledge of his wife's Ojibwe family, he also assumed the uncanny ability to speak for the monuments of the lost race. Perhaps the United States could have taken Indian lands, the material foundation of all its future power, without elaborate myths and alternative histories that placed wandering Celts in prehistoric Ohio. Yet scholars labored to sustain this possibility because it played an important part in securing white resource claims—as archaeologist Berenika Byszewski puts it, "the logic of settler colonialism is embedded in the colonization of antiquity as a national and scientific space."

Promoters of the early oil industry also anchored their new power in the Indigenous past. Most explicitly, Spiritualist mediums claimed to channel Indian spirits from the afterlife, who told them where to drill profitable wells. This book's second section shows how petroleum brought Manifest Destiny into the industrial age. Spiritualists and other faith communities interpreted vast underground oceans of fuel as a gift placed there by God to drive America's endless growth.

By the early 1900s, though there was no shortage of oil, businessmen envisioned a new and spectacular source of energy: damming rivers for hydroelectric power. Eventually, every major river in the United States except for the Yellowstone was dammed in the name of economic development, flooding Native lands and disrupting water-based lifeways. In Conowingo, Maryland, dam construction also threatened massive artworks carved in stone by Native people centuries before colonization. As white residents protested the dam and tried to save the petroglyphs, some of them gained the insight that even their race did not protect them from dispossession by the forces of capital. Some argued that the dam should be publicly owned, so that those who paid the price would also control and benefit from the power. Yet the story that won out arranged the petroglyphs, Indians, settlers, and private industry in a predetermined arc of progress with a divine justification.

The book concludes in the southwestern United States, which in the 1940s and '50s became the most radioactive place in America. This was the site of the Los Alamos National Laboratory, linchpin of the top-secret race to build an atomic bomb during World War II. National defense easily justified the risks and sacrifices of developing an unpredictable new power source, especially when most of those sacrifices came from Native and rural communities around uranium mines and bombing ranges. The birth of the nuclear age forced Americans to reckon with the twisted timeline of power. Despite global dominance, the nation could be obliterated in an instant. Our radiation will outlive us for hundreds of thousands of years. Such uncertain futures further motivate the colonization of the past—the physicists of Los Alamos took refuge from their deadly work by collecting Pueblo pottery.

At each of these sites, new origin stories evolved in tandem with the needs of the moment, always concealing or justifying casualties. Manifest Destiny, the idea that certain deserving white Americans were chosen by God to rule from sea to sea, was not a single policy or campaign—some US leaders opposed territorial expansion, while others schemed to seize the entire North American continent. A belief with many permutations can still converge on the same result. It is completely obvious that this logic served resource extraction and the murder of Indigenous people. Yet it becomes easy to dismiss a simple Oregon Trail version of Manifest Destiny as a thing for history books, which ended with the closing of the Western frontier; another bad, antiquated prejudice. In fact this belief never stopped mutating; it's just one name for a state of anxious consumption. American culture continues to produce new stories that justify the violence of the past and fantasize its recurrence in an apocalyptic future.

• • •

These stories are settler-colonial narratives and narratives of racial capitalism, a term that Cedric J. Robinson coined for the global social-economic system founded on extracting value from non-white people. Despite assurances by European priests and scientists that Indigenous North Americans had no souls or legal standing, settlers felt lingering unease about the high costs of their gambit, whether it could succeed, whether they would be haunted by their crimes. Popular fiction from the early nineteenth century was rife with curses cast by dispossessed Indians; a hostile landscape seemed to swarm with vengeful spirits. Putting to rest this superstitious guilt fell to a motley assortment of scholars, antiquarians, archaeologists, and outright fabulists who offered an alternative history of the continent.

They crafted a redemption narrative, wherein white people got to ancient America first and were subsequently usurped by invading Indians, in terms that frankly mirrored the actual genocide occurring against Native people at that time: a Mound Builder's family is "butchered, amid their shrieks, with all his race," in William Cullen Bryant's poem. Many, like Bryant, openly affirmed that the present conquest was merely cosmic justice. The myth of a lost white race weaves through each of the stories in this book. As historian Jason Colavito has relentlessly documented, this myth is still central to white supremacist conspiracy theories today and often appears in mainstream cable television shows whose audiences would rather speculate about extraterrestrials and Vikings than accept the Indigenous origins of the country's ancient monuments.

Oddly, though, settler narrative has another move that exposes the disingenuousness of the first. In addition to righteously conquering Indians, white people wanted to consume them and become them. The Boston Tea Party featured wealthy merchants in war paint and feathered headdresses, asserting native status before they even had a nation. Philip J. Deloria unfolds this long legacy of appropriation, from elite fraternal societies to the Boy Scouts and Indian Princesses, in his classic book, *Playing Indian*. Nineteenth-century Spiritualists went so far as to don buckskin and channel the spirits of Black Hawk and Tecumseh, who conveyed "deep blessings of the heart" to settlers and graciously forgave all wrongdoing.

The first minting of the "Indian Head" penny from 1859, the same year that the first commercial oil well was opened in western Pennsylvania.

A white Lady Liberty in Indian headdress graced the American penny for half a century, the fulfillment of the Boston Tea Party's demand that elite, white "natives," rather than the British crown, control the wealth of the continent. The desire for symbolic ownership was as real as the drive for material wealth. Throughout the nineteenth and twentieth centuries, from the bleak oil fields of Pennsylvania to the vivid hills of the Painted Desert, white entrepreneurs tried to transmute indigeneity into spiritual currency.

The point of fully flaying out these origin stories is for those who challenge power to know the mutations of the country. We have to go down the obscure paths of haunting and damnation to become unsettled, to recognize the landscape not as a canvas of endless opportunity, but a dense layering of desires, strategies, betrayals, and resistances. This uncanny sediment, supposedly natural yet made by human agency, determines where each of us stands. Recognizing that is not cause for guilt and flagellation on the part of individuals, but for thinking beyond individual causes. It demands a practice of thinking with the land and with the past, something like what Anishinaabe scholar Vanessa Watts calls place-thought, that changes our orientation toward the future.

Reckoning with "hard histories" seems to always leave a wake of reactionary fear, stirring in many white Americans an angry defense of their identity and possessions. Such feelings thrive in a society where justice means punishment and survival is a zero-sum game—any revelation of truth becomes an existential threat, any assertion of wrong a demand for personal retribution. They are feelings inherent to racial capitalism, with its twined logics of individual responsibility and hereditary vice. There's no way to challenge power without excavating these feelings and unspooling their historical permutations, now so embedded in the neutral "common sense" of US political discourse. Bristling at the elusive notion of "social justice," Eve Tuck and C. Ree call for "a different sort of justice—one that dismantles, one that ruins." Snaking through the topographies of domination, seeing from the ground how they accrue their false, towering inevitability, I hope that we can ruin them.

Marxists use the term *hegemony* for the self-reinforcing common sense that justifies the ever-deepening exploitation of land and people, against all rational evidence that this is a path of death. I talk about it with the language of faith, narrative, and prophecy because the ability of any abstract entity—state, society, economic system—to carry this off seems almost supernatural. Understanding how this supernatural aura became so firmly attached to economic calculations and political agendas is a powerful thing in itself. The feeling has teeth, indeed it is geared into our survival, making failure and poverty synonymous with betrayal of national values. It's important to carry around a deep genealogy of that feeling, to understand how it shapes each of our psyches, whether it has allured us or done us violence—and for most people, it does both.

One way of noticing how power works against us is to pay attention to fear. Within narratives of progress, growth, and triumph are instructions about what to fear, usually personified in the enemies whom the United States has overcome. Native peoples, the first enemies of US empire, served as a template for later adversaries, all carefully cataloged by the human sciences based on racial and national characteristics. The hazards of stagnation, degeneracy, and exhaustion that weakened others can always strike at home—must perpetually be guarded against. While the United States extended its military reach overseas, the arrival of immigrants on American soil became a threat of invasion that seeded hereditary weakness into what eugeni-cists thought of as the "breeding stock." This siege mentality has been a hallmark of white supremacy from the Plymouth Plantation to the southern border wall that galvanized voters in the 2016 election.

Threats from outside were directly mapped onto threats from within, of being overrun by deviants who would sap the nation's abil-ity to continue producing and profiting. Perhaps the land's bounty would run out, or God would withdraw his favor. Many people looked at ancient North American earthworks and feared that the United States would fall like the builders of these ruins had fallen. Both at-tracted and repelled by the idea of fateful repetition, they developed a rich fantastical attachment to their imagined predecessors whose world had ended, who vanished with hardly a trace. Imagined kin-ship with a lost white race, or even with "vanishing Indians," pushed out of awareness the fact that the Indigenous world had survived its attempted obliteration, and could well outlive the United States.

At the moment it's easy to believe that the American march of progress has become a march to apocalypse; people of all political stripes are on an end-times footing. Oddly, it's a fantasy common to the powerful and the oppressed of a capitalist system that it would finally go up in a disaster-movie conflagration. This way of think-ing has shaped how settlers read the landscape from the beginning, a flickering shadow of doubt that now blocks the sun. Navigating in this darkness is difficult; the system's compulsive reaction is to conquer more frontiers and leverage more unilateral power, to flee the past through anxious consumption.

I'd like to tell a story about something new that rises out of the ruins of the myth of America, but we also need to know what ground we're standing on, what's beneath the ground and under the water. I don't think it's wrong to dream of hidden things or speak to the dead—these are essential sources of knowledge. This book is a kind of dreaming back over places that were mined for an empire's power, to let different visions and voices surface from all that remains.

PART 1

TONGUES
FROM TOMBS

The myth of
the Mound Builders

The citizens of Elizabethtown, Virginia, began tunneling into a sixty-foot-high earthen mound in the early spring of 1838. Located near the confluence of Grave Creek and the Ohio River, the mound was built by Indigenous Adena people more than two thousand years ago. Overseeing the excavation was a young man named Abelard Tomlinson, a scion of the town's founding family, which had owned the mound for the past half-century. His grandfather, Joseph Tomlinson II, had carefully preserved it from destruction.

During Joseph's time, settlers flooded the fertile Ohio and Mississippi Valleys, fought ruthless wars against the Shawnee, Muskogee, Cherokee, Miami, and other nations, and demolished thousands of Indigenous earthworks as a nuisance. Curiously, these settlers claimed the land as a "terra nullius," an empty place without history, provided for them by God. How did they make sense of this seeming contradiction? Indigenous presence, in towns, farmlands, roads, and earthworks, led European Americans to build an elaborate set of myths that secured their ownership of the continent on the heels of overwhelming military force. Though they had many competing theories about the mounds' non-Indian origins, interpreters found that the sense of mystery itself made the past available to the colonial imagination. Beyond simple possession, there was power in telling and retelling these stories.

The Grave Creek Mound, once the centerpiece of a sprawling earthworks complex, survived long enough to attract tourists who came to marvel at its incredible size. They praised its "great and simple magnificence"—one journalist called it "literally the Pyramid of the

VIEW OF GRAVE CREEK MOUND.

A stylized Grave Creek Mound depicted in 1839.
At the base of the mound stands the farmer with his plow,
a pastoral vision of the hardy pioneer who has cleared the land
and placed it under orderly cultivation.

West." That comparison speaks volumes, as early nineteenth-century Americans often complained that they had no ancient monuments. They pined after Egypt's pyramids, the Greek Acropolis, Europe's castles and cathedrals. The French philosopher Diderot praised "the poetics of ruins" for inspiring grand sentiments, casting the heroic individual into relief against the "ravages of time," but ruins also created feelings of national identity and inheritance. Settlers looked at earthworks with a certain wishfulness, wondering what they were for and who built them. Perhaps there had been civilization in North America, but where was its Rosetta Stone? Why did it not speak from beneath the dust of ages? Abelard Tomlinson and his neighbors saw their chance to capitalize on this mystery.

For Abelard's grandfather Joseph Tomlinson II, the "mammoth mound" was not much of a mystery at all. When he traveled to Grave Creek from Maryland in 1770, he inferred that the mound complex marked the ancestral graves of Native people, possibly the Shawnee, who occupied the area. They were its rightful owners under British law until 1768, when it was signed away in the Treaty of Fort Stanwix—by another group, the Iroquois Six Nations, without Shawnee consent. This made the situation tense when white "pioneers" flooded in. Human bones crunching under the farmer's plow would seem to mock the promise of virgin soil—there was no denying that untold generations had lived and died on the land that guidebooks for settlers promoted as an "unpeopled wilderness." These settlers, promised one guide, "would flow in a current unrivaled . . . into the interior of the country," to lead an "easy, free, and plentiful" life in their solitary log cabins.

This bucolic picture belied that settlers such as Tomlinson were the advance guard of Indian extermination. In the newly independent United States, which declared the Ohio Valley up for grabs, they carried out a style of warfare far beyond the scope of a professional army. Rather than defeat enemy soldiers in battle, the procedure was to send civilian families to live on enemy territory and have them fight off the original population in the name of self-defense. This was by no means a pursuit for solitary cabin dwellers; settlers, moving westward in extended kinship groups, formed militias and ranger patrols that hunted for Indians. They burned Native towns and farms, establishing cycles of mutual retaliation that spared neither women, children, nor the aged.

At Grave Creek, Tomlinson and his neighbors built a private fort in 1774; as violence escalated, state militias and the Continental Army arrived to protect their embattled citizens, taking up the same scorched-earth methods as the frontier rangers. Military men took a scientific interest in Native earthworks, imagining them as ancient fortifications. Major General Richard Butler "went to see 'the Grave,'" that is, the Grave Creek Mound, in 1785, taking thorough measurements and notes, on his way to threaten the Shawnee with annihilation unless they signed a land-cession treaty.

Unified Shawnee, Muskogee, and Cherokee resistance spanned twenty years, until the 1795 Treaty of Greenville banished them west beyond Cincinnati. The settlers' reward for decades of bloodshed was free land, though they were often outsmarted by wealthy investors who had already surveyed and filed claims on their homesteads; the Tomlinsons lost a chunk of land to none other than avid real estate speculator George Washington. In the early United States, "land became the most important exchange commodity for the accumulation of capital and building of the national treasury," writes historian Roxanne Dunbar-Ortiz. "The centrality of land sales in building the economic base of the US wealth and power must be seen."

Perhaps, in moments of reflection, Tomlinson weighed his flimsy land titles against the fact of the Native monuments and saw why those he antagonized would fight to the death rather than abandon their ancestors. He wrote about Cherokee travelers who detoured off their routes to visit the Grave Creek Mound. The Shawnee, Cherokee, Haudenosaunee, and other groups had history at that bend in the Ohio and may have held a living connection to the site. There was no innocent misunderstanding, but rather a cold calculation of what could be taken with enough force. With Indian removal seemingly complete, Tomlinson became committed, perhaps superstitiously, to the preservation of what he previously fought to erase. He refused to demolish the Grave Creek Mound for development. Despite local curiosity, no one was allowed to break its surface.

The past became past very quickly in those times, as if to compensate for the perceived lack of history by stretching living memory out to the horizon. A few decades after the Treaty of Greenville, new arrivals to the Ohio Valley listened to old-timers spin romantic yarns about the "Indian wars." The elaborate earthworks around Grave Creek were leveled and covered with wheat. A magazine illustration shows the Grave Creek Mound towering over Tomlinson's fields, a pleasing contrast between wild ancient ruins and modern civilization. A farmer with his plow rests from his labors at the mound's base. In addition to Native people, others have been erased from this picture: Virginia's settlers did not arrive alone to develop the land. As one historian notes, "The high incidence of slave ownership in western Virginia is remarkable."

What the local chronicles call "homesteads" were in many cases small plantations. The heads of middling families, including Tomlinson, held between three and ten African-descended people in bondage, while the wealthiest held upward of fifty. The events of these people's lives, and even their names, are poorly documented. In 1804, an enslaved man named Mike is said to have crossed the Ohio River to freedom. He belonged to Joseph Tomlinson, who rallied a gang of neighbors to hunt him down, as they had once hunted Indians. Caught in an ambush, Mike stabbed and killed Tomlinson's son, Robert, before he was captured. The next night, while the group camped by a creek, two other travelers reportedly witnessed Joseph Tomlinson execute Mike in retribution; his body, they said, was left unburied. The brutality of the Indian wars, premised on the defense of white property, was neither gone nor forgotten, though it transpired in a twilight realm apart from official memory.

By the 1820s, in Joseph Tomlinson's last years, waves of sightseers and settlers coursed down the Ohio River, which served as a nineteenth-century superhighway to the frontier. His grim investments had paid off: Elizabethtown, which he named for his wife, on the land he staked out five decades earlier, was valuable real estate. The Grave Creek Mound "became one of the standard curiosities of the valley . . . pointed out to travellers by the captains and crews of vessels." "Every tourist mentioned it," wrote one archaeologist of the sensation it caused. Locals began to see the mound as more than an obstruction to progress.

Curiosity proved contagious—a letter to the local paper urged citizens to "Awake! Awake!" and "rally our full force" to discover what treasures lay inside. Joseph Tomlinson died in 1825, among the last residents with any memory, however distorted, of the Indigenous world they had methodically destroyed. Scientific opinion held that Indians were "warlike, indolent, and impoverished" nomads, and arrivals unfamiliar with the recent past argued that there certainly weren't enough of them to build such a massive structure. For many, Grave Creek presented a profound mystery, a blank canvas for the "sublime imaginations" of onlookers.

• • •

This is why, in 1838, Abelard Tomlinson, with the blessing of the uncle who had inherited the site, disobeyed his grandfather's wishes and exposed the mound's contents to an eager public. He would sink $2,500 into the excavation, roughly a year's middle-class wages. This sizable fund came from local doctor James W. Clemens, who in turn borrowed it from neighbors. Abelard was coy about his and Clemens's motives, citing "curiosity or some other cause," but to investors they promised a share of the riches within. Elizabethtown was dreaming of buried treasure, an obsession that swept the country in the early nineteenth century with reports of ancient hoards unearthed in caves, swamps, and Indian mounds. The Mormon prophet Joseph Smith got his start digging for money in the hills of western New York; only when that failed did he come upon the spiritual treasure of the Book of Mormon. This was the settler's fantasy of discovering not just land to be worked, but exponential riches placed there by Providence.

Accounts of the Grave Creek excavation do not mention whether any of the laborers were enslaved; a few could have belonged to the elder Tomlinsons, just like the mound itself. Abelard's generation was, by and large, not wealthy enough to hold slaves, who posed a financial risk because so many emancipated themselves by navigating across the river to the free state of Ohio, and often onward to Canada. On the river's southern bank, Abelard and his crew spent three weeks digging a horizontal shaft into the mound; a hundred feet in, they broke through to a hollow cavern. In the musty, timber-framed chamber, they found shell beads, copper jewelry, and human remains. They reported that the first skeleton was perfectly intact, "not one tooth missing," while another nearby had crumbled, bone fragments mingling with ivory ornaments.

Local doctor Thomas Townsend, who joined the dig as an amateur naturalist, identified the skeletons as "dignified chiefs and renowned kings," given the immense labor required for such a burial. An ancient people "raised this structure, no doubt, for posthumous fame, and for a national monument." There was much debate among naturalists and antiquarians about the racial history of North America—whether "our modern Indians" had been its only inhabitants. Many argued that, because Indians lived in small wandering bands, the Grave Creek Mound was far beyond their capacity to build. Townsend seems to have followed the commonsense thinking of earlier generations in arguing that Native people did build the mounds. Before European invasion, "the population of many of the Indian nations . . . was adequate to the performance of this apparently great work," he asserted, noting that the Osage had constructed a burial mound along the Wabash River within the past fifty years. Townsend sent his report of the excavation to newspapers and magazines, but his would not be the authoritative opinion. His former medical partner, Dr. Clemens, the financial backer of the dig, was an equally learned physician with a reputation as a polymath. One of his scholarly interests was North America's pre-Indian lost race.

Clemens, Tomlinson, and the treasure hunters of Elizabethtown faced a major disappointment: no jewels or gold were in the mound to compensate their effort. Any settler could turn over a field and

An illustration from 1850 shows Tomlinson's pavilion atop the Grave Creek Mound, surrounded by symbols of advancing civilization: the shepherd with his flock, the broad public road, and the snug private home. The museum inside the mound was shuttered in 1846, and the pavilion became a tavern and dance hall.

find Indigenous beads and stone points, perhaps unwelcome evidence of the recently usurped population. The only way to "make the mound 'pay,'" as a cynical archaeologist put it, was to capitalize on its tourism value. Accordingly, Tomlinson turned it into a full-on tourist trap. For ten cents, visitors could walk through a paved tunnel to the mound's center, gaze at the skeletons by candlelight in their vaulted chamber, and ascend a spiral staircase to a three-story pavilion on the precipice with refreshments and souvenirs. It was important not to identify the human remains as Indian; instead, they were the "ancient kings of Grave Creek," entombed in mysterious and mighty splendor. National newspapers trumpeted the discovery. The *Cincinnati Gazette*, turning up its nose at this chintz, bewailed the fate of the "wild wood monument . . . trimmed, tunneled, and cut up into apartments for trinket exhibitions."

Clemens, who was personally on the hook for $2,500, likely had a strong hand in this scheme; his son believed that it was Clemens who prevailed on Tomlinson to open the mound to begin with. Aside from the financial stake, there was the scholarly and political one. The 1830s was the decade of Andrew Jackson's brutal campaign of Indian removal. Jackson won the 1828 presidential election on a wave of populist fervor that he gratified by seizing the last remaining Native lands east of the Mississippi for white settlers. The federal government broke its treaties with the Cherokee, Seminole, Choctaw, Chickasaw, and Muskogee, sending them on deadly forced marches across hundreds of miles to "Indian Territory" in present-day Oklahoma.

Indian removal was not just a military operation. As official policy and as a general patriotic zeitgeist, it shaped how scholars and ordinary citizens thought and wrote about Native people. Just as early investigators were beginning to glimpse the complexity of Native languages and cultures, Jackson's administration incentivized them to cover it up. With the power of research funds and the government printing office, officials boosted scholarship claiming that Indians were naturally doomed to extinction by the superior white race—the army was merely speeding up the inevitable. They also nurtured the widespread belief that North American earthworks were built by an ancient lost civilization. The more science could deduce about this vanished empire, the weaker the argument for Native land rights in the present day.

The theory of a lost race, generally referred to as the Mound Builders, had circulated since the early nineteenth century, even though many authorities, not the least of them Thomas Jefferson, clearly identified the Indigenous origin of earthworks based on archaeological evidence. However, this recognition was double-edged: those in the Indian-builders camp also dismissed mounds as primitive and uncivilized, inherently lacking value because of their makers' race. It's sometimes hard to believe that the two camps are describing the same physical objects, so different are the values and imagined pasts projected onto them. Euro-American opinions would fall into this binary for the next hundred years: mounds were either unremarkable piles of dirt made by Indians, or incredible monuments built by a lost race.

Today's archaeologists see the Mound Builders' immense popularity as a case study in how genocide and dispossession overwrite Indigenous history. Lost-race narratives furnished a usable past for proponents of Manifest Destiny, since if Indians overthrew the ancient Phoenician or Celtic kingdoms of the Ohio Valley, it was only fair play that Europeans, heirs to the mantle of civilization, would overthrow the Indians in turn. These narratives proved so compelling for white Americans that critical archaeologists faced a long battle to debunk them and establish a pre-Columbian history based on their scientific standards. That battle is by no means over today—historian Jason Colavito documents the many recent appearances of lost-race myths in mainstream outlets such as the History Channel, with the shows *America Unearthed* and *Search for Lost Giants*, and in white supremacist groups whose members perversely insist that they are "the real Native Americans."

While archaeologists fought for the scientific authority to reconstruct the past on their terms, Native nations have always preserved the histories of their homelands in spoken and written tradition. Earthworks, including conical mounds such as Grave Creek, animal effigies, and vast geometric forms precisely aligned with the celestial map, are vital to many Native communities today—they are places of origin and of communication between upper and lower worlds. Indigenous studies scholar Chadwick Allen calls them "living earthworks vocabularies," a way of writing "through the medium of the land itself." While the word *sacred* is often used to describe these varied sites, they could have many purposes, from politics to commerce, astronomy to sports. Through external form and layered internal structure, they embody Native science, history, and artistic and spiritual relations with place.

Current archaeologists increasingly cooperate with Native communities to prioritize their knowledge, indeed, many Native people have become archaeologists, reclaiming the power to interpret their own sites. Native community leaders and academics have led the fight for access to earthworks within parks and on private land. In Newark, Ohio, the Moundbuilders Country Club—its name evoking the priority claim of the lost white race—built a golf course atop the Octagon Earthworks in 1910, and, as of 2021, only grants full access to nonmembers on four days each year. Dr. Christine Ballengee-Morris, an arts education professor and member of the Eastern Band of Cherokee, describes golfers yelling and throwing golf balls at her group. A coalition of local activists and archaeologists, including Ballengee-Morris, pressed the state historical society to end the country club's lease, a process which is still playing out in court.

Before archaeology took this turn toward engaging, however unevenly, with Indigenous knowledge, its colonial function meant that experts saw Native North America through the lens of white supremacist racial hierarchies. Until the twentieth century, many professionals were just as invested in Mound Builder myths as amateurs were—indeed, there were fewer distinctions between professional and amateur. For instance, the self-taught surveyor Ephraim George Squier completed a renowned work of systematic archaeology in his 1845-47 survey, *Ancient Monuments of the Mississippi Valley*, published by the Smithsonian Institution. While Squier rejected the idea of lost Phoenician or Assyrian tribes, he too felt the need to genetically distinguish the creators of ancient earthworks from modern Indians. He proposed that a separate race, "Toltecans" from Central America, came to the Mississippi Valley to build mounds. This "extinct race, whose name is lost to tradition itself," was perhaps overthrown by the later savage Indian population. While Squier and his partner, Edwin Davis, were seen as setting a new bar for professional excavations, they also produced science that seemed to affirm the policy of Indian removal.

There was another reason that experts such as Squier could not, or would not, imagine a past where ancestors of North America's present-day Indigenous people built the mounds. The professional study of human societies past and present—as it took form in archaeology, history, linguistics, ethnology, and physical anthropology—was founded on an explicit racial hierarchy widely embraced by nineteenth-century scientists. Often simply termed race science, this guiding principle ranked humanity from primitive to civilized based on traits such as phrenological skull shape, skin color, and historical-geographic origins, bundled together as an immutable natural category that revealed the proper place of enslaved Africans, dispossessed Indians, and European conquerors. Crucially, as Roxanne Dunbar-Ortiz points out, the Indigenous peoples of North America did not share this concept of race at the onset of colonization. For millennia they had lived as many distinct nations, with a wide range of languages, religions, politics, and cultures. The idea of a unitary "Indian" essence was imposed from outside, and the diverse peoples suddenly lumped together as the "red race" could not immediately organize their resistance along this axis.

Race science was a practical tool for governing subjugated populations. It held that physical traits correlated precisely with mental traits, and thus a person's intelligence, virtue, and capability could easily be read at a glance, on a face or in a cranium. Dr. James Clemens sent one of the skulls stolen from the Grave Creek mound to Philadelphia phrenologist Samuel G. Morton for analysis. Morton, a founder of academic race science, collected thousands of skulls pillaged from grave sites, cemeteries, and executions around the world, using their shapes to classify the mental traits of the races to which they belonged. Even before Darwin's theory of evolution made its debut, scientists inspired by animal breeding spoke of human races as "stocks," each with fixed hereditary qualities. Both academics and the public embraced the promise of race science to validate the social order. Museums rushed to build their own archives of racial difference, driving a market in stolen human remains and grave goods.

Only a few dissenters agreed with Frederick Douglass that "pride and selfishness . . . never want for a theory to justify them." "When men oppress their fellow-men," Douglass observed of race science's white promoters, "the oppressor ever finds, in the character of the oppressed, a full justification for his oppression." Just as archaeologists denied that Indians could build the mounds, they also denied that Black Africans built the pyramids of Egypt, a position that Douglass roundly demolished in this 1854 speech.

Another central concept for mound investigators was the law of diffusion, which, in its extreme form, held that a single advanced civilization was the source of all human inventions, transmitted to lesser (that is, nonwhite) cultures by trade, travel, or conquest. Antiquarians who saw a resemblance between the Egyptian pyramids and the mounds of North America did not hesitate to propose that light-skinned Egyptians, the inventors of civilization, had crossed the Atlantic and built an empire in Ohio. Squier protested against the errors of diffusionism, pointing instead to the "inevitable results of similar conditions" that lead disparate peoples to develop in similar ways. Still, as the study of humanity became professionalized in universities and government institutions—the Smithsonian Bureau of Ethnology was established in 1879 to map the "human terrain" of westward expansion—experts continued to fit their observations within the framework of racial hierarchy, even as they dismissed the fantastical voyages of Egyptians or Israelites.

Squier's Smithsonian surveys showed that mound architecture was complex, labor-intensive, and carefully planned, disproving the view that mounds were primitive, maybe even geological accidents. To be plausible, an argument for the mounds as civilization had to include some hint of their racially superior origin. When

Squier reached for the Toltecans of Central America, readers would quickly have recognized the "demi-civilized race" that had, since the early 1800s, become a popular Mound Builder candidate. Renowned naturalist Benjamin Smith Barton first nominated them in a 1787 book where he proposed that Danish Vikings had come to North America, built the mounds, then gone south to become the Toltec civilization of Mexico. Picking up the Toltec thread thus evoked, for many readers, the possibility that Europeans were the true first Americans. Squier was aware of this association and, without endorsing it, threw a bone of credibility to its supporters.

What Squier directly referred to was the recent work of Samuel G. Morton, the avid skull collector known as the father of race science, who carefully distinguished two tiers of the "aboriginal race of America": the "Toltecan stock" with its "civilization and refinement," and their "covetous destroyers . . . a vast multitude of savage tribes" who begot modern Indians. Morton abandoned the European-origin hypothesis and rested content with the distinction between a higher and a lower aboriginal race. This preserved the idea of an inherently superior "lost race" driven from the land by Indians "whose very barbarism is working their destruction from within and without." North America before the European invasions was certainly a place of migrations, conflicts, and transcontinental exchanges, recorded in the histories of many Native nations, but that is not the story archaeologists wanted to tell. The framework of scientific racism structured the imaginations of everyone from armchair speculators to experts such as Squier, requiring them to invent a cataclysmic break rather than a continuous history of Indigenous habitation.

Archaeological thought had its mirror in popular literature, producing a genre we might call the mound romance. An account by journalist Timothy Flint, who toured the frontier in 1827, showcases some of the genre's tropes. Flint began by describing his overwhelming sense of emptiness amid a landscape unbroken by traces of humankind: "No monuments, no ruins, none of the colossal remains of castles . . . nothing to connect the imagination and the heart with the past." Flint then turned to the Indigenous earthworks all around him and declared that they would fill the void, providing the longed-for historical connection. However, that connection took the form of a mystery. "When on an uninhabited prairie we have passed at night-fall a group of Indian mounds . . . [we] asked the phantoms, who and what they were, and why they have left no memorials, but these mounds?" Though he used the standard term *Indian mound*, he did not consider it a potential clue to the mystery.

Instead, Flint received an answer in the form of a "mental echo," which told him that a vanished race, not actually Indian, raised the "inexplicable monuments." Many travelers describe their intuitions about the mounds as the hearing of echoes: "We would interrogate them as to the authors of these mighty works," wrote William Keating in 1823, "but no voice replies to ours, save that of an echo." The travelers don't seem to consider that mistaking an echo of your own ideas for evidence is an odd historical method. It neatly encapsulates how Euro-American visitors sounded the contours of the past, and why they found much there that seemed oddly familiar. Their imaginations were structured by European notions of race and civilization that made the lost-race myth deeply appealing.

It became a commonplace for travel writers and poets to muse upon the silent history contained in the mounds. William Cullen Bryant, in his 1833 poem "The Prairies," eulogized "a race that has long passed away . . . a disciplined and populous race"—of course, the Mound Builders. He imagined them yoking bison to plows to cultivate their "ample fields." Agriculture was another mark of racial superiority, and scholars denied the history of extensive Native American farming prior to colonization. Rather, according to Bryant, it was peaceful white farmers who were overthrown by the "red man . . . warlike and fierce," in epic battles upon the mounds. Bryant, a celebrated poet with a huge popular following, wanted his readers to imagine prehistoric North America as a stage where the drama of their own time had already played out once before. Indian conquest of the Mound Builders would be repaid by European conquest of Indians, and the transformation of the wild landscape (back) into an orderly garden.

ANCIENT AMERICAN BATTLE-MOUND.

The antiquarian William Pidgeon used visionary fantasy to produce his rendering of ancient "battle mounds." The notion of earthworks as military structures was widespread in mound romances. "The visitor . . . can not fail to see, in his imagination, the scenes which have taken place," Pidgeon affirmed.

Bryant gave few specifics about the lost race, but a slew of mound romances soon filled the gaps. These pulpy novels told of royal intrigues, heroic battles, and doomed love between princesses of the lost race and Indian invaders, bringing the distant past to life for eager readers. While highly entertaining, they also hammered home that Indian aggression against the peaceable Mound Builders justified contemporary Manifest Destiny. The books blurred the distinction between fiction and history; some included footnotes to real archaeological literature, some cited made-up Native informants such as De-Coo-Dah, last of the Elk Nation, while others rested their claims on even murkier authority. Cyrus Newcomb, who produced *The Book of Algoonah* in 1884, believed that ancient Assyrians built the mounds. He wanted to "assure the scientific world that [*Algoonah*] is formed from authentic materials," but wouldn't quite specify what those materials were.

Eventually, Newcomb revealed that the text had been "communicated by spirits," with Newcomb as their medium. This helps to explain the rambling, disjointed style: mediums often wrote in a stream of consciousness, letting spirits guide their pen. *Algoonah* could be a satire of the lost-race myth except that its author, a Colorado "pioneer" who mined gold and silver in the San Juan Mountains, seemed to be a good-faith participant in the Spiritualist and antiquarian circles where such theories were embraced. Though it might seem odd for a grizzled silver miner to hold seances, many treasure hunters sought supernatural guidance to the underground realm, dabbling in the occult and mystical arts. Archaeologist Warren K. Moorehead complained, in 1892, of the many "visions, suggestions, etc." sent to him by psychic mediums claiming to see the contents of Native earthworks. *Algoonah*'s reviewers acknowledged that "we may doubt the authenticity of the history," while still recommending it to "men of science and antiquarians." One reader found himself "wishing the story were true"; he "at the end adopts it as a truth—in principle—and dislikes to believe otherwise than that it is a truthful account." This pathway from wish to belief was heavily trafficked.

Such fantastical literature would seem like a poor argument for an archaeological theory. Certainly, those who aspired to make a profession of archaeology hated books such as *Algoonah* and railed against armchair visionaries. But consider the common approach of Flint, Bryant, and Newcomb: they used imagination to fill in the gaps of what they believed was a lost history, and they did so because that lost history contained a galvanizing message for present-day Americans, such as Newcomb, who sought treasure in the newly conquered West. Newcomb's book "SHOULD BE READ BY NATIONALISTS," shouted a reviewer in all caps. "It will infuse them with the spirit that will lead to success." William Cullen Bryant's poem "The Prairies" ends with Bryant hearing a whisper from the future, "The sound of that advancing multitude / Which soon shall fill these deserts. From the ground / Comes up the laugh of children, the soft voice / Of maidens, and the sweet and solemn hymn / Of Sabbath worshippers." The triumph of Christianity over heathen ways was another pillar of lost-race rhetoric and of

Manifest Destiny. Bryant's patriotic prophecy was not founded on material evidence; like *Algoonah*, it was a performance of spiritual channeling. He claimed to speak with the past and future voices of the land itself.

Abelard Tomlinson, failing to find treasure in the Grave Creek Mound, heeded the call to join the advancing westward multitude. By 1850, he and two of his brothers were digging for gold in El Dorado, California, a seamy Gold Rush boomtown. As with Newcomb, treasure in mounds and in mines seemed linked by a peculiar spiritual alchemy. All was not quiet at the mound that Tomlinson left behind, hollowed out, with the remains of its Indigenous dead on display. Though Grave Creek's heyday as a tourist trap was short-lived, his haphazard excavation produced one artifact that would become a valuable piece of evidence for the lost race. It was hardly noticed at first; from Tomlinson and his partner, Clemens, the artifact passed into the hands of various antiquarians, who puzzled over its meaning. An aspiring expert on Indian affairs, Henry Rowe Schoolcraft, waged an all-out battle to turn the disputed object into his own intellectual treasure.

Henry Rowe Schoolcraft
strikes gold

At age twenty-five, Henry Rowe Schoolcraft journeyed west to reinvent himself after an embarrassing business failure. This was the American dream of a second creation—starting anew in a bounteous promised land. Failure, however, dogged his footsteps. First Schoolcraft, trained as a glass manufacturer, bankrupted a glassworks in upstate New York and fled to the Mississippi Valley looking for copper and lead. Demoralized by his fall from grace, he simply wanted to strike it rich—to find a valuable natural resource that he could mine for the rest of his life. Though he found plenty of lead in the ground, he had no capital to get it out, and left behind a pile of unpaid bills. The only way to wring some benefit from the exploit was to publish his geological findings, which eventually drew others to the bountiful lead deposits of the region.

Still promoting himself as a geologist and mineralogist, Schoolcraft next talked his way into an 1820 War Department expedition through the Michigan Territory, where he made his first, failed attempt at reaching the source of the Mississippi River. The following year, on the strength of his frontier service, he landed a post as an agent for the US Indian Bureau. He was hired through personal connections and didn't know much about Indians, but this was typical for the notoriously corrupt bureau. Its agents learned on the job. He was stationed in the western outpost of Sault Ste. Marie, at the mouth of Lake Superior, tasked with distributing government rations, "civilizing" the Native population, and negotiating the surrender of their lands. His agency spanned sixty thousand square miles, with a population of more than seventy-three hun-

Sault Ste. Marie straddles the channel where Lake Superior
empties into the lower Great Lakes, marked here as "St. Mary's
Falls." Schoolcraft was responsible for relations with Native nations
throughout the northern part of the Michigan Territory.

dred Ojibwe people, whom the English called Chippewa, as well
as Odawa, Dakota, and other groups. Schoolcraft did not know a
word of their languages.

This is where he found the treasure upon which he would make
his name. It's not clear that Schoolcraft entered the Ojibwe world
with the intention of packaging and marketing its culture. At first
he continued to promote his own narratives of exploration and discovery, and finally planted the US flag at the Mississippi's source in
1832. He also appears to have genuinely fallen in love with Bamewawagezhikaquay, or Jane Johnston, whose Ojibwe mother and
Scots-Irish father made up the social elite of Sault Ste. Marie. Jane
had a classical education, far superior to Henry's, wrote poetry, and
yet also signified the exotic unknowns of this new milieu, where the

twenty-nine-year-old Henry expected to spend the rest of his life. It was hard to get fired from a patronage job at the Indian Bureau. Cut off from his youthful hopes of profiting from the natural sciences, he began to study the Ojibwe language, Ojibwemowin. Though his language skills were not impressive, Jane Johnston's were: she was known as a talented writer and storyteller in both Ojibwemowin and English. Jane and her family translated hundreds of Ojibwe stories for English readers. Until this time, not many Europeans took Native culture seriously; they'd long assumed that Indians, along with other colonized peoples, had no culture worth comparing with the accomplishments of Western civilization. Knowledge in translation came from missionaries trying to convert Native people, from the US Army's efforts to control and exterminate them, and from the French fur traders who lived among the Indigenous nations of the Great Lakes region. Most white Americans heard only lurid tales of tomahawks and scalping and saw stereotypes of noble savages such as Pocahontas depicted in popular plays. On stage, the "Indian princess" converted to Christianity, saved John Smith from her savage tribesmen, and declared Europeans the rightful inheritors of the land, relieving the audience of any unconscious guilt they may have felt for a century of broken treaties.

As these tropes became ubiquitous in the 1830s, the public, and government officials, craved more substantive insight about the "Indian mind," part of an ongoing effort to catalog racial differences and determine whether the Indigenous population could be "civilized." Paradoxically, such inquiries also tried to claim presumed Indian qualities as fundamentally American ones, inherited by white people as if courage or loyalty came with the land itself. One British writer credited "the psychological influences impressed on the soil, atmosphere, and objects of the country by its former inhabitants."

Schoolcraft promised a scientific portrait of the Indian mind from firsthand observation, though this portrait was carefully crafted to please its white audience, rather than its Native subjects. "As we have no architectural ruins in our landscape," he explained to Jane, "we must take the Indian Character for our fallen columns and our encrusted medals." He's still remembered today as one of the earliest North American folklorists and ethnographers. His timing was ideal: the serious study of "popular antiquities," what came to be known as folklore, was just catching on among leading European scholars and spreading to the United States.

When the brothers Jacob and Wilhelm Grimm began collecting their famous German fairy tales in the early nineteenth century, it was far from children's play. Romantic philosophers saw folklore as the organic basis of national identity, the authentic heritage that united a particular population. This was a convenient way of justifying the newly drawn political boundaries of Europe in an age of revolutions, as monarchies lost their divine claim to legitimacy. This fad for "traditional ways" marked the beginnings of the nationalism that would fuel the cataclysmic European wars of the twentieth century. By the 1930s, the scientific doctrine that each race has essential moral and mental attributes that stretch back to its earliest history became a rationale for Nazi genocide. However, in the 1830s, the scholarly rediscovery—some would say creation—of national cultures was a nascent project where Schoolcraft might carve a place for himself.

Tracing their collective identity back to age-old folk traditions presented an obvious challenge for the white US population. Schoolcraft offered an ingenious solution: first he "discovered" Native folklore, then he made it white. His ethnological writings constructed an image of the brave, loyal, and family-centered Indian as a model for US national identity, an identity rooted in the New World. Like many of his contemporaries, Schoolcraft urged Americans to reject European moral decadence and embrace these homegrown virtues, transmuting stereotypes of Natives into white nativism. At the same time, he maintained that congenital defects in "the Indian mind," such as a lack of self-control, erratic emotions, and poor judgment, slated Indians for eventual replacement by whites. Of Ojibwe song, he warned "not to call these wild exhibitions of passion . . . by the formal terms of poetry and music." Only a white interpreter could extract the durable value from such ephemeral matter. A rugged class of Europeans had come to the New World who shared a spiritual kinship with these Schoolcraft Indians—indeed, their duty was to take the torch from their predecessors and fulfill the noble destiny that Indians never could.

Public interest in Schoolcraft's work was sharpened by political concerns of the moment. Andrew Jackson's Indian Removal Act of 1830 forced tens of thousands of Native people to die or subsist on government rations in the unfamiliar territories west of the Mississippi. Newspaper editorials fretted over the "Indian problem"—as thousands of displaced people starved, the government waffled on whether it had any responsibility for their fate. The question, in all its odious variations, boiled down to whether Native people could become good Christian citizens or whether they were doomed to extinction. The answer could only come from a yet-to-be-born science of colonial management able to diagnose how culture determines human nature, and vice versa—the early version of anthropology that Schoolcraft proffered.

Given the urgent situation, his wares should have been an easy sell. He certainly published many books and secured federal funding for research. However, Schoolcraft's disagreeable personality and tedious prose, plus a tendency to play fast and loose with facts, meant that his position was always precarious, financially and in the scientific community. His influence on US culture came by way of the well-known authors who pirated his material, most famously Henry Wadsworth Longfellow in *The Song of Hiawatha*, which drew heavily on Schoolcraft's 1839 *Algic Researches*. (Schoolcraft often coined words in the hope of sounding educated; *Algic* was his pseudo-Latin term for Algonquin-speaking Indians.) Indeed, Schoolcraft encouraged popular writers to produce a stream of faux-Indian tales inspired by his work, helping white Americans feel an intimate connection with the Indigenous people upon whom their country waged war.

Serving as a resource for others was not a satisfactory endgame for a man struggling to put cash in his pockets. During the 1830s and '40s, Schoolcraft tried to defend his personal monopoly as the authority on Indian culture. The extraction mindset of his lead-mining days carried over into his view of the Ojibwe—he spoke of them with the proprietary air of a discoverer. He believed that he had a right to profit from his discovery, that the nation owed him literary fame, scientific renown, and political power.

In the spring of 1842, Schoolcraft crossed the Atlantic for the next strategic move in his career as an Indian expert. Things weren't going well in the Michigan Territory—he had served the Democratic Party of Andrew Jackson for more than a decade and immediately lost his job when the Whig Party took over the White House in 1841. He would have to parlay his experience into book deals, research money, or an academic post. Schoolcraft sailed for England to court Europe's scientific elite and secure an overseas publisher for his work. Relatively unknown there, he hustled his way to an audience with various scholarly societies. His bluster masked a desperate insecurity—as usual, beneath his veneer of gentility, he was going deeper into debt every day. He worried that his Ojibwe legends wouldn't impress the learned scientific gentlemen—that they would see him for what he was, a self-taught frontier bureaucrat hopelessly out of touch with real scholarship.

To prepare the ground for his arrival, Schoolcraft had sent a raft of letters to these scientific gentlemen promoting his work. He made a fateful decision to bill himself as an expert on the pictographs that Native people inscribed on rock faces and artifacts throughout North America. These reflect diverse, continuous histories of Indigenous literary production—as Louise Erdrich puts it, "People have probably been writing books in North America since at least 2000 BC"—diminished because they did not support the case for Native savagery.

Schoolcraft hoped that a pictograph would stoke the interest of European antiquarians still elated by their triumph over the Rosetta Stone in 1822. That first-ever translation of Egyptian hieroglyphics set off a frenzy for ancient languages, the study of which was known as philology. In their evolutionary ladder, philologists ranked pictographs lowest, followed by hieroglyphics, and then by the highest achievement of an alphabet. Along with this philological frenzy

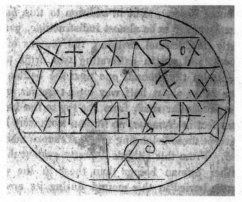

The first published drawing of the Grave Creek stone, submitted by Thomas Townsend in 1839.

came a rash of hoaxes. The mania was so prevalent that, in 1838, Edgar Allan Poe and Charles Dickens both published novels featuring the discovery of supposedly ancient inscriptions carved in stone. The Grave Creek Mound was opened that same year, and Schoolcraft took careful notice of the reports. The news from Elizabethtown, Virginia, briefly mentioned a mysterious stone discovered in the mound, the unheralded prize of Abelard Tomlinson's excavation.

This object was a flat, palm-size tablet made of local sandstone, carved with twenty-four angular symbols. The stone's discovery in 1838 was marked by a few unusual circumstances. Strangely, the witnesses disagreed on who found it and where. If someone planted the stone as a hoax, however, it would not behoove the people of Elizabethtown to squeal; many had chipped in money for Abelard Tomlinson's dig, hoping to profit from buried treasure. Personal letters reveal that Dr. James W. Clemens, who did the fundraising, was most likely the creator of the inscribed stone and tried to promote it as a Mound Builder relic without initial success. His former medical partner, Thomas Townsend, published a report of the dig in the Cincinnati papers that included a sketch of the stone, but did not link the artifact to any lost race; he was rather emphatic that Native people had built the mound. He merely noted that these "hieroglyphics" showed "considerable advancement in the progress of society," for it was well-known that present-day Indians lacked such writing systems.

Clemens's hoax might have been lost to history had it not spoken to Henry Rowe Schoolcraft in his moment of need. Remembering the artifact from Townsend's newspaper sketch, Schoolcraft wrote up a report on the Grave Creek stone and sent it to the prestigious Royal Geographical Society in advance of his visit to London. He confidently translated the inscription as an Indian pictograph meaning "death from an arrow," a grave marker for the warrior whose bones rested inside the mound. Anishinaabe people of the Michigan Territory recorded histories, songs, and messages in pictographic writing on birchbark scrolls and on rock faces. After living with them for almost twenty years, in a region full of Native earthworks, Schoolcraft had no reason to doubt that the Grave Creek mound and stone were made by Indians, rather than a mythical lost race.

The Royal Geographical Society leaped upon this amazing find. They quickly brushed aside Schoolcraft's pictographic translation, however. Instead, they spotted various ancient Indo-European alphabets on the stone, upgrading it to what they considered the most culturally superior type of writing. They followed the diffusionist logic that every alphabet had to trace back to one central wellspring of civilization; reconstructing that lineage was the philologists' dream. Their obsession with finding a single origin for written language ran deeper than Schoolcraft had anticipated. It might just require a ship full of lost Celts to wash up in Virginia in 500 BCE.

Thanks to Schoolcraft, the Grave Creek stone's image made the reverse journey across the Atlantic, spreading from London to Danish and German scientific societies. The Danish were especially keen for any evidence that Vikings had discovered America in ancient times. As Schoolcraft toured Europe in the spring of 1842, he exchanged a flurry of letters with philologists who identified the stone as Phoenician, Celtic, or runic—an antiquarian free-for-all. Most agreed that it marked the shocking appearance of an Old World alphabet in America, centuries before Columbus. Schoolcraft had clearly lost control of the narrative. He would take urgent measures to reclaim it as his own ingenious discovery.

"As I am thinking . . .
My land"

While Henry Schoolcraft courted London's scientific royalty in 1842, his wife's precarious health took a sudden turn for the worse. After taxing journeys from Michigan to New York to Ontario, she would not return again to her home in the Sault. Her fate strangely mirrored that of the Grave Creek stone: both woman and stone were cast as mysterious objects that Henry claimed exclusive authority to interpret and profit from. Yet they were also opposites: the stone's seductive silence lured him deeper into the trap of his own ambition. Unlike the inanimate stone, Bamewawagezhikaquay, Jane Johnston Schoolcraft, used her voice vigorously, in poetry, letters, and stories. These writings outlived her husband's agenda, speaking to later generations of Native poets and readers with all the richness of her experience at a pivotal moment in Anishinaabe history.

During Jane's youth in an Ojibwe and Scots-Irish household, she happily embraced her Ojibwe identity, but over time she came to see herself through Henry's critical eyes. Though he idealized her at first, when the age of Andrew Jackson dawned, Henry's view of Jane shifted with the political winds. He made her into a symbol of the "Indian problem"—the colonizer's dilemma over whether people with Indigenous blood could ever be "civilized." Even while he depended on Jane's knowledge and connections, he knew that the answer his superiors wanted to hear was no.

Henry's consuming anxiety over this question was especially confounding to Jane because she grew up in a society where race was far more complicated than black, or red, and white. Born in 1800, Jane was a product of the "middle ground," an era in the upper Midwest before US rule extended across the Great Lakes and west of the Mississippi. In the 1700s, a unique society arose among French and British settlers and Native people whose lives converged around the fur trade. The powerful fur companies that dictated colonial policy in the heart of the continent wanted pelts rather than territory, and they depended on Native knowledge, labor, and political savvy. European fur traders, many of them young men who'd migrated four thousand miles from home, saw that they had arrived in an Indian world and chose to adapt.

Some courted Native women in what they crudely termed "the custom of the country," leaving unofficial wives and children behind when business took them elsewhere. Others married into Native families, forming alliances that carried on for generations. The children of these marriages were called métis—"mixed"—and played crucial roles managing relations between fur companies, colonial governments, and Native leaders. It was no peaceable kingdom; Europeans were there to extract wealth, and they did so with deceit and violence. Métis families such as the Johnstons enjoyed privileges that full-blooded Indians did not. But at that point a different path, a hybrid society that recognized Indigenous autonomy, was possible. Some Native nations believed they could incorporate Europeans

A drawing of Jane Johnston
Schoolcraft by an unknown artist,
possibly from a trip to New York
in 1825.

into their political and social order. US leaders chose not to take this path. Jane's story is a story of the middle ground's demise.

Jane's grandfather was a respected Ojibwe war chief named Waubojeeg. One summer in the early 1790s, Scotch-Irish fur trader John Johnston reached Waubojeeg's village on Lake Superior. Not long after arriving, Johnston asked to marry Waubojeeg's daughter, Ozhaguscodaywayquay. Waubojeeg was skeptical of the trader's motives and told him to come back in a year. During his travels that winter, Johnston proved his goodwill by sharing scarce food with Waubojeeg's relatives. When Johnston returned, Ozhaguscodaywayquay, seemingly without her consent, became Susan Johnston—at least, to the white world. The couple moved to Sault Ste. Marie, a nerve center of Ojibwe life, where they built the largest house in town and established themselves as its leading family.

Though Ozhaguscodaywayquay had not chosen the marriage, she was well prepared to build a successful business with her new husband, quickly mastering the financial as well as the social ropes of the fur trade. She advised male Ojibwe chiefs on the shifting political situation while carrying on traditional industries, harvesting up to two tons of maple syrup every spring. In the midst of this work she raised eight children. Ozhaguscodaywayquay and John Johnston named their third child Bamewawagezhikaquay, which they translated as "Woman of the Sound the Stars Make Rushing Through the Sky." In English, she was Jane.

Sault Ste. Marie, known as the Sault, was a vivid microcosm of the middle ground, sitting on the only water route between Lake Superior and the lower Great Lakes. Thousands of Ojibwe people, from dozens of far-flung bands with distinctive traditions and leadership, converged there in the summers to fish and hold festivals, while the population dwindled to less than two hundred in the bitter winters. The evergreen landscape infuses Jane's poems—pine trees, wildflowers, "rocks and skies and waters blue." Ozhaguscodaywayquay taught Jane how this natural beauty was entwined with her people's history. At the same time, John Johnston stocked his house with an English and French library. He taught all his children to read and write and was especially intent on teaching Jane European manners.

In the Sault manners counted for a lot: they differentiated the lower-class children of trappers from those such as the Johnstons who moved in white high society, hosting prominent visitors from the East. The town made much of Jane's brief visit to Ireland and England in 1809, which gained her the prestige of a foreign education, though she hardly had time to attend school. She preferred her home country to the gloom of the British Isles. She had everything she needed in the Sault; with free range of her father's library, she studied Shakespeare and Milton, Keats and Wordsworth under his guidance. This study had a purpose; John Johnston was preparing her to marry an educated, powerful white man.

The War of 1812 shattered the balance of the middle ground, as the once-porous border between the United States and British Canada became a battlefield. John Johnston joined many Ojibwe leaders in siding with the British, who, like the French, seemed willing to make alliances with Native nations rather than dominate them and take their land. American soldiers, advancing west, plundered the Johnstons' home and warehouse in retaliation. While Britain had promised to negotiate a peace agreement in the interests of its Native allies, at the close of the war the Ojibwe were "abandoned at their utmost need, and about to be immolated on the altar of American vengeance," according to a British commander.

The victorious US army occupied Sault Ste. Marie in 1820, on a mission to keep out British influence and punish sympathizers. They demanded that Ojibwe leaders give up land for a military outpost. The leaders refused and prepared to fight off the invasion, but Ozhaguscodaywayquay advised them not to risk another war, which they could not win. Twenty-year-old Jane Johnston listened as her mother persuaded the chiefs to compromise for the sake of peace. The Ojibwe negotiated a treaty that preserved their "ancient encamping and burial-ground" from any disturbance. Only a few years later, though, US Army surgeons at the fort were systematically robbing Native bodies from the burial ground, causing horror and outrage among Ojibwe residents. The remains were likely sent to Philadelphia, to the skull collection of Samuel G. Morton, who was at work on his opus of race science, *Crania Americana*. Army surgeons in the western territories were his main source of material.

The Ojibwe of the Sault had little recourse. Authority was confusingly divided between the commander of the fort and the agent of the Indian Bureau. Both reported to the US Department of War; beneath a veneer of diplomacy, Native nations would be treated as captive enemies. As of 1822, the first Indian Bureau agent at the Sault was Henry Rowe Schoolcraft. He was supposed to keep the peace, distribute government annuities, and regulate the fur trade while the army pursued its objectives—to "mildly but firmly" impose US rule.

Schoolcraft denounced the grave robbing as sacrilegious, "an atrocious crime," and wrote to his superiors demanding that the soldiers he accused be discharged. He had no jurisdiction and his requests were ignored. However, he happily covered for the crime's real instigator—the army surgeon Dr. Pitcher, whom Schoolcraft regarded as a gentleman and a fellow man of science. Schoolcraft's loyalties usually broke along these lines: the noble purposes of science took priority over Indian relations. Indeed, Indian relations were a means to that end.

Henry's arrival as the Indian agent at Sault Ste. Marie heralded the closing of the middle ground and the advent of American empire, with its rigid racial hierarchies that had no place for "half-breeds" like Jane Johnston. Yet when Henry first appeared, that impoverished fate lay in the future. He found a thriving culture in the Sault and quickly succumbed to its charms. He'd spent his youth striving and failing and saw the Indian Bureau as his last chance for a respectable career. If that meant living in exile from the great centers of scientific and cultural prestige, he would have to adapt like generations of young white men had adapted before him. His first stop when he got to Sault Ste. Marie was the house of its leading citizen, John Johnston.

Despite the Johnston's British allegiance, both Ozhaguscoday-wayquay and John saw the way the winds were blowing and determined to continue their political influence under the US regime. They invited the new agent to move in with them while American soldiers built his quarters nearby. The Johnstons were used to making strategic compromises—compromise was necessary for peaceful coexistence on the middle ground, though the Americans quickly undermined this custom with repeated betrayals. Henry impressed the literary Johnstons with his intellect, regaling them with stories of scientific adventure. And he immediately noticed the oldest daughter Jane's "refined manners and education."

Historian Robert Dale Parker, who brought Jane's writing to the attention of scholars in the late 1990s, observes that Jane was local nobility, raised to marry a man like Henry, and Henry was an insecure social climber who needed a guide to his unfamiliar new world. "Each of them," writes Parker, "must have looked like the other's best chance." They also fell deeply and earnestly in love. They traded lines from *A Midsummer Night's Dream* and penned sappy sonnets. In a town of fur trappers and soldiers, they felt like two poets in the wilderness, clearly meant for each other.

Jane and Henry married in 1823, and the Johnstons built a new wing on their house for the couple; within a year, Jane gave birth to her first child. Their marriage shored up Henry's wobbly political authority. It also opened a tempestuous spiritual communion that only one of them would survive. They both subscribed to the Romantic ideals of the day, which held that man and wife should feel perfect, harmonious sympathy with each other. Over time, their intimacy revealed deep-seated differences that Henry saw as moral failings. In the beginning, however, he was full of love and admiration for his graceful, talented wife. During his frequent travels to treaty conferences, they exchanged pining verses. "When Henry strays far from my sight," Jane rhymed, "Stranger am I to all delight."

Henry's business came to a halt during the winter, when heavy snow and subzero temperatures battered the Sault. Families relied on storytelling to get through this dreary season, and in 1826, the literary Schoolcrafts decided to put their stories to paper. They started a handwritten magazine that they called *The Muzzeniegun, or Literary Voyager*, combining the Ojibwemowin word for "book" with an image of the French voyageurs who plied the rivers of the upper Midwest trading for furs. The *Voyager* began as a pastime for its authors during long evenings cooped up indoors, but Henry circulated it to officials in Detroit and New York to show off his scholarly activity. Jane and her family translated Ojibwe tales into English, while Henry and Jane added poems, histories, and essays. Henry and Jane did most of the writing. Their process was intimate and collaborative; each page reveals their distinctive scripts in lively conversation. As much as their words and ideas intertwined, they also diverged in crucial ways.

On those pages are the seeds of difference that would blossom into alienation. Draft copies of the *Voyager* contain a tangle of erasure and overwriting, as Henry's pen crossed out and replaced Jane's words, twisting her ideas. She struck back, explained her thinking—but many of her lines are literally scratched over, so that we don't know what she wanted to say. Their disagreements may seem subtle, often a matter of nuances in translation. Henry was hyperattentive to such nuances, both in writing and in behavior, which made him doubt whether he and his wife were truly in perfect sympathy. Since he couldn't possibly be wrong, such deviations suggested that Jane had a problem—most likely, an Indian problem.

Undated engraving of Henry Rowe Schoolcraft.

In one essay, Jane decided to debunk a common white assertion—the claim that Indians had no word for God. This implied that the Indian race was incapable of true Christian faith, a notion that her husband, Henry, was beginning to wrestle with as he questioned his wife's piety. Jane explained that the Cherokee name for God, "or the great being above, is Ga-lun-lak-ti-a-hi"; the Cherokee and many other tribes, she stated, believed in a "supreme spirit." Like other Native Christians in her time, Jane may have fit together her Protestant and Ojibwe beliefs in this way. Though she wrote in a light style, it was clearly a sensitive subject. Henry crossed out parts of her text and changed the argument. Instead of asserting that the Cherokee had a concept of God, the final version states that the Cherokee had words for spirits, "but their spirits are destitute of holiness."

This was not her point at all; Jane suggested that Native religions shared a concept of the sacred with Christianity, and they could meet on this middle ground. Henry saw no middle ground, only Christians bringing the true faith to spiritually "destitute" savages. Perhaps Jane, like other Indians, was congenitally unable to understand this distinction, which called for the total repudiation of their former heathen ways. He became increasingly fixated on his wife's supposed racial traits. Jane's trouble increased after their first child, Willie, died at age three of a sudden illness in March 1827. Both parents were devastated, but Henry's grief turned into suspicion of Jane: God had punished them for her lack of faith. Or perhaps God condemned their interracial marriage because no Indian could become a true Christian.

When the ice melted in spring, Henry traveled to an endless series of war councils and treaty negotiations that marked this period of aggressive Indian removal. His job was to slowly, methodically drive Indigenous people out of the Michigan Territory. In 1836, he would oversee the Treaty of Washington, in which the United States took more than thirteen million acres from Ojibwe and Odawa nations, almost 40 percent of present-day Michigan; at the same time, Henry was speculating on land and had a financial interest in the treaty. Jane waited at home, worried about his safety and burdened with domestic duties; his infrequent letters were no longer romantic but terse, focused on his career, household logistics, and expressions of religious piety.

Despite these fissures, the Schoolcrafts worked together closely and had two more children. They cycled through the intimate, isolated winters and summers of separation. Jane continued to write poems, in English and Ojibwemowin, which Henry sometimes edited and sent to their friends as though showing off her sophistication. Though Henry was proud of her poetry, Jane declined opportunities to publish. Her reasons were complicated. At times she subtly mocked Henry's gender ideals, which included female modesty and avoiding public attention—but she also believed in them and found satisfaction in her way of writing. In domestic matters, she faced Henry's judgment when she asserted her needs. "It is the order of Providence that man should be active, and woman quiescent," Henry wrote from a council meeting in Detroit. "If it is pleasing to you—it is pleasing to me," Jane replied, perhaps with a barely detectable edge of sarcasm, "& I must learn that great virtue of a woman—quiescence."

The *Literary Voyager*, along with other writings he collected from the Sault in the 1820s and '30s, served as source material for the rest of Henry's career. Jane and her community were not merely the subjects of a pioneering ethnologist; they actively collected, translated, and edited the Ojibwe stories that he published under his name. When Henry secured a publisher for his first collection of Indian tales, *Algic Researches*, in 1838, he rejoiced at a major step forward in his scientific career. A man relying on the labor of his uncredited wife was not exceptional in the literary world, and Jane's role was no secret in their social circles. He wrote to her that the book "will bring you up to notice," and urged her to "enrich and encrease my stock of material." Meanwhile, Jane walked a harrowing tightrope, holding on to her Ojibwe identity while trying meet her husband's expectations of white, Christian motherhood. Jane's health had always been precarious; she suffered from coughing fits and was sometimes unable to leave her room for weeks at a time. Under the care of local doctors she became addicted to laudanum, an opium tincture widely prescribed to women with "nervous" ailments.

The stories of the Johnston family and their Ojibwe community, which Henry edited and repackaged over the years under various titles with only moderate commercial success, achieved celebrity in 1855 by way of Longfellow's blockbuster poem *The Song of Hiawatha*. This epic romance spawned a revival of noble-savage-themed plays, songs, and merchandise; more than a hundred towns and geographic features across North America were named directly after characters from the poem. As a result, bits of the Schoolcraft corpus circulated in countless magazines and newspapers, often unattributed, in the omnivorous custom of the nineteenth-century press.

Though it achieved popular recognition, the work's scholarly value was soon cast into doubt by the small but growing community of ethnologists who studied Native languages and customs. Henry claimed to be their progenitor, but was he one of them at all? He never became proficient in Ojibwemowin and depended on the Johnstons for translation. His critics complained, first, that the Johnstons "Europeanized" their stories to please Henry. An esteemed German philologist urged him to "reduce that dress again to the simple children's language of a tale . . . abrupt and unconnected."

This ideal of an "authentic" Native, innocent and timeless, clashes with the Ojibwe practice in which stories vary with the teller and setting. The correspondence of the Johnston family shows various members intentionally cleaning up stories for consumption by outsiders, cutting ribald jokes and clarifying the morals, but also curating what they judged to be the best examples of their traditions. Much subsequent anthropology produced under academic auspices came about in similar ways, through unequal and uncredited collaborations where subjects consciously shaped how they would be represented. The second, undisputable criticism is that Henry rewrote stories and fabricated anecdoes to craft an image of the Indian that *he* believed would appeal to white readers. This Schoolcraft Indian also demonstrated his theories about the minds and morals of Indigenous people. He peddled this newly discovered Indian culture to the reading public as entertainment, and to the Indian Bureau as science.

Jane Johnston Schoolcraft did not seek literary renown, and, like many women of her time, devoted much intellectual energy to her husband's work. When she did write for herself, she used the sentimental verse common to the English poets who filled her library. It was customary to write for small audiences of friends and family, on approved topics such as religion, motherhood, nature, and love. The world she spoke into being through these verses was still undeniably hers, the world of the middle ground. She addressed Ojibwe culture and history as worthy topics in their own right, while also commenting on the painful incursion of US empire. A poem praising the restorative beauty of nature ends with the pointed assertion that nature makes "no laws to treat my people ill." Jane knew where those laws came from—they came from Washington, by way of her husband, and she wrote this line after they surveyed the Ojibwe lands taken in the 1836 treaty. Henry, however, mistook white domination for a law of nature. As her editor, perhaps he saw such expressions as nostalgia for a lost Native past, yet they are equally moral claims about the present.

While Henry and many other scholars saw history as a sequence of violent ruptures that left behind only ruins and artifacts, Jane spoke Ojibwemowin with her children and, raising them in a household filled with the telling and writing of stories, believed that her world would survive into the future. She had no reason to suspect, when she married Henry, that he or anyone else would come to advocate the forced and total extinction of Native culture. After leaving her son and daughter at East Coast boarding schools in 1839, she wrote a short poem in Ojibwemowin. The rhyming translation that Henry published is full of flowery Christian sentiments: "duty commands me, and duty must sway." A new translation, created by Anishinaabe language teachers Dennis Jones, James Vukelich, and Heidi Kiiwetinepinesiik Stark, interprets her words with stark immediacy:

As I am thinking
When I find you
My land
Far in the west
My land

My little daughter
My little son
I leave them behind
Far away land

[emphatically] But soon
It is close however
To my home I shall return
That is the way that I am, my being
My land

My land
To my home I shall return
I begin to make my way home
Ahh but I am sad

"I know it is for their good," Jane wrote half-heartedly about sending her children away. She delivered them to respectable white boarding schools, not the abusive government- and church-run boarding schools established in the years that followed, which aimed to "kill the Indian, and save the man." Both Henry and Jane were status conscious and wanted to instill in their offspring the particular manners required for elite East Coast social life. But Henry also embraced the utility of boarding school to break the chain of cultural transmission represented by Jane's mother, Ozhaguscodaywayquay, a keeper of her nation's stories, who preferred Ojibwemowin to English, whose words Jane recorded and translated, and which Henry sold.

Here is the trap of text and translation: Ozhaguscodaywayquay's traditions, written down in a book, could reach a wide audience.

She and her family had good reasons to share them, making the case for the value of their culture and securing it against an unknown future. Government officials, scholars, and ordinary readers thirsted for this authentic knowledge. But it was too dangerous for Ozhaguscodaywayquay's grandchildren, whom she often cared for when Jane was ill. This is what anthropologists meant, in later years, when they promised to "salvage" Indigenous cultures by recording their beliefs, songs, and rituals to store in archives. With a touch of melancholy, they felt that it was correct and necessary for these cultures to vanish so the next generation could escape their ancestors' backwardness and join modern society. What Ozhaguscodaywayquay told, however, was not meant to sleep in an archive. It depended on the land for its meaning: the place where it was spoken, the relations of the people listening, were part of the history.

When Jane wrote about her love of her native land, she referenced the English landscape poetry of Goldsmith, Pope, and Byron. She also voiced her Ojibwe relation to land as more than a symbol or source of beauty, but as the thing that constituted herself, her family, and her people. "As I am thinking / When I find you / My land" binds the very act of thought into the land. While in Henry's free translation the speaker identifies most strongly as a mother of children, "the dear jewels I love," in this reading by present-day Ojibwemowin speakers she resolutely identifies herself with her home: "That is the way that I am, my being / My land."

The doubling of English and Ojibwemowin meanings and references was another way of sending her ideas forward into a changing world, where future kin might interpret them. Jane's usefulness to Henry ensured that letters, drafts, and fragments of her words would survive in the archives. Theater historian and artist Shannon Epplett, a member of the Sault Ste. Marie Tribe of Chippewa Indians, uses the "competing and sometimes contradictory" archival accounts of Jane in a performance piece that connects her life's west-to-east journey with the east-to-west course of the Anishinaabe migration story. Ojibwemowin speakers can appreciate the full dimensions of her poems in that language; even within the limits of English, new translations evoke a way of thinking that Henry did not grasp. The pieces of Jane's work that Henry saved in overstuffed files were digitized and, as bits of data on the internet, beamed to glowing screens around the world. They can give today's readers an idea of the obligations of living on this land and give Ojibwe writers such as Heid E. Erdrich a "literary ancestor with whom I can identify as a woman, as an Ojibwe with a euro-American father, and as a poet."

At least, in Michigan, Jane had her relatives and the land that was so essential to her being. However, even this slipped away in the election of 1840, when the victorious Whig Party swept Henry Schoolcraft's Democratic patrons out of office. There was no one to protect him from mounting allegations of corruption, related to self-dealing and his general ineptness with money. He was fired from what everyone thought was a secure lifetime post, though the Indian Bureau only became rottener in the years after his departure. He decided to strike out on his own as an Indian expert and returned to the East Coast to seek the renown he desired.

In New York City Jane was reunited with her children, while Henry frenetically attended the meetings of scientific societies. A member of that period's New York literary scene called them "celebrities," remarking on Jane's "vivacity and taste." Yet they were living on credit, and Jane suffered worsening bouts of illness, possibly related to her laudanum addiction. There was no hope of her enduring the arduous trip across the Atlantic, so when Henry set off on his conquest of scientific London in 1842, Jane went to her sister's house in Ontario. One day, soon after Jane's arrival, her sister found her seated upright in a chair, dead.

The letter that Henry wrote to their daughter in boarding school after Jane's unexpected death is painful to read. It begins with a kind of blameful apology: "Reflect, that your mother herself, had not the advantages of a mother (in the refined sense of the term) to bring her up." He can't quite seem to summon authentic grief. "Her taste in literature was chaste," he says by way of praise. "She wrote many pretty pieces, which I have carefully treasured." Henry did treasure Jane's writing; he obsessively archived every piece of paper that passed through his hands. Her words would become especially valuable during the decades to come when Henry worked and reworked his collection of Indian material into thousand-page tomes. Even in life, however, he had treated Jane and her community as silent objects to interpret before the white scientific world. He had her gravestone inscribed JANE, WIFE OF HENRY R. SCHOOLCRAFT, ESQ., leaving off her Ojibwe name, Bamewawagezhikaquay. "Her name splits," writes the poet Heid E. Erdrich, "eclipsed by his." Just when Jane could no longer sustain herself in this painful state, a new object appeared that promised Henry a similar bounty of interpretation.

The news of Jane's death did little to slow Henry's momentum with regard to the Grave Creek stone. He got swept up in the zeal of the English antiquarians, who insisted that the stone was European rather than Native American in origin, in part because of his own changing attitudes about race, religion, and history. He took an increasingly negative view of Native people: Jane was too unruly and passionate, he decided, because of her Ojibwe blood, and the tribal leaders he met as an Indian agent were also irrational, refusing to cooperate with the theft of their land—which, in Schoolcraft's mind, was in their best interest. Though he based his scientific career on his experience in the Michigan Territory, he only went back twice, for his corruption trial in Detroit. In his personal and intellectual life, the Native world was relegated to a static past. Texts and artifacts proved much more compliant with his vision. Like his other enterprises, though, Schoolcraft's effort to make a gold mine out of the Grave Creek stone would end in personal frustration.

In 1842, when British antiquarians identified the stone as Hebrew, Celtic, or Phoenician, Schoolcraft realized that these revered languages held the key to prestige, not just for himself, but for all of prehistoric North America, which might finally "address posterity in an articulate voice." Though he had originally described the stone as an Indian pictograph, he seized on the ancient-alphabets notion and published his own analysis, trying to stay in control of the narrative. It now provided "data of the highest moment, respecting the early visits of European nations to this continent." After the Danish antiquarian society trumpeted his discovery in the press, he favored their theory that the stone contained "ancient Druidical Runes." Though he never explicitly claimed that a white civilization built the mound itself, Schoolcraft saw that the lost-race myth had undeniable popular and scholarly appeal.

Top North American archaeologists, led by Smithsonian surveyor Ephraim George Squier, attacked Schoolcraft's speculative linguistics and dismissed the stone as an obvious fraud. Schoolcraft returned from Europe charged with defending his scientific reputation. He traveled to Elizabethtown in 1843, where he visited Tomlinson's dismal, "damp and acrid" tourist trap inside the mound, choking on the thick smoke of tallow candles. He was allowed to borrow the stone and take it to his hotel room, where he made a copy in wax.

The newspaper sketch he had distributed all over Europe turned out to be incorrect, but he recovered from this embarrassing flub by digging in deeper to the charade. As soon as he saw the stone in person, Schoolcraft claimed to recognize "nearly perfect resemblances" with Anglo-Saxon and the Celtiberic letters of the Norse Vikings. There could be no history or literature without written language, as far as European scholars were concerned, and in their eyes ancient North America had neither of these assets. The Grave Creek stone, declared Schoolcraft, "elevates the history of the Mound Period to a branch of literature." The site also impressed him deeply: "The mound itself is an irrecusable witness" to the work of a lost race. Squier, the preeminent archaeologist of the mounds, became Schoolcraft's sworn enemy, launching a decades-long controversy that would plague later academics desperate to put lost-race fantasies to rest.

Much like *Algic Researches*, and like the Schoolcrafts' marriage, the Grave Creek inscription reveals a pattern of colonial thinking that simultaneously seeks out, appropriates, and erases Native voices, replacing them with an echo of the listener's voice. Schoolcraft grasped an essential truth of showmanship—that people encounter the unknown through their prior ideologies and assumptions. His deep investment in the Grave Creek stone looks like a kind of power madness, a desire to capture "the great unknown void of our aboriginal history" alongside the lands of the West.

On some level, he may have known it was a hoax; an epidemic

of archaeological fakes was raging by the 1840s, and Schoolcraft himself cast doubt on a supposed Native American text called the *Walum Olum*. But the point of that debunking was that Indigenous people had no alphabet or history. The next step was to recover an ancient white history that Euro-Americans would intuitively recognize as their own. The crucial thing was that it didn't have to be true—merely possible, believable, and persistent. His audience was like the reader of *Algoonah* who, "wishing the story were true . . . at the end adopts it as a truth." Schoolcraft later revised his opinion of the Grave Creek mound, adopting the theory of his rival, Squier, who attributed it to the Toltecan race from Central America, which was, in turn, speculatively linked with a European transatlantic migration. The thread of a lost superior civilization remained intact, flexible, and adaptive to the demands of the moment.

Schoolcraft was not a crusader but an opportunist and readily contradicted himself. Most remarkably, he continually republished an anecdote he invented about an "aged Cherokee chief" touring Tomlinson's museum inside the Grave Creek mound. According to Schoolcraft, the chief became "so indignant at the desecration and display of sepulchral secrets" that he brandished a knife in fury and later "was found prostrated, with his senses steeped in the influence of alcohol." This bears all the marks of pedestrian fiction, and no such story appears in the issue of a local newspaper that he cites as his source. The furious chief is a Schoolcraft Indian, passionate and doomed to self-destruct. Such Indians were profitable for popular writers, so Schoolcraft could afford to casually suggest that the great mound held the ancestors of living Cherokee people. He concluded with a curse on white people in the imaginary chief's voice: "Tis not enough! that hated race / should hunt us out, from grove and place . . . / But they must ope our very graves / To tell the dead—they too, are slaves." While entirely accurate, perhaps among the truest things Schoolcraft ever wrote, this tragic sentiment was a generic stock-in-trade. Indian laments and curses flowed from white pens at high velocity in the Jacksonian era. They reflect neither naivete nor repentance, but a cold calculation of what can be taken with enough force.

Seeming contradictions could serve the hierarchy of races perfectly well. Schoolcraft worked to build up "a branch of literature" capacious enough for noble savages and extinct Mound Builders, who were possibly related through the same "racial mixing" so common in Sault Ste. Marie—the replacement of an indigenous population by invaders, as Schoolcraft well knew, involved a great degree of intimacy. Mixed-blood offspring were the tragic heroes of this literature. While, in the middle ground of the upper Midwest, they worked to maintain relations between Native people and settlers in the hope of establishing a sustainable shared world, there was (according to the tragic narrative) no place for them in a white American society obsessed with racial purity.

Henry Schoolcraft's second wife, Mary Howard, epitomized that obsession. From a family of South Carolina slaveholders, Mary referred to Jane as "his Pocahontas wife" and their children as a "dangerous amalgamation of races." In Mary's assessment, the "fixed laws of moral deterioration" dictated the outcome of this "suicidal experiment" for the unfortunate offspring. Henry married her quietly in 1847, leaving the Schoolcraft children, Johnny, seventeen, and Janee, twenty, to flee in the face of Mary's truly evangelical white supremacy. Indians, however, were not lowest on the ladder of race science, and as Mary learned more about them from Henry's stories, she did not hesitate to put them to use.

Mary's true disdain was reserved for the "the savage negro," the subject of her 1860 pro-slavery novel *The Black Gauntlet*, which rehearsed all the era's most twisted arguments for the benevolence of keeping human chattel. There, Mary suggested that abolitionists attend to "the savage Indian in our own country, who is very superior to the blacks, and whose homes we have ruthlessly driven them from. . . . The sufferings of the poor famishing Indians, are ten thousand fold greater than a plantation slave has ever dreamed." As with Henry's lament of the Cherokee chief, this is not a contradiction, but a flexible reality that wraps around the predetermined order of things: sympathy with Indians is merely a literary effect. When Mary's half brother proposed marriage to Janee, Mary was prostrated with horror that her bloodline would be contaminated by "that hateful Indian race." Janee, who moved with her new husband to Richmond, Virginia, tried to revive family connections with her father and stepmother; they occasionally responded to her letters with a few cold formalities. Well aware of Mary's virulent racism, Janee attempted to sympathize. "You can have no idea what it is to live in the South now," she wrote after the Civil War, for "us poor conquered whites."

Despite his best efforts to serve God and empire, Henry's last decade passed under something like a curse. He suffered from progressive paralysis that froze his limbs in painful positions, until he, like Jane in her sickness, could not move from his bed. Unable to write, his voice was filtered through Mary's pen. He died in December 1864, and was buried in frozen ground. Mary wanted a better spot in the cemetery, so she had him disinterred a week later. She brought a photographer, opened the coffin, and took pictures with his corpse, a strange echo of the times when Henry had robbed Native graves for scientific collections. Mary, an adoring, servile, dogmatic wife, represented the curse of the fulfilled ideal. We don't know if he saw anything of Jane about his sickbed—except in his manuscript files. Perhaps he was haunted by the valise full of her writings that disappeared during her final journey from New York to Ontario.

Today's archaeologists have banished the sorry affair of the Grave Creek stone to the dustbin of pseudo-archaeology—frauds from the "bad old days" that they regard as safely in the past. Yet, as Jason Colavito's work makes clear, racially coded frauds and disingenuous mysteries are deeply embedded in popular culture, in television shows and Web forums that cultivate endless intrigue around lost races. They thrive in a world where "every thing may be conjectured, but nothing proved," as a proponent of the Mound Builders remarked wistfully in 1822. Even amid abundant proofs, conjecture is more profitable—it produces endless permutations of media content.

Rather than arguing on the terrain of lost-race theory, we need to understand how antiquarian debates over ancient mounds were part of the ongoing dispossession that Henry, through law and literature, helped perpetrate. We need to understand Jane Johnston Schoolcraft's world, in all of its richness and multiplicity, which

Henry consigned to an "unknown void." No two people, with their particular lives, can stand in for the sweeping forces of history, but it's tempting to read in Henry and Jane's marriage the vampiric core of anthropology, the original sin of cultural appropriation paired with political oppression.

They also shared a twenty-year working partnership that began with real affection, maybe even passion. Henry entered the middle ground with his ideas largely unformed and was welcomed as one who could become a good Ojibwe relative. "Such a fund of fictitious legendary matter is quite a discovery," he rejoiced in his early days of story collecting at Sault Ste. Marie. "Who could have imagined that these wandering foresters should have possessed such a resource?" Soon, Henry turned that resource to his own account, but it wasn't easy creating value from Native stories. He had to shape them into something that could serve power to gain power for himself—he would, for the purposes of colonial management, "lift up a curtain, as it were, upon the Indian mind." Two decades later he concluded, "As a race, there never was one more impracticable; more bent on a nameless principle of tribality; more averse to combinations for their general good; more deaf to the voice of instruction; more determined to pursue all the elements of their own destruction."

This dark alchemy is not a matter of one man's moral deficits, but rather a basic function of settler-colonial science. In the habit of molding his evidence to please white readers, rather than communicating the reality of his Indigenous relations, Henry set himself up to be swindled by a small-town hoax, which the Grave Creek stone ultimately was. Jane's thinking with the land asserts itself against thinking with and for empire—against the idea that the past or future can so easily be claimed. Early ethnologists and later anthropologists could serve as useful instruments in Indigenous projects of thinking the future, and some were changed by it even if Henry was not. If we were to plant another stone inside the Grave Creek Mound as a warning, or perhaps as a curse, the inscription would read, "Don't burrow into empty ciphers; don't burrow into others' graves; the work of forgetting and the work of remembering grapple in every monument."

Spirits released
from human bondage

Today the Grave Creek Mound no longer stands among farms and fields. In 1866, local leaders rechristened the growing town Moundsville, the iconic tourist site trumping the name given by the founding settlers. If those founders assumed that their names on the map were permanent monuments, the land had other thoughts. It has a way of entering into consciousness, even the consciousness of those who would prefer not to remember. Less than two hundred years have passed since Henry Schoolcraft went on his mission to Grave Creek. The short life of Moundsville, with its courthouse, churches, and war memorials, is a passing shadow on the living earthwork.

The state highway runs into town past bleached parking lots and the yellow dollar-store marquee, that ubiquitous gravestone for the prosperity of America's working class. This is a familiar type of small town where polyester flowers in pots hang from wrought-iron porch rails. Its population has declined by 40 percent since 1960, tracking with the demise of coal and steel in the Ohio Valley. Slag heaps still line the river. Next to the elementary school, a tall fence wraps the base of the Grave Creek Mound, just like in the postcards. Facing the mound across Jefferson Avenue, another fence guards a towering Gothic structure easily recognized as an abandoned prison. These paired monuments, the prison and the ancient earthwork, constitute the geographical heart of the town. The prison, a faded banner explains, is terrifyingly haunted and can be toured by day or night.

As much as this has always been a story about haunting, I have tried not to make it about actual ghosts. We rely too much on ghosts to salvage our sense of justice. Was Joseph Tomlinson haunted by the brutality of the Indian wars? Something made him preserve the mound, but he seems not to have suffered for it. Did Jane Schoolcraft torment Henry? She didn't have to; he was trapped in the labyrinth of his own ambition, chasing the Grave Creek stone and other mirages. The notion of the "Indian curse" already pervaded popular culture by the 1830s, giving voice to the nation's uneasy conscience about the brutal theft of Indigenous land and knowledge. Henry Schoolcraft penned a number of Indian curses, including that of the Cherokee chief who conjured the ghosts of his ancestors in the Grave Creek Mound. In one historian's pithy phrasing, white Americans were "heirs through fear": as they imagined and rehearsed the wrath of dead Indians in speeches, poems, and plays, "feeling terrorized by the ground beneath one's feet became, for some, a hallmark of being an authentic American." This feeling, though, is not justice. I would never deny that ghosts exist, but in the premier US tales about ghosts, the living are the heroes, fighting to banish what torments them. In a different kind of story, the ghosts take their house back, and the frame of the story falls away: they had never been dead.

A view of the West Virginia Penitentiary from the 1930s.

In June of 1866, the year that Elizabethtown became Moundsville, Moundsville became the home of West Virginia's first state prison. The state had split from Virginia, finally rejecting slavery and fighting for the Union in the Civil War. With peace came a number of municipal challenges, including the containment of criminals, who routinely escaped from local jails—indeed, the war's upheaval created a mobile population of landless poor people, many formerly enslaved, whose supposed disorder caused rising public alarm. The West Virginia Board of Public Works decided to build the new prison on ten acres of land, previously a Union Army encampment, in the shadow of the Grave Creek Mound. The prison's future inmates, including an African American man known as Big John, spent the summer of 1866 in wooden barracks, digging a foundation and cutting stone for the crenellated battlements that would mark the horizon of their world. With walls literally closing in, they set fire to the barracks in the first of many escape attempts.

There's no record of what these prisoners found during construction. The ancient Grave Creek complex extended for a mile around, including many smaller burial mounds and three circular enclosures, each up to five hundred feet in diameter. Raised roads may have connected the central mound to the river and the hills on either side. A brochure published by prisoners decades later reflected that "at many places near the mound human bones have been found; relics in large numbers and great variety have been picked up."

This was the case not just on the prison grounds, but throughout Moundsville, which hobbyists combed for Indigenous artifacts. While the experts Schoolcraft and Squier feuded over a fraudulent tablet, they displayed little interest in the mound's archaeological context, which became a bald prison yard gushing rivers of mud in the spring thaw. Drainage was so bad that inmates petitioned to have the prison cemetery moved off-site; the bodies of the recent, as well as the ancient, dead kept reappearing in the runoff.

When the building was finished, complete with an escape-proof rotating entry gate, the prisoners were made available on contract to private companies. Both contracting and convict leasing, which placed prisoners directly under company management, became widespread after the Civil War. They followed on the heels of slavery as a tool for labor extraction and social control targeting Black Americans and the poor. In 1890 about 4 percent of West Virginians were Black; they made up 30 percent of the prison population. People landed behind bars for increasingly petty offenses: the inmate-run prison newsletter, *Work & Hope*, noted that "a 14 year old Negro here committed the heinous crime of overdrawing his bank account." The largest enterprise in the Moundsville prison was the Webster Wagon Works; trapped behind bars, inmates hewed wheels and yokes for the westward-rolling empire.

The racial typing so prevalent in this period, which presumed that inherited qualities determine individual behavior, explained why the Mound Builders were not Indians, and why Indians could not become Americans. Proponents also believed that the science of human types explained the country's rapidly growing prison population. The criminal problem, like the "Indian problem," forced the question of whether people can truly change—or, seen from another vantage, whether they can become trustworthy agents of a system that subjugates and brutalizes them. In the case of Native nations, following the rules meant cooperating with the obliteration of their culture; in the case of the "criminal class," following the rules meant accepting a yoke of moral puritanism (birth control, for instance, was illegal) and economic exploitation (state police and militias were violently brought to bear against striking workers). "Prisoners want to be freed," declared the newsletter editors. "Some people may ask; why, so they can commit more crime? No dear reader, the great majority of the prisoners are just like you, they fell from the elevation upon which you are now standing. One little slip and down you will come too."

From the perspective of law enforcement and social reformers, though, the problem lay with deviant people, not with an oppressive system. Could they be fixed? Italian criminologist Cesare Lombroso famously championed the view that criminals are born, not made, and can never be cured of their evil nature, but a long line of prison reformers argued the contrary. From Baptist minister Francis Wayland to mental-health advocate Dorothea Dix, they asserted that modern, rationally engineered routines of penitence could bend human nature. The West Virginia State Penitentiary was modeled on Wayland's favored Auburn system, first implemented in Auburn, New York, which combined the benefits of industrious communal labor by day and solitary meditation by night. Talking, except when necessary for work, was entirely forbidden. The prisoner who emerged from this regimen was reborn as a law-abiding citizen. Before rebirth, however, the prisoner passed through civic death, losing the right to property and the vote. Literary scholar Caleb Smith points out that this penalty of civic death makes all prisons, Gothic or modern, already haunted by the ghosts of suspended personhood. "This was not discipline," wrote a former inmate in his memoir, "it was damnation."

Despite prison reformers' high hopes, in 1886 a reporter for the *Wheeling Register* described the Moundsville penitentiary not as a house of rebirth, but as a self-contained and admirably efficient city of the damned, where "the ex-minister and pick-pocket work side by side, while the ex-legislator marks time with the sneak thief." The reporter's position on the nature-versus-nurture question is abundantly clear. Though industrious inside the walls, Moundsville's inmates "glide back to their old haunts and old companions with a fatal facility.... The frost work of new habits appears to melt away at the first fire of temptation."

The American public avidly followed new theories and debates over criminal reform, developing a deep fascination with prisons as microcosms of the human struggle between good and evil—a psychological laboratory rather than the instrument of a violent social order. Prison tours were an ordinary middle-class leisure activity, both informative and edifying. "Shades of purgatory!" exclaimed one visitor to the Moundsville prison. "We don't think we will ever do anything bad in our lives!" Wardens and superintendents became friendly guides. "Our storm of questions," the visitor wrote, "were answered courteously and fully." In this vein, the *Wheeling Register* ran periodic bulletins from the penitentiary, a sort of virtual tourism that indulged readers' curiosity about the criminal underworld while reassuring nervous neighbors. Moundsville's armed residents

Inmates seated shoulder to shoulder at sewing machines
in the "tailor shop" of the West Virginia Penitentiary,
watched from above by an armed guard.

had been summoned on multiple occasions to help the guards put
down inmate revolts.

According to many reformers, physical labor was the pathway
to moral redemption, a fortunate coincidence for chronically un-
derfunded prisons. The *Register* praised model inmates such as Big
John, the Black man who laid the original masonry, for their loyal
service to the institution. An especially "valuable" prisoner, Big
John's years of work added up to at least $10,000 worth of labor
for the state of West Virginia—more than $300,000 today. Local
trade unions protested the penitentiary's contracts, complaining
that "plenty of good men walk our streets with their hands in
their pockets, their right to labor denied them." As poverty drove
people to crime, and then into prison sweatshops, unions alleged
that "the insatiate greed for wealth by selfish capitalists" was "fast
ruining our country." Moundsville's prisoners also noticed this
"inevitable logic": "Wonder how long it will be until they are all in
here?" one writer mused. Big John was serving a life sentence for
a crime that would only merit fourteen years under legal reforms

of the 1880s. Locked up soon after Emancipation, John was still enslaved.

Another face in the *Register*'s gallery of rogues was Charley Thomas, dubbed Thomas the Cherokee, imprisoned with three companions for murdering whites on the frontier. Perhaps this was the unnamed man listed as an inmate at Moundsville in an 1878 Bureau of Indian Affairs report; he was a member of the Arapaho Nation, but newspapers cared little for such distinctions. The reporter spares no flourish in painting a Schoolcraftian tableau of Thomas's silent agonies, his "memory of broad plains, the wild free life of the nation." Indeed, we learn that Thomas's fellow Cherokees died in prison of "broken hearts," perishing as all Indians were expected to perish in the face of advancing civilization. Thomas's survival is linked to his being a "half-breed"; whiteness allowed him to labor by the clock. Yet his Indian half, according to our reporter, still yearned to join his friends "released from human bondage, started for the happy hunting grounds." While free people commonly imagined prisoners longing for death's release, this romantic notion shared with the "vanishing Indian" an assumption that social deviants saw no future for themselves in this world. Such unfortunates were already ghosts. The words and actions of the Moundsville prison population—many decades of organized revolts and mutinies—suggest that they did not want the freedom of death, but actual bodily freedom.

It's a ubiquitous horror-movie trope that poltergeists appear in houses built on an "Indian burial ground," but white writers in the nineteenth century preferred to evoke the "happy hunting ground," a segregated heaven for Indians, who were easily dispersed from their earthly real estate. This neat separation of body and soul, echoed in the *Register*'s comment on Thomas the Cherokee, badly distorted Indigenous beliefs about death. These beliefs vary widely among the Native nations of North America, but often involve ongoing care for physical remains, which are interred in a respected place. For an example, the reporter might have looked to the two-thousand-year-old Adena burial monument across the street from the prison. It seems unlikely that Thomas, or anyone else, wished for death knowing that their bones would lie in a corner of the prison yard, resurfacing with every rain. Henry Schoolcraft, in his two-faced fashion, praised the Ojibwe for "the scrupulous regard with which they are found to remember the burial-grounds of their ancestors," while also deriding this as a superstitious "form of eastern idolatry." The white horror of Native burials that emerged in the twentieth century reflects this persistent refusal to see non-Christian, nonwhite lives and afterlives as human; when their spirits haunt the land, they are demonic or monstrous enemies, however justified their revenge might be.

The mound and prison were not such a dissonant pairing. Tomlinson's gaudy display of the Grave Creek remains—"To tell the dead—they too, are slaves"—anticipated the display of undead inmates to carceral tourists two decades later. In 1909, their fates became legally intertwined. The mound faced demolition after the death of its last owner, former prison warden George McFadden, who bought it hoping to place a water tower on top. The Daughters of the American Revolution, keen on preserving the monuments "built by a pre-historic race, presumably the Mound Builders," launched a campaign to save the massive earthwork. West Virginia's governor agreed to purchase it for the state. Rather than turning it into a park, he put the penitentiary in charge of the site, promising that convict labor, not taxpayer funds, would maintain the mound—just as convict labor, not taxpayer funds, maintained the convicts.

This stewardship marks a reversal of previous encounters between unfree labor and Indigenous sites. Enslaved people and impoverished workers were often made to excavate mounds, at times over their objections to desecrating burial places. The men who dug into the Grave Creek Mound were described as paid laborers; it's possible that some were enslaved and working for a wage. Their views of the act went unrecorded. Antiquarian Montroville Dickeson used enslaved Black workers to open up nearly a thousand mounds throughout the Ohio and Mississippi Valleys in the 1830s; they had firsthand knowledge of the relics that lay below the region's soil, but no real means of registering complaint. A mound romance set before the Civil War describes the reluctance of the Southern Black population to disturb earthworks as a "tradition,

Huge Mound and the Manner of Opening Them, an image of Montroville Dickeson's mound excavations created for his traveling panorama show, *The Monumental Grandeur of the Mississippi Valley*, which toured the United States in the 1850s. Enslaved laborers dig in the foreground.

from time beyond memory." "I shall pay you well for digging into that mound," the book's heroic antiquarian promises his men. "I will not only make you rich presents, but I will do more; I will set every one of you free!" The author scornfully contrasts the superstition of the enslaved with the rational mind of their enslaver, who is, of course, seeking the buried treasure of the lost race. Black Americans were often promised freedom in exchange for serving white supremacy, yet their reward remained elusive.

The first recorded hints of resistance at an excavation come in 1903, when archaeologist Charles Peabody, of Harvard's Peabody Museum, hired Black laborers to open mounds in Coahoma County, Mississippi—at least one man was leased from a local jail. Peabody was also interested in folk music, so while the men toiled in the heat, he wrote down the words of their working songs:

> Some folks say preachers won't steal;
> But I found two in my cornfield.
> One with a shovel and t'other with a hoe,
> A-diggin' up my taters row by row.

It didn't occur to Peabody that he was the thieving preacher, digging up somebody else's field. Literary scholar Jodi Byrd, a member of the Chickasaw Nation, whose monuments Peabody plundered, sees "resistant traces" in the laborers' songs: they "acknowledge the desecration that is occurring . . . positioning themselves as tied to the people buried in the mounds." Byrd believes that the lyrics slyly reference Peabody's theft of Native remains—bones become potatoes—and show local knowledge and care for the site, even if the singers couldn't refuse to dig. African-descended laborers may have thought of their own mound burial traditions, practiced widely throughout the South, meant to "both enclose and appease the spirits of the deceased." Black and Native communities had complicated histories of relation and opposition: Black freedom-seekers found refuge in Native-controlled lands; at the same time, elites among the Cherokee and other nations owned slaves, while Black "Buffalo soldiers" served in the wars against Plains Indians. Each at times turned the shifting racial hierarchies of US society against the other. They didn't need a shared political identity to recognize that none of their dead were safe.

Only a few years after Peabody's dig, West Virginia prisoners marched across the street to landscape and groom the badly eroded Grave Creek Mound, which some had seen through barred windows for many years. Its current shape is a result of choices they made, moving tons of dirt to stabilize the collapsed shaft where Tomlinson's spiral staircase descended and filling pits left by decades of curiosity seekers. Inmates built a shop where tourists could buy souvenirs and handicrafts. This work detail may have been preferable to the prison coal mine. At least some inmates became interested in the enigma of Moundsville's ancient past: Who built the mound, for what purpose, and where did they go?

A local Methodist pastor named Compton, who took notice of the mound when he married into the Tomlinson family, wrote up his explanation of the mystery and shared it with curious prisoners. They were so impressed that they featured it in a 1929 souvenir brochure created by the incarcerated staff of the newsletter *Work & Hope*. Perhaps Moundsville's prisoners were more inclined than ordinary citizens to appreciate the homegrown wonder in their front yard. "Go to Europe to see ancient things?" they scoffed—as though they were in any position to take a European tour. "Look at this American mound, the storms of thirty centuries have passed over it!" They mostly copied chunks of the Reverend Compton's text, recounting local history and Tomlinson's excavation. They shared Compton's low opinion of the Grave Creek stone: its "mysterious charades were never deciphered to the satisfaction of those versed in such things." Schoolcraft, they insinuate, was a dupe, and his claims to translate the stone were pure bluster. "The statement that the inscription on the engraved stone tells us where the Mound Builders came from, their number and the cause of their disappearance is untrue, there is not a particle of truth in any such assertion."

The newsletter staff followed Compton in debunking these more fanciful conspiracy theories; their take on the mound seems in tune with the archaeological consensus of the 1920s. However, the enduring myth of a lost race is scattered in small clues throughout their story, denoted in a shorthand that readers today might not even recognize: when they write that the mound was built by "a departed people," they don't mean dispossessed Native Americans. The skeleton found in the mound, "and especially the nose, were distinctly Roman"; in 1880, someone is said to have stuck a pole into the mound and "drew out a large tuft of coarse, reddish hair." These hints of Vikings and Aryans don't have to be consistent or coherent, they merely have to keep possibility alive.

The Reverend Compton believed that "our so-called 'Indian mound' is not an Indian mound, but was built long before the Indians came to America.... This work was not done by savages." As if on cue, he conjures the old logic that Indians usurped the peaceful, enlightened Mound Builders and so deserved their fate. "We often hear about how the white man drove the Indian out of his inheritance and that our land belongs to the Indian. The fact is that the white man . . . has come into possession of the land held by the Indians, but the red man . . . drove out the people who were before him." This is the inevitable march of progress, Compton insists— no hard feelings, and no haunted Indian graveyards.

However, as Compton elaborates his theory, the march of progress seems to go in a circle. He describes a Mound Builder society not so different from the American society of his lifetime, which spanned the Civil War, the Gilded Age, and the Great Depression. "The people were not free," he writes, "but in a condition of servitude to their rulers." Only a nation that sentenced certain classes to forced labor could erect such a "useless and gigantic" monument as the mound, he explains. The same could be said for the nation that built a massive penitentiary in the mound's shadow. *Work & Hope* deemed the United States "a prison ridden Country." One wonders what the inmates thought about the Mound Builders' toil. Perhaps understandably they didn't drop any hints in their tourist pamphlet. They couldn't have anticipated that their own prison walls would become just as much an object of myth and speculation as the mound that they cared for, and in a much shorter time.

During the Progressive 1920s the penitentiary had a newsletter and an orchestra but was also becoming massively overcrowded. Across the country, in the service of Jim Crow and managing the immigrant threat, states expanded their definition of crime. Two and eventually three people wound up in Moundsville cells meant for solitary confinement. The following decade they ran out of space for cottage industries, with 2,000 people in a facility built for 650. Violence ruled the day amid disciplinary beatings and "germ-festered filth."

Ironically, as the prison became a dark blot on the landscape, the mound across the street finally won national designation as a historic site. In 1975, state archaeologists began the first professional excavation. Local self-taught archaeologist Delf Norona spearheaded the construction of a museum to shed scientific light on this long-exploited mystery. An orderly, rational arrangement of facts would put the lost-race tales to rest once and for all, or so Norona hoped. The blocky modernist interpretive center is topped by a glass pyramid that echoes the mound's slope. Its wall text and dioramas explain how the Indigenous Adena people moved sixty thousand tons of earth two millennia ago. The interpretive center hasn't changed much since the 1980s; a narrow parking lot buffers this modest tribute from the ghastly spectacle across the street.

The West Virginia State Penitentiary wasn't decommissioned until 1995, after two major uprisings and multiple escapes brought national attention to its decrepit, overcrowded facilities. One riot was prompted by a broken pipe that leaked raw sewage into the cafeteria for months. When the last inmates transferred out, the town of Moundsville took another economic blow: prison jobs had been a lifeline in the wake of deindustrialization. Moundsville was also left to manage a massive historic structure without any support from the state. To keep it from crumbling—and also, in a sense, to fill an open wound with a bit of ghostly gauze—the town embraced dark tourism. Within a year of losing their jobs, former guards returned to the penitentiary to guide visitors through its now-haunted cellblocks. One wonders if something more than economic desperation drew them back, if this is a kind of compulsion to return to the site of trauma.

Today's Moundsville ghost hunters are transfixed by 1930s gangsters and 1980s gang violence, more vivid to the imagination than the mundane property crimes that landed the majority of inmates behind bars. Celebrity psychics, doing obligatory investigations for reality TV, froth at the mouth over the brutality of the place, its violent routine of rape and murder, and the sensational crimes of serial killers. Amazingly, their intuitive powers reveal that the building was once a prison. The greatest selling point for the $75 overnight "paranormal experience" is that 104 executions were carried out on the site, 9 of them in an electric chair dubbed Old Sparky. Before the prison newsletter was defunded in 1931, it ran multiple protests against this punishment. Such a high density of violent death guarantees abundant ghost readings on any instrument.

Tapping into Americans' morbid fascination with serial killers and capital punishment turns a modest profit for Moundsville, which expects some repayment after a century of housing society's most unwanted. Over generations, those laborers whose work was devalued by convict leasing, union busting, and globalization became prison guards. The guards doled out the systematic traumas of prison life until they too were rendered obsolete and told to reinvent themselves again. Some would reinvent themselves as the stewards of angry ghosts. No former prisoner is invited to tell their side of the story. They are treated as silent objects, spoken for by those who had power over them, who feared them most. "When punishment is administered with vengeance," asked *Work & Hope*, "who is the criminal?" If these voices of inmates were heard, the haunted prison could command the abolition of prisons; instead it justifies the necessity of evil. One has a right to become a monster when dealing with monsters. The tangle of human guilt and suffering becomes a satisfying hit of terror followed by relief, then terror again, and relief again, until you reach the gift shop.

Ghostly repetition tends to abstract real events into universal tropes, recasting them with stock characters; after a few haunted tours, all ghost stories sound the same. One paranormal website writes of the Moundsville penitentiary, "According to popular legend, the prison buildings were built on an old Native American burial ground. Some believe that the legend coupled with its violent past is why it is haunted." The burial ground, in this case, is not a legend. The whole town stands on an earthworks complex containing many interments. That the descendants of the mound's architects are quite alive is not the type of thrill that audiences are looking for. In ghost-hunting TV shows, exterior shots of the prison carefully keep the Grave Creek Mound out of the frame.

Strategic forgetting also requires strategic remembering, such that when the mound is included in the frame, it still represents the unsolved mystery of ancient America's inhabitants. A local historian and ghost-tour guide, who notes that she is a card-carrying Daughter of the Confederacy, sees the mound as the key to the West Virginia Penitentiary hauntings. The secret, in her view, is ley lines, spiritual energy fields used by ancient people to align their monuments with the sacred "paths of the dead," according to New Age philosophy. She elaborates that if the mound's ley line "runs through the West Virginia Penitentiary, it could possibly fuel all the paranormal activity that happens there."

Though she identifies Grave Creek with the Adena people of the Woodland period, she follows this with the seeming contradiction that "the mound is not Native American Indian; it goes all the way back to the Mound Builders." Insistence on this distinction is the hallmark of lost-race theories. Amid contradictory vagueness, only the initiated can glimpse the hidden truth. In conspiratorial tones, some New Age believers bemoan the cosmic spiritual wisdom that's been lost in the modern era, and which they seek to unlock through ley lines or crystals. This framing of ancient mysteries glosses over the project of colonization, which tried to cut off Indigenous people from their pasts and extract whatever value lay there in the form of knowledge and power for European science. Undoing this destructive project and recentering the continuous relation between Indigenous people and their lands includes confronting the recent history of sites such as the Grave Creek Mound, understanding how narratives of silence and ghostliness were produced.

The enterprising prisoners of the Moundsville penitentiary, not imagining that their own ghosts would become the town's main tourist attraction, argued in 1929 to restore the interior of the mound as it was in Tomlinson's day: "Again it would become a center of interest and when the good roads are completed hundreds of visitors would come from the east, west, north, and south to view this great monument of a departed people." The state used their labor to build those good roads, rather than tunnel through the mound a second time. It stands today, for any such visitors, more or less the way they preserved it. A paved trail spirals up the slope to the flat, grassy peak, where the viewing pavilion used to stand, enclosed by a low stone wall. The town spreads out on all sides, resting in the Ohio River's bend. The air on a hot day sits over the place with pressure and lightness. Into the blazing vacuum of the present rushes the steady time and space of continuous life that stretches into a future beyond seeing.

From even farther above, the shadow of the mound and the shadow of the penitentiary move in overlapping circles like twin sundials—twin clocks of honor and shame, persistent memory and willful oblivion. Their shadows interlock on what most would consider neutral ground: simply another American town that's seen better days. I would argue that there is no neutral ground. As Roxanne Dunbar-Ortiz emphasizes, the land itself was the first basis of US wealth and power. The way settlers and scientists made sense and value from earthworks reflects an effort to secure that power. This work presented opportunities to those, such as Abelard Tomlinson and Henry Schoolcraft, who positioned themselves as gatekeepers to the mysteries of the past. It even gave a sense of ownership to people who owned nothing besides the trinkets in their prison cells.

The prison also speaks to the exploitation of those who willingly and unwillingly serve a nationalistic power. Inmates and guards, the living and the dead, become a resource for narratives that sustain fear. Fear of disorder, fear of revenge, fear of degeneration or collapse, are carried along in our contradictory stories about lost races and haunted ground. Excavating ghost stories offers a different set of possibilities, mobilizing the powerful anger of a curse while rejecting the false assurance that anything is finished or fated. Moundsville's inmates fought back repeatedly against the living death of incarceration; Black laborers marked the evil of stealing Native remains even as they were made to dig them from burial mounds.

Today, Native people across North America are building new earthworks, revitalizing the practice of writing with the land. Some earthworks are printed words, including the poetry and fiction of Monique Mojica, Allison Hedge Coke, Geary Hobson, and Lara Mann. Others, such as the Chickasaw Cultural Center and the First Americans Museum in Oklahoma, are what Choctaw writer and intellectual LeAnne Howe calls "twenty-first-century mound cities," gathering places that embody the changing architectures of contemporary Native life. Howe, Mojica, and a group of collaborators are generating, from experimental movement at ancient mound sites, a form of theater that reflects the mounds' layering of knowledge and expression.

Contemporary earthworks tell about the formation of specific peoples from the earth of specific places, and also foster Indigenous connections across North and South America and beyond. They can include grieving for countless pillaged sites: "We are left among ruins / to save what we can," writes Monacan poet Karenne

Wood. They militate for access to sites, such as the Octagon Earthworks, still in private hands. Howe proposes that Native architects "emplotted the land with meaning" long ago to ensure these cycles of return and renewal, "continuances rather than disappearances." Continuance is also buried in language. Reflecting on a strange line in the 1829 *Choctaw Hymn Book*, Howe sees a message that predates the arrival of Christian missionaries. She asks, "Could '*Issa halali haatoko iksa illok isha shkii*, because you are holding onto me, I am not dead yet' be a mnemonic that ancient Choctawans chanted while looking at the mounds they built?"

The refusal to let go of the dead, and of the land, is a refusal to be made an object or a resource. It is also a demand for just relations that we can still read through her husband's scribbles in Jane Johnston Schoolcraft's manuscripts. Holding on to these relations, dangerous and undeniable, allows the living to connect people, land, and memory, rather than consume them. The Grave Creek stone, incidentally, has vanished; a "ghost of the counterfeit," no one knows where it went.

PART 2

HARMONIAL WELLS

The Pithole at
the end of the world

S ome origins, like the engineered Lake Itasca, make themselves plain; they want you to come and see where things all began. The oil region of northwestern Pennsylvania, stretching from the juncture of French Creek and the Allegheny River north to the border with New York, promotes itself as the birthplace of the American oil industry. Colonel Edwin Drake, who was not a colonel, drilled the world's first commercial oil well there, near the town of Titusville, in 1859, though origins are never as simple as they seem. The region quickly became known as Petrolia, a destination for fortune hunters from around the nation. Highlights of the frenzy that followed included a five-hundred-foot-high fireball rolling downriver to engulf Oil City's main street. Today, on the same street, the local history museum tells this and other boomtown tales; its rack of brochures beckons the tourist to roam across a landscape scarred not just by extractive industry, but also by its unceremonious exit. A lifelong resident offered enthusiasm for all the local sights except for a place called Pithole. "Don't go to Pithole, there's nothing there," she warned knowingly. The name could give you that impression.

She's right that nothing is there: Pithole boomed and went bust in three years, between 1864 and 1867. A town of fifteen thousand people at its peak, there was hardly anyone left to be counted in the decennial US census. Pithole's founders bought the land on a hunch, hoping to strike oil far from the beaten path. When they hit an unprecedented gusher, a flood of fortune seekers appeared to stake claims nearby. Hotels, blacksmiths, brothels, and what was briefly the third-busiest post office in America popped up overnight in flimsy wood-frame buildings, a transient domain known

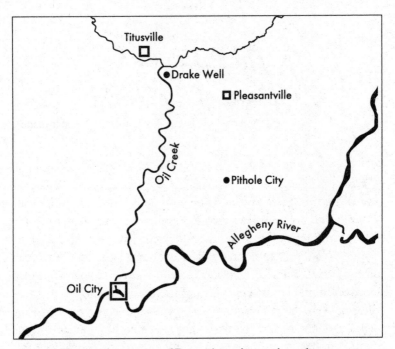

The early epicenter of Pennsylvania's petroleum boom
extended out from Titusville to Pleasantville, Oil City, and Pithole,
with extensive drilling along Oil Creek. The site of Oil City belonged
to the Seneca leader Cornplanter until 1818, and its purchasers never
made full payment for the land title.

for its particularly heedless debauchery. No one had plans for this
to last.

The place is now a monument to the disposability at the heart
of capitalism. All its structures melted into air—or were disassem-
bled and carted to the next boomtown—yet Pithole is carefully
memorialized. Americans have a strange impulse to hold on to the
ephemeral, interchangeable sites and experiences conjured by the
vast machine. In this case, the State of Pennsylvania maintains a
display of emptiness. Groundskeepers mow a grid where the streets
of Pithole used to be, while trees more than a century old stand in
the footprints of buildings. Informational plaques gesture at ghostly

The gusher that made Pithole's fleeting fortune was named the United States Well, shown here in 1865.

routines—from the hotel to the saloon, to the post office with another plea for credit from long-gone associates—repetitions in the ruins of linear time. The green-carpeted streets are mostly empty of people, except for the occasional school field trip. Birds make an airy racket. Ghost towns are supposed to feel uncanny, but Pithole exudes a deep sense of peace, as though we had come to the end of the world and found that it continues.

In this vision it continues without us. Pithole is a carefully staged time-travel vignette, in which we fast-forward to nature reclaiming what humans have ravaged, our subtle traces barely detectable. Pennsylvania's oil region helped to launch the petroleum epoch, which we now expect will, sooner or later, lead to planetary upheaval on a scale that defies imagination. By disappearing, Pithole also makes a claim to showing us our future. Gazing upon ruins reminds would-be conquerors that their time is transitory, but what if there aren't even ruins? For people who feel ashamed of the plastic islands and nuclear waste we will inevitably leave behind, the ease with which Pithole vanished is aspirational.

Fredric Jameson's quip that "it's easier to imagine the end of the world than to imagine the end of capitalism" has been the twenty-first century's brand, the brand of dystopian climate-change fiction and financialized water scarcity. It's true that the no-place of Pithole—a utopia, in its way—is more welcoming to the imagination than the inhabited towns of Petrolia. Residents have trouble envisioning a future in which things get better for them. Though the boom years ended by the 1890s, they depended on the oil economy until the 1980s. Falling crude prices finally led the industry to seek better profits in Texas. "Inside Oil City, Hope Runs Dry" was the rueful headline when the last big company, Quaker State, left in 1995. Most jobs in Oil City, once Petrolia's nerve center, are in retail, hospitality, health care, and human services, a pattern that tracks with industrial decline nationwide. We should question why this represents decline, why the declarations of hopelessness: meeting the community's needs is important work. It's not, however, profitable in the way that taking oil out of the ground is profitable. Low wages and precarity are the norm in these sectors whose product is the continuation of social life. A fourth-grade teacher was grateful to have one of the last good jobs in town, but this didn't bode well for his students. "The best case," he said, "is that the kids move away."

Like many postindustrial places, the oil region has heritage sites, arts districts, and a tourism bureau. With oil slowed to a trickle, towns are told to conjure their own value in the form of creative experiences. Unfortunately, Oil City is tucked into the hills two hours from Pittsburgh and ninety minutes from Youngstown, Ohio. Only a modest stream of outdoor enthusiasts and obsessives seeking the origins of the petroleum industry are planning their vacations to Venango County. This vision of self-help, that communities must polish themselves up and market the last resource they have left—stories of what the place used to be—makes it easy to blame those communities when it doesn't work. The demand for innovation is how free market partisans have dispensed with the human misery that the market leaves in its wake.

Oil City has already glimpsed the end of capitalism, it's just that America's imagination hasn't caught up. Communities don't always melt into air when they fail to conjure the magic of economic development. People and places need to be cared for; care workers should have more, not less power than that lucky generation of industrial workers who reaped the benefits of unionized shops—benefits designed, after World War II, to build a docile white middle class. While Americans have constantly migrated to new sites of production, with an equal fervor we venerate the hometown, and many view it as a tragedy that neighborhoods should be sacrificed in the name of often-illusory progress. The last half dozen residents of Centralia, the Pennsylvania town on top of a coal mine that's been on fire since 1962, are macabre folk heroes, refusing to abandon their houses to the infernal fumes. Like Pithole, Centralia is a nearly empty street grid with vegetation reclaiming its vacant lots.

What kind of resource is a home? To keep us moving, we're encouraged to see it as an investment—a starter home, a retirement fund. While we're there, our politics are the politics of whatever increases property values. Where property values bottom out, people are trapped, dropped from the frictionless stream of economic mobility. But a home has other qualities relevant to survival in the eddies of the market. Home means community support, family and church networks, strategies for getting by learned over a lifetime. More than survival, it can mean the freedom to make stuff that doesn't have a resale value—that nurtures the community where it's made.

To economists, the people who live in homes are labor and consumption; they too must flow across the terrain of capital. A Brookings Institution study showed that states recover from the loss of major industries "not because employment picks up, but because workers leave." Such mobility has fallen by half since the 1990s, a maddening phenomenon for conservatives, who blame welfare for dulling the prod of financial desperation. Economist Michael R. Strain urges, paradoxically given conservative scorn for public programs, that the government should pay the unemployed to relocate with every economic cycle—a subsidy to businesses who can't attract their own workers. Migrating for upward mobility might be the American dream, but even with a cash incentive it carries severe risks; there's no place of refuge with stable work, health care, and a pension. If people don't want to liquidate the durable bonds of their community, why should the market dictate that they must? They're not wrong about the danger of starting over somewhere new in a country without a safety net.

Oil City is hardly a ghost town. On the steep hills above Oil Creek, the split-level houses with driveways full of children's toys suggest that life there isn't coming to an end. The National Transit Building, once the ornate nerve center of John D. Rockefeller's petroleum monopoly, houses art studios and concerts. Retirees craft complicated fishing lures. It's true there are "deaths of despair," that is, some people do dangerous things in a context of lacking necessities for a dignified life or any hope of getting them. Working at Dollar General, a corporation that nets more than $2 billion per year, you might need food stamps to shop at Dollar General. This is the final form that extraction takes, tapping the meager trickle of public benefits in a bare-bones, penny-ante racket. Abolish the racket, and one can imagine a society that needs no engine of profit to justify human purpose and pleasure. But no town by itself can engineer this redesign. Leaders instead promise revitalization through tax incentives meant to attract bold, but possibly mythical, technology companies. I've seen many nostalgic imitations of Oil City's main street in suburban developments built for white-collar workers who prefer a fresh canvas. It's not a story unique to Venango County.

In each town where people mull over decline, they grapple with feelings of powerlessness. Petrolia is the symbolic origin of the power behind modern industrial society. Its residents poured their lives into jobs and communities, and then power flowed elsewhere, turned out to have always been in someone else's service. Indeed, what they thought were investments in a particular place were more like externalized operating costs for industries that no longer need them, though oil companies did pitch in to erect a series of historical markers telling this not entirely flattering story. The great and small forces of history that brought people to western Pennsylvania's oil region, which still proudly calls itself "the valley that changed the world," have drained away and left people stranded. Yet the memory of those forces is a pillar of local identity and a crucial form of explanation for all of us who live in the tumultuous grip of oil.

In pristine-looking woodlands around Oil City, one can stumble over the end of a cast-iron pipe sticking out of the leaf litter, like the spine of a primeval being still anchored somewhere hundreds or thousands of feet below. Bringing oil out of the ground is an uncanny fold in time: fossil fuels were the flora and fauna of eons past, transformed by stupendous pressure and heat. Oil spent eternities percolating through the infernal spaces that many cultures regard as the land of the dead. The philosopher of horror Eugene Thacker describes oil as "an ancient and enigmatic manifestation of the hidden world." Others suggest that oil is the form of time thinking—a more-than-human consciousness, a brain of accumulated matter. From the vantage point of our present difficulties, it's easy to see this substance as possessing us, rather than humans possessing it.

Petroleum is more than a source of combustion energy; early acolytes were transfixed by its spiritual power, declaring that it was put on earth to "mould society into a more beautiful character." It's proper to question the forces with which we have communed. Is there something occult about oil, some benevolent or sinister intent? Or is it animated by the human desires of a particular place and time? Many people have felt it pull like a magnet on their bodies or heard it whisper in the silence of their minds. Throughout Petrolia, prospectors dreamed of oil and even came back from the dead to get it. We don't know how long it's been issuing these strange communications, but they only reached a violent pitch once people understood oil's vast subterranean kingdom exclusively through the lens of profit.

In human time, oil has always seeped to the surface in small amounts, often mixed with water from underground streams. These natural oil springs occurred around the globe, from Ontario to Azerbaijan. People found many uses for it: medicine, ceremonies, light, heat, and even weapons. Some dug seeking more of it, establishing industries which Western observers studied, but did not dignify with that name. Though oil's properties were remarkable, it never became central to societies moved by water, wind, and muscle power. Chemists in the medieval Islamic world refined crude into a clean-burning lamp oil, an idea that reemerged in American industry hundreds of years later.

In what is now western Pennsylvania and New York, Indigenous people built thousands of timber-lined pits or troughs, up to ten feet deep, to harvest petroleum that seeped up from the earth. Whether used for medicine, light, or another purpose, it was likely part of a far-ranging trade, collected by groups who traveled from the Mississippi Valley to summer villages by Lake Erie. Phillip Carroll Morgan, a Chickasaw historian and novelist, paints a vivid picture of the cosmopolitan mound cities of the fourteenth-century Mississippi Valley, where this oil may have circulated. The earlierst known villages near the oil springs are almost two thousand years old; some troughs date to the 1400s, but archaeologists don't know how long this process was used. There's a history of North American oil that isn't available for European science to catalog, or for settlers to claim as their own prehistory, as they would attempt to do in Petrolia.

It was after 1600 that the Onöndawa´ga:´, known to settlers as the Seneca, expanded their territory from their original lands west of Lake Canandaigua to what is now northwestern Pennsylvania, spurred by conflicts with the French military and other Native groups over the expanding fur trade. This is the land they defended through the onslaught of European invasion. Perhaps the Seneca were familiar with the uses of oil and could now gather it at the source. Later-arriving settlers denied that Seneca people knew anything about the timber-lined troughs and intensive oil harvesting of prior centuries, for "the Indian . . . would scorn to bend his strength to rude toil in excavating multitudinous pits for the reception of oil, or in bearing it from place to place after it had been secured." They emphasized that Native use of petroleum was haphazard, "without labor and without much forethought."

However, as late as 1770, Moravian missionary David Zeisberger had described an annual March gathering of Senecas at Oil Creek, where they collected petroleum from "the hundreds of oil-pits on the flats," boiled maple sugar, and hewed canoes. A century before, a Franciscan visiting the Neutral Nation also alluded to the use of oil, and this became a point of interest for white travelers already mapping potential revenue streams. Though missionary accounts are by no means authoritative, and the sources that survive in the historical record often exclude or warp Native perspectives, Zeisberger and others noted that the Seneca stored oil and used it in their networks of trade. Popular accounts of Indians and oil leapt over these observations of ordinary life and conjured more exotic scenarios.

J. T. Henry, a chronicler of Pennsylvania's oil region, wrote in 1873, "The oil springs . . . formed a part of the religious ceremony of the Seneca Indians, who formerly lived on these wild hills." He then poured out the sensational details of a savage fire ritual, noting the "hideous appearance" of the natives who set a torch to Oil Creek, which "burst into a complete conflagration" while the gathered crowd howled and cheered. For the white observer, this inferno conjured the exotic forces of oil's hidden world, something out of the primeval past like "the ancient fire worship of the East."

This fire-ritual story appears in nearly every nineteenth-century report on Pennsylvania oil. All cite the same source, a letter from a French commander who witnessed the ritual in 1750. However, the French commander's letter was likely a hoax. At the close of the nineteenth century, under the heading "How History Is Manufactured," journalist John McLaurin revealed that a local newspaper made up the story in the 1840s, "to whet the public appetite for historic and legendary lore." No original copy of the letter exists. A taken-for-granted ethnographic fact may have started as a kind of local tourism stunt.

McLaurin himself should not necessarily be trusted, and if Native people burned oil in a ritual, their intentions can't be assumed—they could equally have meant to inform or confound white observers. At issue is the way the elusive French commander, Henry, and McLaurin all make a particular use of oil into a diagnostic test of savagery or civilization, emphasizing the failure of Native people to "correctly" use a commodity for technological progress. Inquiring minds, then and now, are not entitled to an accounting of Native people's knowledge about oil, mounds, or any other feature of their world. By declining to talk about oil in the desired detail, the Seneca may have protected their relationship with it. In a familiar pattern, Europeans filled the silence with something profitable, an echo of their own fantasies.

When Henry says the Seneca "formerly lived on these wild hills," he means that a scorched-earth US military campaign nearly drove them from their land. The Seneca were part of the Hodinöhsö:ni´, or Haudenosaunee, known to the English as the Iroquois Six Nations, a confederacy that united the Iroquoian-speaking Seneca, Cayuga, Ondondaga, and Oneida nations under a democratic government that spanned their homelands from the Hudson River west to Lake Ontario and the Niagara River. The Tuscarora people, fleeing wars with North Carolina colonists, were adopted as the sixth member of this confederacy in the 1720s. After decades of costly engagement in proxy wars between the French and British, the Haudenosaunee wanted nothing to do with the American Revolution, but many among the Seneca, Mohawk, Onondaga, and Cayuga reluctantly took up arms for their British allies. They knew that this war erupted, in part, over settlers' desire for Indian land. The British crown had negotiated a western boundary for its colonies at the Appalachian Mountains; rather than live as neighbors with Indigenous nations who had already given them ample space, colonists wanted the natives gone. Even before the Declaration of Independence, squatters and armed militias had established a pattern of frontier violence, acting as shock troops who cleared the way for wealthy land speculators.

The British strategy on the western front of the war was to have its Indian allies raid these illegal white settlements. It appears that a majority of the "barbaric" raiders, in some cases, were British loyalists dressed as Indians, but this did not lessen the demand for the new American government to extinguish the savage threat. In 1779, the American general George Washington ordered "the total destruction and devastation of [Iroquois] settlements and the capture of as many prisoners of every age and sex as possible." More than forty Haudenosaunee towns were burned, leaving refugees to freeze in the coming winter; 160,000 bushels of corn were de-

Portrait of George Washington in the home of an impoverished western New York farmer, 1937. This territory was seized under General Washington's direction during the 1779 US offensive against the Iroquois.

stroyed, and thousands starved. Washington specifically instructed troops "to ruin their crops now in the ground and prevent their planting more"—a scorched-earth strategy of extermination that became the gold standard in US warfare.

Some members of the Haudenosaunee fled to Canada or to the west; those who stayed lost most of their land in coerced treaties and sales. The Seneca were something of an exception: Pennsylvania granted sixteen hundred acres to the Seneca leader Kaiiontwa'kon, known as Cornplanter, for his work keeping the peace after the US invasion. In New York, hard-won treaties established Seneca territories at Allegany, Cattaraugus, and Tonawanda, though other territories such as Buffalo Creek were lost to later land grabs. Both Cornplanter and the New York Seneca, their once-continuous territory now parceled into small islands, negotiated to keep their oil springs as an important source of medicine. Cornplanter secured land at the mouth of Oil Creek in Venango County—the future site of Oil City. In New York, Senecas reserved one square mile around a different waterway called Oil Spring. Both places would become centers of the first oil boom, but even before the rush for black gold, guarding Native land rights took constant vigilance and wasn't always successful.

Cornplanter's brother, the religious visionary Sga:nyodai:yoh, or Handsome Lake, saw the New York Oil Spring as a sacred site—this rocky, one-square-mile territory lay far from the main communities where the Seneca lived, yet it mattered enough that Handsome Lake demanded a map from white officials as proof of ownership. Handsome Lake's Longhouse religion, which combined ancient traditions with adaptation to European ways, played an important role in Haudenosaunee cultural revitalization. In 1856, the Seneca Nation went to court to defend the Oil Spring Territory from squatters and won with this map as evidence. Meanwhile, in Pennsylvania, Cornplanter's land on Oil Creek passed into white hands. He agreed to sell to two men named Connelly and Kinnear, but they took the title without paying what they owed. Pennsylvania officials declared it a shameful matter and declined to intervene when Cornplanter's descendants continued to claim Oil City decades later.

Surveyors were at the ready when Seneca leaders signed land-cession treaties, often under conditions of threat and duplicity. Land companies chartered by wealthy financiers divvied up the terrain for an influx of settlers. These companies courted customers far and wide, targeting those in desperate circumstances: advertisements circulated to the hardscrabble farmers of New England, and to "multitudes of poor people from England, Ireland, Scotland and Germany." They presented an idyllic picture of agricultural life, glossing over its constant labor and precarity. Settlers often bought their acreage sight unseen and wound up with rocky terrain that couldn't be planted, but this region was unusually productive precisely because it had been so carefully managed for centuries. The Holland Land Company boasted the "uncommon excellence and fertility of the Soil" and even the great "variety of Fruit Trees . . .

which were planted by the Indians." It's striking that occupying the orchards of a dispossessed people was part of the promotion. Oil was not among the advertised features of this new Eden. However, by the early nineteenth century, settlers began bottling and selling it as a cure-all home remedy. They called it Seneca Oil, based on the loose understanding that Indians had used it as medicine and left it behind, like the fruit trees, for white enjoyment. In the teachings of Handsome Lake and other Seneca practitioners, being healed by medicines was spiritual as well as physical, requiring respect for the materials used. Confident that spiritual powers could be purchased, white Americans attached a great mystique to supposed Indian remedies. By the late nineteenth century, when the patent medicine industry reached its fullest flowering, quacks even recruited members of the Haudenosaunee for their traveling medicine shows. These actors joined an ensemble dressed in fanciful costume, performing a routine that they likely regarded as farce. It was, however, good business, and some Native entrepreneurs left white-run medicine shows to start their own competing product lines.

Until the 1850s, oil was mainly bottled as an elixir, applied to the skin or taken by mouth—the purgative effects proved that it was working. The idea of tapping into its underground source arose after chemists analyzed Seneca Oil and suggested burning it for light, to replace whale oil in the nation's lamps. This would take huge quantities of petroleum. As the story goes, there was no reliable procedure to extract it until Edwin Drake, on what seemed a fool's errand, bored beneath the bedrock of Oil Creek. Unfathomable depths of time burst into the accelerating human time of the nineteenth century. With Drake's well, a barrier was broken and a force unleashed that would rearrange the world. Though no supernatural voices guided his drill, the popular mythology of "Colonel" Drake casts him as an instrument of fate.

In 1858, Drake stepped off the train in Erie and boarded a mail coach for the jolting ride to Titusville, Pennsylvania. A group of investors, incorporated as the Seneca Oil Company, sent him to test their idea of extracting the product from the earth. Other, disconnected efforts were already afoot, in West Virginia, Ontario, Poland, and Romania, throughout the 1840s and '50s—a strong contender for the true first commercial oil well is the one drilled by the American Merrimac Oil Company in the British colony of Trinidad in 1857. This well didn't produce enough to gain much notice, or to keep the company from bankruptcy, but it marks the beginning of a pattern in US oil ideology: a focus on the bounty beneath American soil, while overseas exploits were pushed out of view to hide a growing global empire. The industry would choose Drake's well as its origin story, a heroic drama of one man's struggle to unleash wealth from the land. Drake made quite the underdog: he had no qualifications for oil exploration besides a free train pass from his previous job as a railroad conductor. The company gave him a military title and a top hat in the hope that locals would take him seriously. This was unsuccessful; when he arrived in the town of Titusville and explained his mission, the townspeople dubbed him Crazy Drake and refused to work for him, at least according to later recollections.

Until the 1840s most Americans lit their homes with whale oil, but the world's whales had been hunted nearly to extinction. Camphene, a blend of alcohols distilled from pine trees, became the next cheap lighting source, but it was so much more volatile than any previous fuel that users frequently perished in explosions. The Seneca Oil Company was part of a small petrochemical vanguard hoping to replace blubber and camphene with the flammable substance that burbled up from beneath Oil Creek—if they could figure out how to reach it. In the salt industry, deep wells for salt water were opened up using a steam-powered drill on a long pole to pierce the bedrock, and Drake enlisted an expert salt-driller for this purpose. Crucially, he chose a location a dozen yards away from a cluster of Indigenous oil pits; he relied on this Indigenous infrastructure for his supposed discovery, as earlier settlers had eaten from Indian orchards. For a year hired workmen drilled fruitlessly, until the company cut off Drake's funds in the summer of 1859. Here, writers from the period wax prophetic about the "mysterious guidance" that kept alive his "grand idea struggling to the light." Drake had

GRAND BALL GIVEN BY THE WHALES IN HONOR OF THE DISCOVERY OF THE OIL WELLS IN PENNSYLVANIA.

In an 1861 *Vanity Fair* cartoon, whales throw a ball in honor of Drake's discovery and the demise of whaling. Their banner, THE OIL WELLS OF OUR NATIVE LAND, MAY THEY NEVER SECEDE, refers to oil's strategic role in the Civil War. Both whales and oil wells seem to be active Union supporters.

also sunk his entire personal savings into the quest. Locals claimed that they loaned him money to continue, and a few weeks later he finally hit oil at seventy feet below the ground.

This world-changing reward for perseverance was the foundational legend of the oil boom. Drake became both an everyman and a visionary who put his doubters to shame. "Some mysterious power had got possession of the man's heart, urging him forward," gushed local pastor Samuel Eaton, "to realms of wealth hitherto unknown." In Drake's case this wealth was fleeting; his well soon ran dry and he died in poverty. But perhaps he sacrificed so that others could enter the holy land. The press, which played a crucial role in promoting the Pennsylvania oil region, canonized him as a literal bringer of light to the nation—"Light from the Rock," as one headline proclaimed. In the scramble for cheap lighting fuel, someone else would have hit oil in the late 1850s if Drake had not, and writers would have molded the details of that person's life into an equally inspirational story. Indeed, it's still unclear why the Seneca Oil investors chose the completely unqualified train conductor to search for petroleum; it seems to have been the result of a chance encounter in a hotel restaurant.

More transparent is the investors' choice of a name for their business: *Seneca Oil* needed no explanation, since many people were familiar with the elixir sold in drugstores as an Indian remedy. The oil boom not only changed the future of Petrolia, but also its past. Settlers took another look at the thousands of timber-lined troughs and realized that someone had already harvested large quantities of oil there. Now that white people saw oil as an icon of modernity, they felt that Indians could not be responsible for a large-scale oil enterprise. They "never even dreamed of trade or commerce," wrote the Reverend Samuel Eaton, and "never employed themselves in manual labor of any kind." He and others demanded a more fitting, a more civilized, history for petroleum.

They reached for the popular myth of a lost white race. The vanished white empire most certainly extended from the mounds of the Mississippi Valley to the oil fields of northwest Pennsylvania. Writers frequently alluded to the lost race in their narratives about early oil. J. T. Henry hinted, "At some former period in the history of the American continent, the existence and use of petroleum had been better understood . . . [and] development comparatively extensive." Eaton envisioned "thousands of towns and cities" teeming with millions of inhabitants, a market for petroleum "similar to our own," complete with financial speculation and joint stock companies. This development must belong "to a race of people, who occupied the country prior to the advent of those aborigines, found here by our Latin or Saxon ancestors." Oil troughs, Henry concluded, "were probably the work of that mysterious people who left the traces of their rude civilization in . . . the mounds of the South-West."

This assertion, with the rest of the lost-race mythos, carried forward for more than a century. A 1940 ad for Pennsylvania crude lured customers with the mystery of the oil pits: "Who dug them? Scientists disagree. But most evidence points to the Mound Builders who preceded Indians in North America." *Popular Science* repeated in 1959 that the oil pits "may have been the work of a race preceding the Indians," built with "a construction Indians did not use." The idea persists today in alternative-history conspiracy theories insisting that Greek "oil tycoons" extracted petroleum for their great civilization from North America.

Henry was correct that a different group of people preceded the Seneca in western Pennsylvania, and that their sphere of influence spanned the Great Lakes to the Mississippi Valley. Eaton was right that North America had populous cities and transcontinental trade. It might seem as if these quaint chroniclers were close enough to the truth, given the limitations of their time. But they loudly insisted on a racial distinction that had already been disproved. They praised the superior Mound Builders' "development" as evidence against Indigenous claims to the land. As Henry and his fellow historians tell it, savage Indians drove out their industrious predecessors, and the use of oil degenerated to the primitive rituals that Henry derides as "fire worship"—never mind that published accounts of these rituals were likely white inventions. By this reasoning, white people had fulfilled their Christian duty in reclaiming Seneca oil for civilization.

The contrast that Henry painted between Native and white uses of oil was an ironic reversal. The Seneca, whatever their preferences for its application, seemed to maintain good relations with oil, while speculators surely did not. Henry assured readers that the precious substance, "which careful, prudent men now guard against conflagration, flows into peaceable tanks, and, instead of lighting up the wilderness for exhibitions of uncouth savages, sends joy and comfort into thousands of distant homes." In fact, the oil boom unleashed incredible death and destruction, an onslaught of uncontrollable fires and explosions that historian Brian Black calls a "harbinger of the thinking that guided American industry and land use." Newspapers reported from the inferno of Petrolia with a truly savage relish. They breathlessly recounted the dying moments of victims who fled "shrieking and screaming in their anguish" from jets of flaming oil. Speculators used nitroglycerin torpedoes to widen their wells, igniting entire towns. Fires raged for weeks at a time because even the water that could have extinguished them had oil in it. What followed Drake's discovery was a mass sacrifice to the gods of fuel.

Petrolia's
spiritual awakening

Venango County's many Methodist and Presbyterian churches are a testament to the wildfire spread of religious revivals across the frontier in the early 1800s. Circuit riders would travel from town to town urging the faithful to let God into their hearts—to abandon old doctrines and make a direct connection with the divine. Settlers were often adrift from their old communities and churches. Summer tent revivals drew thousands to outdoor sermons, where audience members seized by the "glorious outpouring of the Spirit" testified with tears and shouts. Roiled by religious fervor, people also opened their hearts to the voices of the dead in Spiritualist séances. The discovery of oil only heightened the feeling that another world was close at hand, just below the surface of things. The earth was teeming with invisible forces, if one only tapped in.

In a field behind Pleasantville's Presbyterian church, a dignified clapboard building on a quiet street, one of the strangest oil strikes of the nineteenth century occurred, guided by powers that claimed to be divine. In telling and retelling the story of Colonel Drake, the press had already established an expectation that God would lead the faithful to oil, but Harmonial Well No. 1 represented a new way of putting that faith into practice. The field has now returned to woodland, the underbrush strewn with bricks, car parts, and splintered lawn furniture—nothing to memorialize where the veil between worlds once parted, allowing a lucky prospector to see through the earth to the ocean of oil below. The whole oil business was ephemeral. Once a well went dry, heavy equipment was sold and wooden derricks rotted, leaving nothing more than a pipe sticking

Triumph Hill, denuded of trees and bristling with dozens of derricks, was typical of Petrolia's muddy and oil-choked landscape.

out of the ground. Even the famous Drake Well, a state historic site with a working steam pump, is a modern reconstruction. Instead of a unique place, it commemorates a ubiquitous process.

Thousands of identical derricks once bristled from the muck of a deforested Petrolia. In grainy photographs, they nestle together on steep hillsides. The procedure developed in these hills would repeat in Texas, California, Russia, Saudi Arabia, and onward around the world. However, deciding where to drill was more idiosyncratic. With an up-front investment of $100,000 in today's money, operators didn't want to strike out. They were desperate for a way to predict the location of oil. Scientific models of the underlying rock formations were unreliable, though geologists could be induced to guess. Cheaper than a geologist, and just as accurate, was what J. T. Henry called an "oil wizard." This motley class of diviners, penetrating the earth with occult energies and elaborate visions, claimed to sense the crevices and caverns where oil lurked.

The most popular method of wizardry was dowsing: dowsers held a forked stick from a hazel or peach tree and walked until the stick dipped and lurched, pointing like a compass needle to oil. Journalist William Wright, touring Petrolia, witnessed the dowsing stick "in the hands of a gentleman of much intelligence and utmost veracity." This gentleman "was not a believer" in folksy superstitions. Despite his skepticism, he "had to acknowledge the existence of the phenomenon for which he could not account," explaining it as "magnetic influence, or some other cause." What mattered to him were practical results. Some professional dowsers, such as Jacob Long, advertised all the famous wells they'd located, predicting "the exact depth that oil would be encountered," but they tended not to record the number of times they had missed entirely.

If a forked stick didn't inspire confidence, others developed more elaborate devices, known as doodlebugs. These ranged from wands to mechanical contraptions with literal bells and whistles. As with dowsing rods, doodlebugs became popular because sometimes they worked. In the oil fields there was no bookish distinction between superstition and science. Seeing was believing. Wright emphasized that the people of Petrolia were no dupes; they were "as keenly inquisitive and practical as are to be found." Groping in the unseeable depths, many embraced spiritual modes of sensing oil.

This longing to commune with the invisible was especially widespread in the 1850s and '60s, not just in remote oil fields but in churches, rowdy theaters, and refined upper-crust parlors. It swept the United States in strange new forms, fusing religious awakenings with the occult sciences of mesmerism and animal magnetism. A motley array of experimenters held that people could influence each other, and the external world, using a mysterious energy that flowed through the human body. It seems inevitable that renegade Christian sects would embrace these fringe scientific theories: rejecting old religious authority, they looked to physical science for proof of the immortality of the soul. The best-known result was a movement called Spiritualism, based on direct communication between the living and the dead. Most recognizable today are the spirit photographs it produced, purporting to capture the energetic imprint of disembodied souls in the new medium of film.

The idea that the dead are present and active in our world is central to many religious traditions, but was not endorsed by mainstream Christianity when the Fox sisters of Hydesville, New York, began delivering messages from spirits in 1848. These spirits were different from ghosts, demons, and other supernatural characters, in that they communicated long-distance from heaven. It began with loud rapping noises echoing through the sisters' bedroom. Soon, they were performing for audiences, translating the raps into letters of the alphabet. The sisters became instruments for the clamoring souls of the dead, who eagerly identified themselves and brought solace to mourning relatives, and to anyone who needed reassurance about the immortal glory of heaven.

This direct line to the spirit world appeared just as new technologies—namely, the telegraph—enabled instant communication across vast distances. Given the remarkable achievements of nineteenth-century science, even heaven seemed within reach. The Fox sisters inspired other Christian religious seekers to become mediums too—they gave the name Spiritualism to this new evidence-based religious practice. Spiritualists developed a range of methods to turn their bodies into "spiritual telegraphs." Entering a trance state, they allowed spirits to "control" them as they wrote, talked, or performed. Though Spiritualism never had an organized structure, followers produced a vast body of literature mapping the landscape of heaven and the pursuits of the afterlife.

Mediums accessed the heavenly spheres with the help of spirit guides who had not yet ascended to the highest, most exalted levels. Though Spiritualists saw their religion as one of progress and liberation, their heaven tended to re-create the unequal landscape of earth. A tradition quickly developed that the lowest levels of the spirit world were inhabited by Native and Black people. According to Andrew Jackson Davis, Spiritualist patriarch and proud namesake of the US president responsible for the Trail of Tears, people of color were bound to their physical forms, while whites could gradually ascend as pure soul-matter.

White mediums often channeled stereotypical "Indian spirits" to serve as guides, reenacting the mythologized service of Sacagawea, Pocahontas, and Squanto. Unlike Ozaawindib, the Ojibwe Two-Spirit woman who may have looked with amusement or scorn on the egomaniacal Henry Schoolcraft as they trekked to the source of the Mississippi, these Indian guides were authored by the white imagination, avatars of guilt, fantasy, and desire. Because of their presumed connection with the earth, and the oft-repeated tale of the Seneca fire ritual, it followed that they would have a nose for oil. "Were the red men drawn to these locations by some mystic attraction? Was petroleum their lodestone?" marveled an oil industry journal. A rhetorical question; the answer was self-evident because "practically every important oil field in North America was once a favorite stomping ground for some Indian tribe." Quite a suggestive correlation, if one overlooks that all of North America belonged to Indians.

On Halloween day in 1866, four men rode a horse-drawn buggy heading south from Pleasantville, Pennsylvania, about four miles east of Oil Creek. One of them was Abraham James, a lanky, pale man with an absentminded look about him. The legend goes that James, "violently influenced" by Indian spirits, suddenly leaped out of the moving buggy, jumped over a fence, and ran into a field. Completely entranced, he paced in circles until the spirits controlling his body threw him to the ground. As his concerned friends gathered by his side, James went on an out-of-body voyage beneath the surface of the earth. A cavern opened up before him, and spirits led him down a long tunnel until they reached a vast lake of petroleum. He gazed in wonder upon an "apparently boundless store of wealth." When James awoke, he explained his vision and planted a penny in the place where he would drill for oil—a small buried treasure to mark the spot of far greater treasure to come.

This and other origin stories of Harmonial Well No. 1 come to us second- and thirdhand, from pamphlets, newspaper reports, and speeches. We can't know what really happened in the field outside Pleasantville that day, but the accounts that circulated were the work of certain Spiritualists with a strong desire to get into the oil business. The men in the buggy were investors who had already leased the field where James happened to be moved by the spirits, and James was renowned as a powerful medium with some geological knowledge from a stint in the California Gold Rush. The tale of James's spirit possession formed the sales pitch for an exclusive stock offering that targeted wealthy Spiritualists. To raise start-up funds, he traveled the country giving lectures, hyping the "hidden treasure" revealed to him through "the counsels of his heavenly teachers."

This was a brash strategy—James took people's money on the promise of authentic revelations. If he didn't find oil, then Spiritualism was false. He must have believed in his own vision, for he kept raising the stakes. In lectures that winter, he made more prophecies: he saw Pleasantville with "an almost innumerable number of derricks shooting up like mainmasts," while belowground oil coursed through "streams and bright veins shining like liquid fire." This wasn't pure fancy; geologists at the time believed that oil either flowed in horizontal streams or filled vertical crevices, like gold veins. James evoked these theories "in strict harmony with the principles of geological science." He claimed that many of his spirit guides were geologists pursuing their studies in the afterlife. This marriage of science with exalted religious vision was a hit with his target audience. James even claimed that the spirits screened each investor to make sure their motives were pure.

Drilling soon began on the spot where an entranced James had placed a penny in the earth. Seasoned oilmen doubted that petroleum could be found so far from Oil Creek. Throughout the yearlong process, James made ecstatic prophecies of coming triumph. Naturally, the locals mocked him as a charlatan until the day in February 1868 when James's Harmonial Well—named for the Harmonial philosophy of Spiritualist patriarch Andrew Jackson Davis—began to draw oil from a depth of 835 feet. A thousand people from nearby towns flocked to see the miracle firsthand.

"There is one good thing—success," gloated the *Spiritual Magazine*; "everyone appreciates that." Practical businessmen immediately snapped up leases on adjacent properties. After a period of market downturn, Harmonial Well No. 1 kicked off a new boom and expanded the quest for oil far beyond its previous territory. "The people from Pithole and other dead towns are tearing down their houses," the *New York Tribune* reported, "and rushing off with them to Pleasantville." Investors lined up for shares of Harmonial Wells Nos. 2 through 5, with the land valued at up to $6,000 per acre. The Spiritualist victory was broadcast in newspaper headlines far and wide as "a prophecy verified," a strange and wonderful achievement of this modern scientific religion.

James Peebles, a leading Spiritualist who had known Abraham James before the oil days, was pivotal in this promotion. He rushed a glowing biography of James to press only seven months after Harmonial Well No. 1 started flowing: *The Practical of Spiritualism* was both a puff piece on James and an impassioned argument for the unity of science and religion in the great march of human progress. Peebles first visited James's Chicago office in 1863, where he found the medium surrounded by large, elaborate geological drawings that he made while controlled by spirits. In a competitive market, mediums had to specialize, and James's specialty was all things mineral. He certainly could have read illustrated books about the "rocky strata" he depicted with such convincing detail. However, Peebles maintained that this knowledge came not from books, but from the spirits of dead geologists. It's an odd distinction, meant to insert Spiritualism into scientific discovery. According to Peebles, "the future life is one of intense activity and progress." Forget eternal rest; heaven is a busy laboratory. There was no need to fear the products of science because wise and pure spirits would only allow it to be used for moral purposes; namely, for the promotion of Spiritualism.

These dead geologists, chemists, and other exalted experts were often called wisdom spirits, who communicated with mediums through words and visions. Yet for James to go from sketching rocks in Chicago to lying facedown in a western Pennsylvania field something more physical had to intervene. A skeptic might say that a desire for money moved Abraham James to the oil region; Peebles maintained that it was the spirits of Indians who "controlled his body mechanically."

Though Peebles did not witness the momentous events of Halloween 1866 that led to the drilling of Harmonial Well No. 1, he visited Petrolia two years later and was honored with a reenactment. James "was seized by an Indian control and rushed for the forests," Peebles reported. "Using the Indian vernacular, attended with violent gesticulations, he traced with his finger the oil veins . . . and there thrust his cane into the earth." According to Peebles, this site too became a productive well. This was a typical show of Spiritualist mediumship, featuring dramatic pantomime and made-up languages. Peebles himself claimed to channel the spirit of "Powhatan," that is, Wahunsenacawh, leader of the seventeenth-century Powhatan Confederacy, for medical advice. Healing was another skill of Indian spirits who inhabited the lower spheres of heaven, intimately connected with the earth and eager to give its medicinal secrets to whites.

The racial logic of the Spiritualist afterlife is obvious enough, justifying worldly white supremacy by stealing and speaking with stereotyped Native voices. Dakota historian Philip J. Deloria writes that this phenomenon of white people "playing Indian" "rests on the ability to wield power against Native people—social, military, economic, and political—while simultaneously drawing power from them." However, Peebles, like many other Spiritualists, considered himself an advocate for Indian welfare. Spiritualists, Quakers, and other Christians with missionary interests were often the sole white advocates for Native nations during decades of intense anti-Indian hatred, when mainstream newspapers depicted Native people as bloodthirsty savages to justify their slaughter. Spiritualists ventured to speak the truth, that "whites have cruelly and unjustly usurped" the continent, and adamantly opposed the "exterminating war upon the Western tribes." On top of their reformist politics, Spiritualists acted from a strange form of self-interest: they feared that their Indian guides to the spirit world, angered by genocide, would abandon them in the metaphysical wilderness. Peebles believed that Indian spirits had saved him from death with their medical prescriptions and felt a strong debt of gratitude founded on this illusory brotherhood.

Peebles was so outraged by the increasing brutality of the Indian wars that he traveled to Washington, DC, to personally lobby members of Congress, some of whom were fellow Spiritualists. He got himself attached to the government's Indian Peace Commission, which toured the Great Plains from the winter of 1867 to the summer of 1868 to resolve conflicts which they admitted "traced to the aggressions of lawless white men." Unsurprisingly, the commission's ideas for helping Indians were not what Native leaders wanted. The commission called for confining Native people on reservations and converting them to a lifestyle of farming, manufacturing, and nuclear families—and relinquishing their land to the influx of settlers which the government claimed it was helpless to stop.

This was the most enlightened position that most white Americans could imagine. Self-appointed advocates such as Peebles assumed that Indians would have to become white to survive, while Native people sought political and cultural independence. The Peace Commission brought no remedy; indeed, it led to a worst-case scenario: many Plains tribes signed treaties and moved to reservations, but the government failed to supply the promised rations. The Lakota, Kiowa, Comanche, and others were forced to hunt for food and pillage from settlers, and were punished with another brutal military crackdown. In 1871, Congress ended the centuries-old practice of making treaties between Europeans and Native nations. Denied political sovereignty, Native people would be managed as wards of the state.

Eastern Spiritualists rarely encountered actual Native people, and their obsession with Indian spirits reflects the common trope of the "vanishing Indian," the idea that what they called the "red race" was doomed to extinction. Peebles wrote chillingly that their "soul-grandeur" "will shine out more clearly in the hunting-grounds of heaven"—practically stating that they were better off dead. Yet a few months later, after meeting with Cherokee and Iroquois Six Nations leaders, Peebles turned around and condemned this trope: "We had been cloyed with selfish talk that the Indian must necessarily perish—perish by law of destiny. Away with your theories about destiny!" Upon returning from the Peace Commission, he reported that the tribal delegations were more "civilized" than the white settlers and generals. "I sometimes feel like flying away from this Christian civilization, so false to justice and benevolence," wrote Peebles, "and going off alone into their country." It's as though he stumbled close to seeing the Indigenous perspective but instead fell into a pit of sentimental self-indulgence.

Peebles's ability to call out "selfish talk" and then perpetrate it captures Spiritualists' unreliable views on the "Indian question." Sometimes they acted as if Native peoples were already gone, at other times they cried out for justice. They often contrasted noble Indians to corrupted, greedy Christians. These ideas were complementary, since the disappearance of Indians made it natural for Spiritualists to receive their wisdom and carry it forward.

Back in the east, the Seneca Nation, and its allies in the Haudenosaunee Confederacy, were certainly not gone, though each group went through its own complex struggles to secure sovereign territory in the US and Canada. The Seneca had significant land holdings near the new oil fields of western Pennsylvania and New York, including Oil Spring, which the prophet Handsome Lake had designated a sacred site. Peebles traveled to Petrolia in 1868, right on the heels of his Peace Commission tour. His interest in petroleum was so keen that it made the living Seneca vanish before his eyes. It was during that 1868 visit to Pleasantville that Peebles witnessed Abraham James running around the woods in search of oil, spouting a made-up "Indian" dialect. Next, Peebles traveled from Pleasantville to the town of North Collins, New York, for an annual meeting of Spiritualists and Quakers. At this meeting, white mediums again channeled Indian spirits. On August 23, Peebles sat in his seat, waiting to deliver one of his celebrated inspirational lectures. A speaker approached the podium who "intensified in diversity" the day's proceedings: he was actually Indian.

Dr. Peter Wilson, a member of the Cayuga Nation who lived for much of his life in a Seneca community, had agreed to address the gathered Spiritualists. Dr. Wilson was the first Native graduate of the Geneva Medical College and a renowned public speaker. He may have endured a long session of white mediums delivering the purported words of Indian chiefs. Then he let them know that they had everything wrong. Unfortunately, the only record of

Wilson's words that day are the few lines that James Peebles wrote down. Wilson himself was mediated by what he felt that he could say, what his audience could understand, and what Peebles would publish. Even so, it seems that he objected strongly to the Spiritualist performances. Peebles describes the beginning of the speech as "playful criticism." Did Wilson find the North Collins mediums laughable, infuriating, or both?

Spiritualists tended to assume that Native people were proto-Spiritualists, focusing their ethnological gaze on Native traditions of communication with ancestors and nature spirits. Just as Indians intuited the value of oil that whites would fully realize, they also anticipated the breakthrough of spirit communication. Wilson tried to push back against the homogenizing assumptions of his audience; perhaps he told them about the role of ancestors in his community and his understanding of what happened after death. All Peebles noted from this section of the speech was that "spirits continually come back." While Wilson may have specified how his faith was different from Spiritualism, Peebles, the medium, wanted to affirm that they were the same.

This outlook was part of a larger, pseudohumanitarian effort to Christianize Indians. During centuries of violent pressure from missionaries and officials, Native people had to exercise great care with their public religious expressions. Each group and individual had different ways of embracing, adapting, or rejecting Christianity. William Apess, a Pequot and ordained Methodist minister in antebellum Massachusetts, used deeply-held Christian identity and values to support his demands for Native rights. Indigenous dances and religious ceremonies were banned under US law, and those who kept their traditions alive, or took up new ones such as the Ghost Dance, ran great risks—starvation and military crackdowns on reservations, brutal punishment in boarding schools. Meanwhile, bizarre misrepresentations of Native ceremonies circulated in American popular culture, including at the North Collins meeting. Spiritualists and other sympathetic Christians often claimed that Indians worshipped a "Great Spirit" who was identical with the Christian God. While many Native people, including

Jane Johnston Schoolcraft, did find compatibility between these two traditions, Dr. Wilson took his chance to reject the demand for religious brotherhood.

"None of us desire to go to the Christian's heaven!" he told the North Collins crowd, so vociferously that even Peebles took note. "Why should we? They'd turn us out, if possible! See how they've used us in this world; and they preach, there's 'no change after death.'" Here, Wilson pinned the Spiritualists on their segregated heaven, where race continued to determine destiny. Dr. Wilson, to the extent that we can identify these as his words, held that it was false to lump together Indigenous worldviews with Spiritualism developed in a white, Christian, colonial context. He strongly suggested that he was a "pagan Indian," that is, a follower of the Longhouse religion of Handsome Lake. The Native leaders whom Peebles met on his tour with the Peace Commission wanted sovereignty over their land, and perhaps Wilson demanded spiritual sovereignty. Somehow, Peebles could listen to and record these assertions of sovereignty and immediately go back to channeling Indian spirits in his usual way.

This selective blindness is a testament that sympathy is not solidarity and can indeed produce its opposite. Sympathy was Spiritualists' cardinal virtue, the key to talking with the dead. More than a feeling, sympathy evoked a deep, resonant connection between souls. Spiritualism attracted hundreds of thousands of followers because it promised that the sympathetic bonds of love could overcome death, a notion that helped many to heal from loss. Yet Peebles's sympathy with the Indian cause was a perfect mirror of his own assumptions and yearnings. When Dr. Peter Wilson stood up to speak for himself, he was simply not recognized. "There was hardly a ripple of inharmony," Peebles reported.

Sympathy can come close to subverting the order of things: white mediums seized by Indian spirits fiercely condemned America's "crimes as red as blood." The mediums' performance was offensive to Native people, and also traitorous to many white people—one critic suggested that Spiritualists should face the Ninth Cavalry if they truly sided with the "dirty, thieving, dissolute" Indians. Actually switching sides in a military conflict was far past the limit of reformist politics. Some Spiritualists did turn their sympathy into meaningful political action. The same group of heterodox Quakers who hosted the North Collins meeting had led a nationwide protest to overturn the fraudulent 1838 Treaty of Buffalo Creek, which nearly robbed the Seneca of all their land. In the end, however, playing Indian reinforced the order of things. Indian spirits, projections of the white desire for forgiveness, accepted their place in the lower rungs of heaven and, with cartoon vernacular and bawdy jokes, showed that racial difference transcended death.

Abraham James's search for oil followed this order, with Indian spirits working "mechanically" on his body while white "wisdom spirits" enlightened his soul. In the higher spheres of heaven, geologists were hard at work mapping oil deposits. Surprisingly, Peebles revealed that certain wisdom spirits had an ancestral claim to the oil region. "These controlling intelligences are the spirits, (some of them) of an ancient race, that inhabited this country many thousand years ago," Peebles wrote, referring to the mythical Mound Builders, whose "unmistakable evidences of art, science, and manufactures" proved to so many Americans that Indigenous nations were the usurpers of a previous white civilization. Always trying to claim the authority of science, Peebles endorsed the antiquarian timeline of the lost race. Despite his sympathies with the Native cause, he eagerly repeated the idea that the Mound Builders had "dug wells . . . and speculated in oil" long before the arrival of "red men." Applied to Petrolia, this theory helped to undermine the land rights and sacred sites of the Seneca Nation when their land became a target for extraction.

No one knew where oil would next be found. Major development was concentrated near existing wells in Venango County, where the odds seemed best. Wildcatters with their doodlebugs roamed the hills from Oil City north past the New York border. Immediately after Drake's strike the Seneca Nation acted to lease its Oil Spring and Allegany territories, but the wells were unproductive. In the 1870s, deeper drilling led to the discovery of another vast oilfield. In 1871, near the town of Bradford, Pennsylvania, a well drilled to eleven hundred feet heralded the opening of this new field, which would, for a brief time, produce almost three-fourths of the world's oil. Thousands of workers and speculators brought with them the usual explosive tendencies, eventually engulfing the Seneca Nation's Allegany and Oil Spring territories on all sides in oil fever. While they had successfully defended the Oil Spring territory from white squatters, by the 1890s, Seneca leaders faced overwhelming political pressure and financial need to lease land for renewed drilling. "Many envious eyes have been turned to the direction of the reservation," wrote an industry magazine, practically drooling over the prospect. Oil companies aggressively bribed and swindled Seneca officials into exploitative leases. The corruption was so egregious that Congress launched an investigation in 1897; it concluded that the deals were unfair but should go ahead anyway. If the Senecas delayed to get a fair price, someone would steal their oil by drilling just outside their borders.

The oil industry quickly left its mark on Seneca territories. Contrary to the superstition that Indians must be sitting atop buried treasure, dozens of wells drilled on the Allegany and Oil Spring territories failed to produce. Controversies smoldered over whether

Burning oil tanks at Olean, New York, between 1880 and 1890.

Seneca people had the right to seek the treasure themselves or by cutting individual deals with white firms. In January of 1897, an oil company chopped down a derrick that a Seneca engineer, Daniel Shongo, had erected on land for which both parties claimed the lease. By October, a fire swept the territory, destroying "a large number of oil well rigs and a great deal of oil property"; reports made no mention of what happened to Seneca homes and crops. This strife was but a preview of the price that Indigenous people paid when they tried to benefit from their own mineral resources. Two decades later, in the oil fields of Oklahoma, more than a hundred Osage people were murdered by their white husbands and guardians for oil royalties. Though without the same financial motive, gender-based violence against Indigenous women and girls remains endemic to extraction boomtowns into the present day. The Osage murders shock because of their intimacy, but like the continental process of genocide, they stemmed from the elaborate European myth that the land was meant for white people, who were backed by a higher law that overruled even God's commandment not to kill.

In the wake of Abraham James's success in 1868, Spiritualist mediums joined the array of occult oil-finders at large in Petrolia. A Pittsburgh newspaper described a Spiritualist who "had been sleeping at his home . . . when the spirit of an Indian chief came and beckoned him." The apocryphal chief, Old Tonahauqua, led the man to a place in the woods and declared that "far down in the earth's crust . . . there was water that would burn." Again, the spot was drilled and yielded a hundred barrels a day. This work could be done remotely by correspondence, a signature skill of the renowned medium and mystic Edgar Cayce. After locating wells for others in the Texas boom, Cayce decided to establish his own oil company. Like the earlier Harmonial Wells, his "Mother Pool" was supposed to fund the advancement of spiritual enlightenment, though Cayce had less luck than James. Other mediums located oil by channeling the ancient memories stored within rocks. As always, skeptics amused themselves by making fun of these enterprises, unless they worked.

High-minded Spiritualists such as Peebles took a huge risk by associating their religion with a dirty industry. It seems incongruous that a crowd so focused on the joys of heaven would descend to the inferno of Petrolia, a place known for ruthless greed where prospectors quipped that they were drilling "to oil or hell." Peebles had initially approached with caution. In January of 1867, when he first visited Spiritualist friends in Titusville, he resisted their pressure and "did not invest" in oil. "'Tis better to dig up than down," he proclaimed, gesturing at the heavenly kingdom. However, a year later, after witnessing Abraham James's miracle, he joined his friends in asserting that petroleum was part of a divine plan to "illumine distant cities, and spiritually enlighten human minds." He realized that oil could do something for Spiritualists, and they could do something for oil.

Spiritualists knew how to seize a narrative. Their movement had grown with astonishing speed since 1848, with followers numbering in the millions, thanks to powerful performances and widely circulated newspapers. Petroleum was on a similar trajectory. In the decade after Drake struck oil in Titusville, poor farmers became millionaires overnight, kerosene became America's main artificial light source, and a Northern oil monopoly aided the Union victory in the Civil War. The unstoppable flow of oil became a metaphor for the onward rush of modernity, also signified by railroads, telegraphs, factories, and mushrooming cities. The eyes of the nation were especially riveted on the drama in western Pennsylvania, due to the sheer novelty of the substance gushing from deep within the earth. Newspapers, books, and magazines covered every twist and turn of the nascent industry so that even distant readers felt immersed in the thrill of a new era.

The narrative was one of glorious and fearsome progress. If some Americans felt uneasy about technology, Spiritualists had the special ability to bless it with the voices of the past. They soothed the violent shock of the new, for the spirits "had long been aware of these petroleum deposits, and had patiently awaited the opportunity and conditions to develop them." Peebles also emphasized that oil was a healing substance inherited from Indians. "Many years ago, as the Seneca Indians have the tradition, the Great Spirit appeared to one of their chiefs in a dream," Peebles claimed; the Great Spirit foretold "a liquid which would prove a balm for the cure of many ailments to which red men as well as white men were heirs."

This prophecy hints at the political meaning of oil at a pivotal moment in the 1860s. What were these "ailments" afflicting white men, which petroleum promised to cure? To many Northern Spiritualists, the ailment was slavery, which they had long railed against as part of the abolitionist movement. In retrospect, they thought it no coincidence that oil appeared just in time for the Civil War and was both geographically and metaphorically on the Union side. Kerosene replaced camphene, a lamp oil produced in the South using slave labor. As one company prospectus put it, oil was "a great gift of God, held in store for ages, and recently given to us in our day of national trial." It literally greased the gears of the factories and railroads that kept supplies flowing to Federal troops. The less savory reverse of this narrative was also true: war created the oil boom, with massive inflation driving investors to seek hard assets, namely oil lands and infrastructure.

Spiritualist believers were said to be abundant in the Union ranks, including the "regiment of Spiritualists," the Fourteenth Massachusetts Volunteers, and Colonel Nathan W. Daniels, who led one of the Union Army's first Black regiments, the Second Louisiana Native Guard Volunteers. James Peebles, citing his delicate health, served as a quartermaster's clerk. As abolitionists noted with unease, the war's official purpose was to defeat the Confederacy, not to free the enslaved. The mass resistance of enslaved people who stopped work and escaped bondage led to Emancipation as a military strategy. Still, many who served under the Union flag did so in the name of freedom, and a Republican Congress enacted Black citizenship and suffrage on the strength of their sacrifices. Spiritualist papers boasted that war's purifying flames, beyond just ending slavery, could burn off all the evils corrupting society, North and South. In this they were sadly mistaken; especially because they often accepted racial subjugation so long as Black people weren't bound in actual chains. Meanwhile, the Union army had already begun a war of extermination against Native nations west of the Mississippi.

Despite their general support for Emancipation and a fervent role in radical Reconstruction, white Spiritualists were hardly immune to the view that racial inequality was a fact of nature. Black spirits were relegated to the lower spheres of heaven, alongside or inferior to Native ones. As Black ex-Spiritualist Paschal Beverly Randolph could attest, living African Americans had rarely been welcomed in the movement, though a few, such as Harriet E. Wilson in Boston and Henry Louis Rey in New Orleans, were successful mediums and used the voices of spirits to assert their own demands. Rey's spirits became increasingly pessimistic as Reconstruction faltered and the dream of Black political power was dashed by reactionary violence. The spirits could only look on in horror as former enslavers reinstated white supremacy, despite "the lessons of the Past which ought to have enlightened you, for they have been written in letters of blood." Anti-slavery Spiritualists in the North seemed equally helpless. Paschal Beverly Randolph labeled their "Northern philanthropy" a "hollow pretense." They spouted platitudes of healing and forgiveness, averting their eyes so that North and South could enjoy a sentimental reunion. If oil was a "balm for the cure of many ailments"—meant to aid Northern victory—the cure had been even less than skin-deep.

Thousands of Civil War veterans went straight from the battlefield to the oil fields as soon as they were mustered out, having closely followed the oil boom in the newspapers. This oil rush helped Americans forget the recent crisis and rally around the market as a source of identity and opportunity. The Reverend Eaton called it "the solution of the mighty problem of the nation's destiny." Science-loving Spiritualists were proud of Northern factories, railroads, steam power—it was easy to see industrial growth as God's plan for the triumphant Union. Upon closer inspection, this balm too merely concealed the ailment: the war had enriched profiteers and laid the groundwork for an era of inequality, corruption, and genocidal westward expansion. Racial politics held the contradictions of industrial capitalism in place, pitting poor whites against Black and Indigenous people for land and resources. The question for Spiritualists was whether they would again let a narrative of divine progress justify these evils.

Spiritualists had no illusions about the virtues of the market. They constantly inveighed against the worship of money as the cardinal sin of the nineteenth century: "the rich get richer" by preying on the increasingly miserable poor. Celebrity medium Cora Richmond described the post–Civil War decades as "one continuous tide of ruinous 'prosperity' . . . the prosperity born of speculation, of gambling in all the natural products of the country." Many, outraged by the iron rule of exploitation, combined Spiritualism with socialism and radical politics. Perhaps a real remaking of society would come through cooperative farms, mutual aid societies, or communal banks, ideas that filled the pages of the Spiritualist press. In the Midwest, working-class "prairie socialists" circulated their own small newspapers espousing heterodox religion and revolution under the banner of "free thought." The medium Victoria Woodhull, a socialist and women's rights advocate who briefly ran for president in 1873, with Frederick Douglass in the vice-presidential slot, suggests the mass politics that some envisioned.

There was also a strong impulse to retreat from an unsympathetic world and build separate, self-sufficient communities, "so as to be a light unto others." The founder of a Spiritualist colony in California promised, "the good that bloodshed could not gain, your peaceful zeal shall find." He held up a forty-five-pound beet grown by a resident as proof that God had favored their endeavors. Spiritualism was so multifarious and broadly popular that its followers did not cohere beyond a general reformist mood and desire for moral reckoning. Finding fault with actually existing unions and political parties, many concluded that enlightenment had to happen individually and put faith in the intervention of spirits, rather than strikes, to peacefully "reconcile capital and labor."

Even for Spiritualists who bemoaned the evils of industrial capitalism, oil held a powerful attraction. It was new and seemingly democratic, since anyone could, according to popular depictions, strike it rich. The Spiritualist colony called Summerland, home of the forty-five-pound beet, in fact derived its wealth from an oil boom after its founder invented offshore drilling. The moral criticism sometimes levied against oil—that it broke the link between hard work and wealth with its spontaneous effulgence—actually helped its image in comparison with coal, an unglamorous fuel that was far more important than petroleum for the nation's economy. Coal miners, recruited from the most desperate classes at home and abroad, worked under notoriously authoritarian, dehumanizing conditions that reeked "more of feudalism than of freedom," in the view of Spiritualists. Yet when miners went on strike, middle-class Spiritualists complained that coal prices were too high and called union leaders "reckless, ignorant demagogues."

The labor situation in the oil fields was extremely violent in its own way, with tremendous hardship inflicted on the lowest rungs of the workforce—teamsters, boatmen, and railroad men like forty-seven-year-old Jeff Martin, whose cause of death was first listed as "exhaustion," then corrected in another hand to "skull crushed by fall of rock." Unlike in coal mines, labor organizing was rare among oil's nomadic workforce. The industry's dominant narrative, which centered white middle-class prospectors rather than Black workers like Martin, was one of bootstrapping individual heroism. Spiritualists could indulge a harmonious vision that the earth revealed its secrets to worthy souls, for worthy causes. They saw petroleum as a natural product harvested from the earth in a rustic frontier— and placed there by God for a cosmic purpose. Perhaps they had a chance, by getting into the business, to convert greedy oil operators to the Golden Rule—"love thy neighbor as thyself." Finally, the powerful symbolism of light and illumination had been central to Spiritualist faith from the beginning. Cheap kerosene lamps burning in every home were beacons of populist uplift, just as ubiquitous smartphones are today held as proof of technology's virtue.

The movement was often torn between its vision of a just society and its fetish for technological progress. The leap into oil prospecting reflects that, like many of their fellow Americans, a number of Spiritualists simply decided to pretend these were the same thing. Peebles promised that "petroleum as the basis of national prosperity" would quickly "mould society into a more beautiful character." The testimony of the spirits forged an enduring link between prophecy and profit.

Ruinous prosperity

It might seem inevitable that the discovery of oil leads to a frenzied boom like the one in western Pennsylvania—who doesn't want to get rich overnight? But the unique nature of oil made the boom faster, messier, and more dangerous than anything seen before. A liquid commodity that gushed from the ground, but could dry out just as suddenly, fed the American economy's volatile swings. Indeed, oil embodied that growing volatility. Most previous forms of production were anchored to a specific place, whether to farms, mills, factories, or coal mines. Oil was process based, sweeping from site to site at a stunning pace. Even people in the industry compared it to the onslaught of an invading army. The power of markets to mold landscapes wasn't new, but oil did so at a nearly unprecedented scale.

Some observers compared the oil boom to the California Gold Rush of 1849. Though both triggered large migrations of fortune seekers, the forty-niners were artisans compared to the oil operators, whose product was so abundant and cheap that they often wasted more of it than they sold. In 1862, one observer estimated the losses at three-quarters of total production. Thousands of gallons of oil spilled from pumps and leaked from shoddy barrels or burned in fires and explosions. This may seem like madness, but people acted quite rationally; writing the chaos off as "oil fever" obscures that the market dictated such behavior.

The master logic of the oil boom was the rule of capture. This rule, enshrined in the property law of the time, meant that whoever owned surface land had an unlimited right to harvest resources from it, even if those resources might extend to another person's property. The classic example is water: if I draw water from a stream on my farm that flows to my neighbor's farm, the law of capture allows me to slurp all the water before it reaches my neighbor. Once someone struck oil, competitors bought up nearby land and raced to tap the same deposit. Like a soda with ten straws in it, the oil would soon run dry. The winner was the person who drilled first and fastest, but victory was fleeting. Nine months after Abraham James's miracle, reports noted a "steady decrease in the production" of the Harmonial Well because it had too many new neighbors.

The rule of capture determined the fate of the oil region. Speed was the overwhelming imperative, sweeping aside concerns for safety or efficiency. The need for immediate action to seize available oil "gave the industry the right to have no rules restricting its development," writes historian Brian Black. Ironically, this speed led to wild fluctuations in the price of oil that bankrupted many prospectors. In 1861, a promising entrepreneur named Henry Rouse hit the first "gushing well"—previous wells needed a pump to bring oil to the surface, but this one spouted forth uncontrollably. Tens of thousands of barrels flooded the market and caused a crash that put many out of business.

The gusher left in its wake a graveyard of abandoned derricks, plus the grave of Henry Rouse and sixteen other people. Rouse had been standing with a crowd near the spouting well on the day of its discovery, celebrating his wild success, when a spark from a distant engine ignited the volatile gas in the air, and then the oil itself, which fell from the sky in a rain of fire. Newspapers described him staggering from the flames, clothes burned off and "eyeballs crisped to nothing." Rather than repent his sins as he died, Rouse reportedly said, "My account is already made up. If I am a debtor, it would be cowardly to ask for credits now." Even his soul had submitted to the unforgiving balance sheet of the oil fields.

When the price of oil was way down, as in the aftermath of Rouse's gushing well, operators did the math to see if it was worth the cost to them of tanks, barrels, and shipping. Sometimes it wasn't. However, as Black writes, "the corporate priority remained to pump all the oil out of the ground before someone else could get it." One spiteful operator, asked why he was pouring a hundred barrels an hour down the creek, replied, "You won't give five cents a barrel for it, and I can stand a loss rather than let you have it at that price!" In the race against competitors, some stored oil in shoddy tanks, or in standing pools, which fueled more infernos and loss of life.

For locals, petroleum swept through like an invading army. Indeed, many workers came directly from the battlefields of the Civil War. Geologist Stephen F. Peckham called them a "floating and unsettled class," masses of men seeking their fortune in reckless and ruthless competition. Peckham could have said much the same about himself, though his interests were more scientific than most. Peckham was discharged from the Union Army on May 26, 1865, weeks after the Confederate surrender. Before the war, he had barely left Rhode Island, but afterward he pursued oil across continents and oceans, hardly living in the same place for more than a few years. As a sort of petroleum scout, he saw how the industry repeated its characteristic procedure at each new site.

Peckham mournfully described this scorched-earth process: "The farms, fields, orchards, or gardens alike are lost to agriculture and given to oil. . . . Beautiful and valuable timber is ruthlessly cut and left to rot in huge heaps. . . . The vast storage tanks stand, a perpetual menace to everything near them that will burn." The land had been sacrificed. "Nothing that I have ever beheld reminded me so forcibly of the dire destruction of war . . . and nothing else but the necessity of an army commands such a complete sacrifice of every other interest or leaves such a scene of ruin and desolation." Having survived the horror of the Civil War, he was compelled, ghost-like, to revisit it at each new oil frontier. For many New Englanders such as Peckham, the war had been a grand crusade to end slavery and restore the Union, but what was the purpose of this new violence?

It's easy to view the sacrifice of Petrolia as a "tragedy of the commons" situation. In that famous parable, instinctive selfishness leads people to plunder a shared resource, such as a common pasture, until nothing is left—even though more modest use would allow the resource to last in the long term. Indeed, the tragedy of the commons explains all environmental damage and scarcity as inevitable consequences of human nature. This story is still taught in science classes today and has an intuitive appeal, but it's important to consider the source. The essay "The Tragedy of the Commons" was written in 1968 by an ecologist named Garrett Hardin, who also pursued a career as a right-wing eugenicist ideologue. Hardin lent scientific credibility to eugenic and anti-immigrant crusades, warning that other races would outcompete whites for limited resources. His factual claims about human nature justified the conservative worldview that produced those very claims.

We don't have to rely on the thought experiments of eugenicists; history suggests that people do not always decimate the commons. Indeed, the commons once sustained collective life in many places. English peasants shared common land for centuries before it was seized by a wealthy elite starting in the sixteenth century. The wealthy pushed forward laws that gave "sacred status" to their new property, leaving masses of peasants to starve. Writes Roxanne Dunbar-Ortiz, "The traumatized souls thrown off the land, as well as their descendants, became the land-hungry settlers enticed to cross a vast ocean," where they committed unfathomable violence against Native Americans, Aboriginal Australians, and others. Indigenous groups often had their own communal land ethics, based on upholding good relations between human and nonhuman life, which European invaders tried to stamp out. These acts were protected by the Doctrine of Discovery, a legal invention of Christian rulers that allowed them to claim land inhabited by "heathens." This is not a timeless tragedy of human nature, but one driven by new legal and political tools enabling unprecedented exploitation of land and people. The Supreme Court continues to uphold the "discovery doctrine" as the basis of US authority over Indigenous lands.

Similarly, there's more to the story of oil than primal human nature unleashed. The oil boom was constructed by systems far from some imagined "natural" state. Historian Brian Black reminds us that the tragedy of the commons models "human nature, as a capitalist society rewards it." The rule of capture was supported by laws, court rulings, financial instruments, and corporate imperatives, to which individuals only responded. The need for ever-greater quantities of oil was itself manufactured, partly by the round-the-clock production schedule forced upon the urban working classes—kerosene light was cheap and safer than the alternatives, but "dependency didn't mean desire, or even consent," as one historian puts it. "Independent, rational free enterprise" only appeared a timeless urge within a social and economic system built for exploitation.

The support of a top-notch legal team, and huge bribes to government officials, was crucial as the oil industry consolidated in the 1870s and '80s. John D. Rockefeller, an ambitious former clerk who bought his first oil refinery in 1863, moved quickly to monopolize the railroads that transported his product from western Pennsylvania to Cleveland. Rockefeller's genius lay in exploiting the elaborate inner workings of the market, in pulling hidden levers of this machine too fast for anyone to stop him. The rise of Rockefeller's Standard Oil Company brought shipping and refining under monopoly control, but this new corporate order didn't make life in Petrolia any more humane. Rockefeller gained the power to set prices, squeezing oil producers and justifying their reckless practices. When they tried to outsmart him by building pipelines that would bypass his railroad network, Rockefeller simply laid his own pipelines. Journalist Ida Tarbell made these outrages public in her famous 1904 exposé, *The History of the Standard Oil Company*. Among many embittered by the monopoly, one oil producer told her, "The people of the Oil Regions have by slow degrees been brought into a condition of bondage and serfdom."

Tarbell's obsession with taking down Rockefeller grew out of personal experience; she came of age in Petrolia amid his rise to domination. Standard Oil put Tarbell's father out of business, and he was among the small producers calling themselves "independents" who sabotaged Rockefeller's supply lines in protest. At stake was oil's democratic-entrepreneurial ethos, the idea that anyone could strike treasure and reap the profits, a promise at the core of American identity. Resistance also drew from the religious revivals that swept the region—if both the Bible and oil came directly from God, the independents wanted no church or monopoly to intervene. They saw the rule of capture, its rugged individualism, unpredictability, and danger as aligned with their fiery faith.

However, for outside observers during those decades, a narrative of progress prevailed. Rockefeller portrayed himself as "an angel of mercy reaching down from the sky" to heal the chaotic oil fields. Perhaps controlling the country's supply of this highly spiritual substance made him feel like a messiah: he compared himself to "Moses who delivered [oilmen] from their folly" and spoke of his endeavors as "godlike." By the 1890s, it looked as if oil had evolved into a mature, steady industry, as Petrolia settled in to the production pattern set by "the Standard." Even before Rockefeller intervened, the expectation of progress from thrilling chaos to pious order was already in place, promoted in part by Spiritualists seeking their own toehold in the industry.

The Spiritualist propagandizer James Peebles had asserted, "There is a vast difference between a wild oil-excitement fever . . . and a steady legitimate business" of the sort that Abraham James was running. Peebles didn't deny that oil speculation was driven by sinful greed. But he, along with other moralists of every stripe, felt that oil itself was not sinful; indeed, it was the redemption of the American project. "It is said that faith will remove mountains," remarked one commentator; "in this case . . . it penetrated the flinty rock and caused the earth to yield up her oily treasures, as a fitting reward for the indomitable energy and perseverance" of the oil operators. This foul-smelling, corrosive, highly flammable substance was proof of God's grace. Many churches invested in oil leases—some even drilled in their own cemeteries, on the hunch that God would be more likely to put oil under holy ground. It took a lot of Manifest Destiny to make desecrating graves into a virtue.

Though Spiritualists were not the first religious group to profit from oil, they made the Harmonial Wells a public proof of their religion in a new way. Their mission all along was a merger of science and faith—replacing mysteries with evidence, making the invisible world visible. Rather than ancient scripture, Spiritualists had real-time testimony. "Liquid treasures are flowing under [your] feet," the spirits of the dead proclaimed, urging the living to "enter into your reward!" Given the widespread longing for directly revealed religious truth, not to mention mineral wealth, many church-going people delved into occultism and psychic mediumship. The revelations that Spiritualists such as James used to promote the fuel of the future shaped the outlook of other Christians who might have hesitated on the precipice of Petrolia's muddy hellscape.

Among those Christians who fused religion with the frantic search for buried treasure was Lyman Stewart, founder of the Union Oil Company and an engineer of the Christian fundamentalist movement. Born in Titusville, Stewart came of age amid the religious revivals and abolitionist meetings that grew in the same soil as Spiritualism. He returned from his Union regiment in 1865 to find his hometown ravaged by oil extraction. However, he interpreted the situation through the lens of his vigorous faith: God had hidden the keys to heaven, and to find oil was to find salvation. Like James, he saw that spreading one's religion required money. If he struck it rich, he could deploy an army of missionaries around the globe—far more effective than becoming a missionary himself. With the help of investors from his church, Stewart bought land a few miles from Pleasantville and opened his first well in 1867. It produced 750,000 barrels for the cause before running dry. Though he never identified as a Spiritualist, Stewart's method for finding oil belonged to the supernatural tradition of Abraham James and other diviners. He crept over the hills of Petrolia, his senses open to signs, portents, and intuitions. Like James, he saw his soul as an instrument moved by divine forces to detect blessings below the ground.

In the years that followed, more conventional Christian sects gathered around the divine fountain of crude. Oil baron John D. Rockefeller led them there with his lavish donations, funding a Baptist college (the University of Chicago), overseas missions, and scientific research. Rockefeller declared, "The power to make money is a gift from God," justifying his ruthless business practices with philanthropy. "I believe it is my duty to make money and still more money," he told a reporter, "and to use the money I make for the good of my fellow man according to the dictates of my conscience." The Spiritualist script echoed here as well: Rockefeller and his foundation trumpeted reason, progress, and oil as part of God's plan to elevate humankind. While Spiritualists confirmed this directly in their dramatic séances, mainstream Protestants preferred a quieter God whose will manifested in the stock ticker.

Though both Rockefeller and Lyman Stewart merged their spirituality with capitalism, they were archrivals in everything else. While Stewart fought to end slavery, Rockefeller sat it out, donating money to the Union and spending the war years accumulating what one admirer called "God's gold." By the time Stewart got established in the oil business, Rockefeller's iron grip on western Pennsylvania was tightening, driving independent operators to ruin. Technically, it wasn't Rockefeller who caused Stewart's bankruptcy—Stewart simply made and lost some risky bets—but he would never forgive Standard Oil's dirty tactics. In 1882, Stewart joined the westward migration of oilmen to unproven fields in Texas and California. He believed that God would lead him through trial to a bounteous promised land. This vision proved accurate: Stewart indeed found oil in California, and this time invested wisely in a refinery, pipelines, and a laboratory to develop new uses for his product, such as the oil-burning locomotive. He named his enterprise the Union Oil Company, which rose to challenge Rockefeller in the name of small, independent producers.

Stewart also challenged Rockefeller's liberal Christianity, which purported to soothe the ravages of capitalism with uplift for the poor. Instead, Stewart poured his money into a new movement called fundamentalism, which celebrated those ravages as a herald of the end-times. His pamphlets *The Fundamentals*, distributed by the millions around the world, asserted that the Bible was literal truth, God's will was active in the world, the rapture was near at hand, and everything depended on saving souls before that fateful moment. Stewart built up fundamentalism through his publications, Bible schools, and missions—just as in the oil fields, there was no time to waste. Charity was senseless, since only embracing the true faith could lift people out of misery and ultimately into heaven.

Theology had a direct impact on the oil business, just as the oil business shaped Rockefeller's and Stewart's theology. Historian of religion Darren Dochuk details how Stewart, an industry underdog fighting the Standard Oil behemoth, rallied his fellow "independent producers" around a fusion of rugged free enterprise and strict fundamentalist morals. Within their companies and in the consumer marketplace, they imposed a vision of America as a Christian nation built on the divine bounty of crude—in oil's family, labor serves management at work, and women serve men at home, to keep humanity's house in order for the great day of reckoning. The churches they supported, now broadly labeled evangelical, have come to dominate American Christianity.

The rule of capture that governed the oil fields, where taking as much as you could as quickly as you could was a virtue, flowed into the modern prosperity gospel that celebrates the rich as God's chosen. Religious scholar Brendan Pietsch calls it "millennial capitalism," arbitrary and unsustainable by design, where wealth is "a product of supernatural blessing instead of a product of labor." Lyman Stewart set the mold for the twentieth century's evangelical oilmen, such as Sun Oil founder J. Howard Pew, who plowed their fortunes into conservative schools, foundations, and media outlets to fight the liberal trends of the New Deal and civil rights eras—which Pew blamed on "witch doctors abroad in the land, teaching communism." Perhaps it's natural that these evangelicals joined forces with free-market economists in the rise of the new political right that began in the 1950s.

Stewart's and Pew's individualistic evangelism and Rockefeller's corporate liberalism were hardly opposite poles on a political spectrum, just two different strategies for protecting the powerful. Despite profound disagreements, Rockefeller and the independents both concluded that the wealthy were uniquely entitled to mold society according to their visions. Previous robber barons had done charitable deeds, endowing hospitals and museums to placate the rabble, but this new form of corporate power aimed at the nation's political soul. Pew called for a "strong and fervent faith in the superiority of our American competitive enterprise system as a means of raising the standard of living for all." This had the advantage of protecting his wealth from democratic control. Winning access to classrooms with free lesson plans and books, oil-sponsored curricula taught generations of children that the personal "freedom to dream, to think, to experiment" was synonymous with economic "free enterprise." To regulate or tax, to organize for labor rights, or to build public programs defied the supreme intentions revealed in things as they are.

This would seem like a very different outcome from the dream of Spiritualist oil entrepreneurs in the early days of the industry. The most radical among them, socialists and utopians of many stripes, imagined a new world where power was shared for the benefit of all. Yet enterprising Spiritualists, just like Stewart and Rockefeller, felt that their path to changing the world lay through "accumulating sufficient wealth" to build libraries, schools, and lecture halls— spreading the commodity of enlightenment along with the light of oil lamps. These utopias were loyal to the liberal ideal that social progress inevitably followed scientific and economic advancement. Despite the mockery Spiritualists endured for channeling "offensive and unpleasant" Indian spirits, they seldom had to doubt that they were included in the great national destiny, one contingent on Black and Indigenous dispossession as well as periodic crackdowns on working-class unrest.

In their eagerness to fuse their religion with modernity itself, Spiritualists such as Abraham James helped to deify the market as a mysterious instrument that converted divine insight into material wealth and eventually to social betterment. They wanted to be the market's mediums, to animate it with their progressive agenda. Against the ruthless maneuverings of Rockefeller and the brimstone of Lyman Stewart, the humble Harmonial Wells never had a chance at that monopoly. Just as the Standard absorbed its competitors, the industry as a whole absorbed the renegade visions of oil-channelers into its celebratory folklore. By 1915, a tribute to oil pioneers in the *New York Times* asserted that Abraham James was guided by the spirit of "Mountain Bear, a Seneca Indian chief," collapsing the specifically Seneca history of Oil Creek into the generic myth of the "Indian gift" that fueled American progress. The tribute also turned James into a generic spirit medium, misnamed as "William F. James" and conflated with other Spiritualist prospectors. The imprint of Spiritualism on petroleum's flows is a ghostly but real one. Like oil extraction, we can think of it as a process rather than a product, a way of moving across the land that claims the voices of the past as a justification for future reward.

Not everyone bought in to the sacred oil narrative. From the beginning in 1859 a small minority of observers saw oil as a trick of the devil, a portent of doom, or a creeping evil wrapping its tendrils around humanity. Any resident of Petrolia's boomtowns could confirm that oil did not produce exemplary behavior in its worshippers. The dreaded vices of drinking, gambling, and sex work were rampant; moreover, innocent people far beyond Petrolia were swept up in bad investments that left them broke and vulnerable to moral decay. The notorious flammability that afflicted the oil region was exported to cities and towns across the nation via kerosene. By 1871, when kerosene dominated the market for lighting, one popular magazine called it "an engine of destruction." More Americans were killed in household explosions "than have been scalped by the Indians on this whole continent"—the most horrifying comparison the editors could think of. The broader fossil fuel economy of oil, coal, and natural gas, with its stoves, boilers, and steam engines, made cities into battlefields. Finally, transporting oil in pipelines and tankers "threatens more evil to districts through which it passes," the editors warned, "than the passage of the most destructive engines of war."

In the first years of the oil rush, a few clergymen fixated on petroleum's infernal origins as a literal sign of the end-times. According to an industry magazine from 1862, some were preaching that gushers and fireballs are "merely a measure preparatory to the arrival of the great and notable day when . . . the earth, and all the things that are therein shall be burned up." The author made light of this apocalypse. "Even if their theory were correct there would be no terror in it," he quipped, "for when the appointed time comes, the world might as well burn quickly as be long about it."

Lyman Stewart, the Christian fundamentalist, believed this in earnest: amid the brimstone of the oil fields, the end-times seemed near at hand; pure souls should rejoice rather than tremble. Moderate Christians simply accepted oil's dangers as a growing pain of modernity, no more or less terrible than the explosions of coal mines or the spectacular train crashes that reaped a yearly harvest of lives. It was unreasonable to insist on moral absolutes; the benefits outweighed the costs, for those who survived. Rather than demanding that the merchants of destruction face public accountability, concerned citizens called upon science to aid "burned and blistered humanity"—science, they had to trust, would turn the curse it had unleashed into a blessing.

The idea that oil rewarded the faithful was so persistent that it drove many prospectors and investors to their ruin. It gripped the nation's consciousness well into the twentieth century, sustained by the discovery of new western oil fields and popular tales of rugged independents who, like Lyman Stewart, sensed that they had a destiny to fulfill. Of course, for every Lyman Stewart, there were countless Jonathan Watsons: unremembered losers caught in the clutches of a cruel dream, chasing signs and portents that led nowhere. A native of Petrolia, Watson became its first oil millionaire by buying cheap leases from his neighbors before they knew how much their land was worth. From this unscrupulous beginning, he got rich enough to lavish donations on every church in town—perhaps he realized that his soul was in peril. He became a devoted believer in Spiritualism, marrying the medium and feminist reformer Elizabeth Lowe. Watson shared the mystical ethos of Stewart and Abraham James, roaming the hills until he sensed the presence of oil below. When this failed repeatedly, he brought in Spiritualist mediums to locate wells. That too failed, and Watson eventually lost everything drilling dry holes.

In 1889, the destitute Jonathan Watson had a vision. While writing a letter at his desk, he was visited by the ghost of Henry Rouse, the prospector whose eyeballs were "crisped to nothing" in the explosion of his own gushing oil well three decades earlier. Rouse seemed to have no regrets, nor any concerns whatsoever besides getting back to business. He knew where to find oil. Watson was desperate, but wary from his previous failures. "Spirit

Rouse . . . urged me to go at once and buy this land," Watson recalled, "and for a whole month kept urging me." Watson delayed, perhaps reflecting on the unpleasant fate that had befallen his spirit guide, but Rouse "told me I would make $100,000 clear money." Watson needed that $100,000 more than his life. The well was soon drilled on credit, and papers reported that it gave 280 barrels in its early days.

What can we make of this strange visitation? Why did Rouse return to earth to badger his old acquaintance into yet another high-risk speculation? Perhaps, like all ghosts, he was simply compelled to repeat things. In this regard the living are also ghosts. Watson's faith compelled him to drill yet another well using borrowed money. It was not as "phenomenal" as the papers claimed; this was more hype from an unscrupulous press, compelled to repeat rosy stories of redemption. Watson admitted that the well was mostly spitting salt water, but he intended to keep drilling deeper—thousands of feet deeper, to a new geological stratum. "The spirits sent me to find deep oil," he insisted in a tone of prophecy. "In that horizon I will yet find oil in abundance."

Watson was never rewarded for his faith. This phenomenal well, like all the others, did not produce, and he died penniless five years later. His obituary painted a sad picture of a man possessed by a single desire: "Up to within a short time of his death he still had hopes for, and his sole ambition was, to once more become affluent." One wonders if he was ever released from this nightmare, or if he looks for oil still. The strange substance that punctured time, itself made of accumulated death, had rearranged the world into an ever-widening circuit of devotion. As it hurtled into the twentieth century, its blessings proliferated: from light, heat, and electricity to the astonishing engines of flight. If these blessings required a dimly perceived sacrifice, Americans barely paused to mourn. Like Watson encountering Rouse's ghost, they read all signs and portents as opportunities.

God's gold

The belief that spiritual forces could bestow vast wealth upon ordinary people was not exclusive to the oil fields. It was part of a larger spiritualization of capitalism that justified the power of the rich, the misery of the poor, and the violence with which a godlike market scoured the land. Perhaps it's strange to speak of the economist's dusty calculations as enchanted. Yet over the twentieth century, evangelicals and conservative businessmen led by Sun Oil's J. Howard Pew worked to popularize and sanctify the tenets of neoliberal economists. In the words of historian Quinn Slobodian, these economists portrayed the global market as "sublime, beyond representation and quantification"; their claim to speak for this mysterious force had an air of divination about it, perhaps an echo of the Spiritualist medium communing with the dead.

Abraham James and Jonathan Watson may shrewdly or wishfully have doctored their prophetic visions of oil. We don't know how much they believed—without a confession of fraud, mediums stand in a gray zone between faith and deception. It's much clearer that neoliberal economists did not entirely buy the mythos of a supreme, omnipotent market that they preached. Rather, like many mediums, they had a spectacle for the public and a dark cabinet where the technical maneuvers were executed: their followers gradually built a system of corporate law and economic policy that upheld the illusion of the market as a wise "invisible hand," protecting it from measures that might harness resources to the public will. The intellectual tradition of Ludwig von Mises and Friedrich Hayek, through alliances with business tycoons and evangelical leaders, merged into a movement for what Pew called "faith and freedom," uniting capitalism with Christian morals. Pew invested

A spirit manifestation and the apparatus used to produce
the illusion of ghostly hands in a darkened room.

heavily in this effort; he once considered sending copies of *The Road
to Serfdom*, Hayek's manifesto against central economic planning,
to every Protestant minister in the United States.

In the broad strokes of history textbooks, the age of Enlightenment and revolutions purportedly vanquished the religious
worldview that upheld monarchy and the church, replacing it with
democracy, science, and secularism. Max Weber theorized that
a capitalist ethic in which each person "strives systematically for
profit for its own sake" had evolved from, but ultimately replaced,
old notions of Christian virtue. As God receded from the picture,
the calculating quest for material wealth became the ultimate purpose of human action. At least, this story is often repeated as fact: a
narrative of disenchantment.

That narrative has not held up under scrutiny, and mid-
twentieth-century free-market acolytes were hardly the first to in-

fuse capitalism itself with divine and mystical powers. Throughout the nineteenth century, certain economists and intellectuals embraced the divine order of the market. Perhaps the most notorious is Thomas Malthus: many readers concluded from his early work that human population would increase unsustainably if everyone's basic needs were met—therefore, starvation was part of the Almighty's plan. The poor man, he wrote, "has no claim of right to the smallest portion of food." Malthus, a professor at the East India Company College, noted regretfully that this competition would not be fair, as Western European elites were hoarding the world's resources through colonial plunder. The classical economists who followed this school of thought concluded that the market had the best interests of humanity in mind, if people accepted and molded themselves to its dictates.

Divining the market's reason was especially difficult as it became more complex and prone to sudden shocks. Yet trying to predict its whims—that is, investing in stocks—was also a new form of digging for buried treasure. The oil mania of the early 1860s lured many ordinary people into the stock exchange for the first time, extending oil's psychic reach into homes and offices around the country. "Ceaseless sensationalism beguiled the public," reported Edmund Morris. Unsavory promoters sold "low-budget stock for as little as 25 cents a share," so that cooks and chambermaids became oil speculators, losing their humble savings to crooked schemes. Samuel P. Irvin, who worked as an agent for such schemes, repented the many customers "reduced to extreme poverty or driven to desperation" through his actions. When an inflated bubble bursts, "the money appears to be gone," he wrote mournfully, "and no one can tell whither." Nevertheless, newspapers continually showcased fresh-minted petroleum millionaires who had gambled on the market and won.

These new ways of transmuting money into more money were strangely detached from the material world. Even for those on the inside, the market's workings took on a force of their own, beyond direct human control. Yet, like the whisperings of spirits, it seemed almost legible, just on the other side of the veil. And some people, like Abraham James, became possessed by it, if only momentarily. This numinous force was an obsession for the turn-of-the-century novelist Frank Norris, who tried to put his finger on the pulse of the new market society, the ecstatic, vital, but dangerous power that courses through railroads, stock exchanges, and the global supply chain. Those who channel it may become rich, but they also risk their sanity.

The market is a "primeval energy" in Norris's 1903 novel, *The Pit*, and it possesses real estate tycoon Curtis Jadwin as he begins to dabble in commodity trading. Entering the amphitheater called the Pit in the Chicago Board of Trade for the first time, Jadwin feels a rush of exhilaration: his very body "stirred and answered to its centripetal force . . . felt the mysterious tugging of its undertow." His trance is only broken months later after he loses every penny on a failed scheme to corner the wheat market. Jadwin insists there is nothing supernatural about the market's monstrous power, merely "ordered and predetermined" laws of nature. Yet these laws defy the control and the comprehension of any individual. Jadwin pleads, "The wheat cornered me, not I the wheat."

Spiritualists also claimed that there was nothing supernatural about their communion with the spirit world. They saw it as a natural phenomenon, similar to magnetism, electricity, or "the forces of demand and supply" that science had not yet mastered. They even acknowledged that spirit communion could drive its mediums to madness, as the "ungovernable torrents" of wheat did to Jadwin. Both mediums and market speculators were delicate instruments picking up powerful, invisible currents that others could not perceive, not unlike the prospectors who scoured the hills of Petrolia. Traders darkly called the New York Stock Exchange "the lunatic asylum"; men who lost their fortunes in sudden shocks often also lost their minds. The key to successful mediumship, financial or spiritual, was learning to harness these "elemental forces," to moderate and direct them to useful ends.

That's why Spiritualists perfected the interesting trick of channeling dead experts, who upon passing to the other side gained more complete knowledge of such mysterious phenomena as petroleum geology and commodity trading. In addition to locating oil, Abraham James's spirit circle monitored the stock market, warning him when the value of crude was about to rise or fall. In a turbulent economy, he stored up his oil until the spirits told him "there will soon be an advance in the price." Countless "business mediums" around the country advertised similar abilities, and they served everyone from small-time hustlers to the Wall Street elite. Victoria Woodhull, the women's rights firebrand who ran for president in 1873, and her sister Tennessee Claflin, served as psychic advisers to railroad tycoon Cornelius Vanderbilt and built on their clairvoyant reputation by opening Wall Street's first female-owned brokerage. Both mediums and stockbrokers were criticized as charlatans, yet whenever they struck on extravagant riches, public interest surged. The market had an air of enchantment about it. Here was a way of locating God's word within the economy, assigning meaning to a process that, per one stock exchange observer, "is, and always has been, a sort of maelstrom."

When we talk about the mysterious force of the market today, amid stagnant incomes and declining life expectancy in the United States, we refer to the airy realm of corporate profits. Workers strive to become more productive, and the benefits flow upward to the wealthiest few. Though many people are aware of this disconnect and may remark on it cynically, we maintain a collective belief in "the market" as a real, autonomous thing that sets rules for our behavior. This belief is a center of American political and spiritual life. As such, it has very material power. Perhaps we're suspended in a web of illusions, but if the web is shaken, those above us will panic and cut the strings. Consider the daily recitation of stock market numbers on the news: it's both a ritual call to prayer and an oracle. What little security we have seems to depend on keeping the faith. Each of us is alone in our thrall to this wrathful deity. Like the ruined oilman Jonathan Watson, whose only thought until his death was "to once more become affluent," many whom the market casts out will never be redeemed.

We're all locals of Petrolia now, fleeing fires, floods, and other apocalyptic portents unleashed by distant investors and complicit governments. It's possible we'll continue to pay until there's nothing left. Oil is not special in that other commodities have deeply shaped US capitalism, with stolen land and chattel slavery shrouded at its foundation. These were entwined with coal, oil, and natural gas in the rise of the fossil fuel economy. However, oil's liquid form and spiritual nature made it easy to separate from morally-troubling histories of power. In a kind of narrative distillation, its impurities were burned off to produce a national symbol, or perhaps an idol, often declared the "lifeblood" of America's twentieth-century prosperity. Petroleum came to embody the market with its scale and frantic momentum, the fantasy of treasure below the feet of a sleeping world, waiting for a visionary entrepreneur to release the gusher of wealth. Actual oil receded in importance compared to these ideas. The barrels that floated down Oil Creek often arrived at their destination nearly empty, and it didn't matter; what mattered was the belief that more oil would come, the value that kept rising, the dispensability of the labor and the land through which it flowed.

The modern re-creation of Drake's well in Titusville, Pennsylvania, still pumps oil, though there's none in the ground. It circulates in a loop between the pump, the barrel, and a buried tank. In the past, this was a well-known trick for selling shares in a dry well. It feels like as good an origin as any for our dream of infinite growth. Even with all the trappings of a staged reenactment that repeats on the hour, the first spurt of oil has a revelatory power; the audience murmurs and cheers before demanding, as at a magic show, to know how the trick works. The pump's metallic, percussive din fills the otherwise bucolic park, drowning out the chatter of picnicking families. The strange bellow pierces through time to a different landscape, one where no grass grows and bleeding pack mules struggle with their wagons through belly-deep, oleaginous mud.

Stephen Peckham, the surveyor whose Civil War memories floated over his view of the oil fields, took solace in nature's ability to reclaim the land. "The wave of desolation passes," he wrote, "and nature changes the scene. . . . Along Oil Creek, for the most part, the derricks have disappeared, and the brambles and the young forest are fast removing even a trace of their former presence." It's true that little remains of sites such as the Harmonial Wells. Much of mountainous Petrolia, unsuited for modern enterprise, has returned to woodlands. To the untrained eye, one forest looks just like another. Isn't there a difference, though, between oblivion and peace? Forgetting has been the indispensable tool of those who plunge us forward into ever greater violence.

Born in freedom

The oil industry has long told and retold the story of its origins with a consistent message. In 1954, theaters around the U.S. received film reels of *Born in Freedom*, starring Vincent Price as the upstanding Colonel Drake. The film, which likely reached more than 12 million viewers, closes with swelling music and a voiceover proclaiming that Drake "made use of a great American right: the freedom to explore, invent, and discover." Never mind that Drake wound up penniless in the end—he stood for the "independent businessman," the wilderness prophet of postwar America's "high standard of living," its global "mastery over land, sea, and air." The film was produced by the American Petroleum Institute (API), which formed in 1919 as an unprecedented alliance between the Standard Oil network and independent producers. After decades as sworn enemies, Rockefeller and independents like Lyman Stewart came together to ensure that their industry would enjoy secure long-term profits.

They confronted a number of threats that boiled down to the problem of democracy: if the public felt exploited and held hostage in their growing dependence on oil, voters could use the political process to gain control over this national resource. Supply disruptions during World War I had made it clear that oil for heat and transportation was essential to everyday life, especially as car ownership rose sharply. Rampant price gouging—the cost of oil doubled between 1914 and 1918—didn't help the industry's case for civic responsibility. The government came close to nationalizing the coal industry in 1918, and petroleum companies feared the same fate: that the state would establish production limits, rationing, and price setting to ensure fair access. If the public came out of the war convinced that they had a right to fuels such as coal and oil, companies saw the looming threat of regulation or, worse, state control, as had happened in Europe. In fact the government had no intention of nationalizing petroleum; instead, federally mandated private cooperation in wartime laid the foundation for the American Petroleum Institute and a century of unprecedented industrial power.

In another irksome development, both government and industry scientists began to raise concerns about the limits of America's petroleum reserves. As the rule of capture again drove environmental chaos and wild gluts in the western oil fields, experts worried that the domestic supply would soon run out. Sun Oil executive J. Howard Pew coolly informed Congress that he was "not in favor of preserving supplies of petroleum for the use of generations yet unborn." Americans had to have faith that God, not Howard Pew, would provide for them. Once a bringer of light, oil took on a dark cast amid ever-widening inequality in the 1920s, and especially in the Great Depression. Homemakers, many now dependent on petroleum products for cooking and heat, began to agitate against "the high cost of living," forming consumers' leagues that urged strikes and boycotts. If it continued to toy with prices, the industry was "treading on dangerous ground," warned one investor. Meanwhile, oil field workers labored and lived amid a perilous hellscape, whose tendrils penetrated cities such as Los Angeles, where thousands of wells operated in densely populated neighborhoods. Socialist muckraker Upton Sinclair took aim at this reckless frenzy in his 1927 novel, simply titled *Oil!*, which cast the greasy fuel as a font of financial and spiritual corruption.

With his usual didactic fervor, Sinclair skewered those who would yoke together religion and profit, incarnated in the young preacher Eli Watkins. Eli seems to conjure crude when he prays over the sinking of an oil well on his family's ranch; after summoning the "treasures of the earth," he rockets to fame as a radio evangelist. For the workers who suffer horrific accidents at the well and try to unionize, Eli preaches saintly endurance: "If they would only have faith in the holy spirit, they need not worry about their wages"—a sentiment straight from the union-busting heart of Howard Pew. The contrast could not be greater between Eli's opulent tabernacle

Oil derricks line a road in Venice Beach in the 1930s.
The West Coast oil boom slammed residential communities
throughout Southern California, and many wells continue
to operate in densely populated areas.

in Angel City, aka Los Angeles, and the muddy, scarred landscape
where the oil workers toil and perish. Sinclair asserts that the agent
of their suffering is not a wise God, but "an evil Power which roams
the earth . . . luring the nations to destruction by visions of unearned
wealth," that is, the "black and cruel demon" oil.

Sinclair, though censored and slandered for his political views,
had a loud public voice; when he denounced a social evil, people
listened. Yet any counternarrative of oil as a demonic force was hard
to sustain, given the seductive convenience of home heating and appliances, not to mention the growing popularity of the automobile.
How could something so mundane and domestic be as bad as Sinclair claimed? Communicating oil's uncanniness fell to the likes of
horror writer Fritz Leiber, who cast it as a sentient, diabolical agent

in his tale "The Black Gondolier," set in Venice Beach, California, of the 1950s. The story's protagonist, Daloway, lives in a shack next to a massive oil pump, which begins to haunt his dreams. Daloway's visions are like a sinister mirror of Abraham James's Spiritualist prophecies. In sleep he travels to vast subterranean lakes of oil, but instead of an exalted holiness, Daloway feels certain that he has "received the Black Baptism." "Like some black collective unconscious," oil itself has possessed him—perhaps, Daloway speculates, because he has "a touch of Indian blood" that makes him sensitive to nature's revelations. From these infernal voyages, he concludes that petroleum "truly had a dim life and will of its own . . . that we were all its puppets." The great Spiritualist beacon of light unto the masses is revealed as a "hellish light visible only to [oil's] servitors, or to those who become its slaves."

Such dreadful visions, along with public demands for regulation, loomed large in the minds of oilmen, who saw government intervention, rather than the exhaustion of the oil supply, as their apocalypse. They didn't want Americans to feel enslaved by petroleum, but rather freed by it. By shelving their differences and joining together, oil companies were able to claim that they, not the government with its "political clap-trap," actually represented the public interest, and they gained the power to regulate themselves. In the 1920s and '30s, small and large producers closed ranks to protect their profits, which swelled by orders of magnitude when World War II brought a bounty of military contracts.

The API soon produced the science and statistics, set the standards, and bought the political influence to protect the flow of this substance they equated with freedom. Leading oilmen especially opposed the New Deal, with its limited redistribution of wealth to the working classes, as a lunge toward communism—"the road to serfdom," in the words of the economics text that so moved Howard Pew. Employing Hayek's advice about mystification, the industry's complex planning was represented to the public as a spontaneous market phenomenon, "America's thousands of privately-managed oil businesses" reaching perfect equilibrium without the need for draconian government oversight. At the height of the prosperous "American Century," a triumphant petroleum industry wrote the story of oil as the lifeblood of a Christian, democratic nation.

Ironically, they did so with advertising and educational content that kept the image of their old rivalries alive. "We have little time to lose" in persuading the public, one executive warned, suggesting the real peril of popular demand for regulation. In 1947, they launched an "unprecedented" PR campaign asserting that "Americans thrive on rivalry. Example? You couldn't find a better one than the oil industry." Competition produced better products, lower prices, and scientific innovations—never mind that the rhetoric of rugged independence was increasingly a front for a powerful industry that enlisted its employees, local businesses, civic clubs, and schools to spread its gospel. To the public, oil would represent the opposite of collectivity, its promotions extolling homespun, masculine competition—"win that girl—win that game—win that job—win those customers!" Rivalry was the essence of America itself—"we are lost without it"—and the harder people opposed each other, the more everyone would have. The word *more* is like an incantation that pushes back all doubts: "more ... more ... constantly more for you." Such miraculous abundance was the master narrative of Cold War America.

At the celebration of oil's centennial in 1959, physicist Edward Teller warned the gathered members of the American Petroleum Institute about a greenhouse effect caused by fossil fuels "sufficient to melt the icecap and submerge New York. All the coastal cities would be covered." Teller, a hawkish promoter of nuclear weapons, was at the API symposium to rain on their parade and boost nuclear energy, which might have made the audience skeptical of his nightmare scenario. However, the API had already funded research on atmospheric carbon dioxide concentrations in 1955 and knew he was correct. They quantified a roughly 5 percent increase in CO_2 as a result of burning coal, oil, and gas over the past century. The trend would "possibly cause marked changes in climate," API president Frank Ikard told the membership a few years later. Despite this flicker of concern, the API soon became adept at turning any mention of limits into an ideological clash between capitalism and communism.

The white middle class, beneficiaries of GI Bill funds and generous lending, flocked to segregated suburbs in which cars and cheap fuel really were the basic tools of individual freedom. Their newly mobile, atomized existence fostered what Matthew Huber calls "entrepreneurial life," an illusion of self-created power rather like the magic trick of the Drake's Well reenactment. As with a séance or magic show, the audience was hardly passive, but played an active role, whether by using an API-sponsored science lesson in the classroom or buying a house with an hour-long commute. The narrowing field of common sense in which these choices seemed natural and good, not like choices at all, is a hidden origin of the world we have today.

In 1931, in the depths of the Great Depression, the thriving API purchased the long-neglected site of Drake's well. Historic preservation was not a part of oil field culture, where everything burned or was used for scrap; all that remained was a pipe and

The ruins of the Drake Well in 1926, before its revitalization as a tourist site. The boulder on the left is a monument to Drake erected by the Daughters of the American Revolution in 1914.

a pile of rocks. The API recreated Drake's pioneering derrick, as if promising renewed prosperity around the corner. They built a museum and library, then gifted this heritage site to the state. Such civic-mindedness ensured that their myth has its sacred place, their story has the blessing of history. The modern museum, its interactive exhibits bathed in the glow of nostalgic neon gas station signs, wraps up the narrative with vague allusions to the industry becoming "green" and "sustainable" somewhere in the undefined future; the book display in the gift shop showcases both sides of the climate change debate. Given that most visitors won't come from more than a couple hours away, one wonders what the return on investment is for corporate donors. They didn't want to do business in Venango County—executives at Quaker State complained that it was too hard to get there by private jet—but they care about keeping this identity alive among the people they left behind.

Another feature of the Drake Well's historical displays is a remote pumping system that radiates out across the site from a large engine house, a system known as a central power. Central powers appeared in western Pennsylvania in the 1880s, as leaseholders tried to suck the dregs from thousands of dwindling wells. Long metal rod lines extend from a gigantic wheel, running through the trees like strands of a great web. In this way, a single engine drives

An abandoned central power of the South Penn Oil Company in the Bradford field, Warren County, Pennsylvania, c. 1960s.

many pumps. With these slow, spidery devices, companies such as Quaker State kept some Pennsylvania crude flowing through the 1970s. Even after the big companies left town, small businesses could make a modest living from milking old wells or drilling them deeper, especially with state subsidies. Some families have held on to leases from the nineteenth century. One reporter calls it "a culture around which they've built their lives," the strange American conflation between a way of surviving and a treasured heritage. According to the Pennsylvania Department of Environmental Protection, the state had fifty-one thousand active petroleum wells in 2020, some producing only a few dozen barrels per year.

Stephen Peckham's idea that nature had reclaimed the land—the feeling one indulges in Pithole—gives way to the uncanny motion of these pumps driven by a hidden power. In a few places this skeleton infrastructure persists like a hungry phantom, moving through the trees with metallic creaks and sighs. It could be the sound of Henry Rouse's restless spirit, still speculating on oil from beyond the grave, compelled to repetition. His spirit, or something more sinister that was once mistaken for it, creeps through the apparatus, which is in turn threaded to the global oil market. Marginal extraction balances just on the edge of profitability; when it costs more than it's worth to run a pump, the phantom unlatches and the well is abandoned.

Though leaving only a pipe in the ground, these "orphan wells" leak oil into the water supply and belch greenhouse gasses, up to 10 percent of Pennsylvania's human-caused methane emissions. They've been discovered below schools, churches, roads, and apartment buildings. Fracking, the new boom industry, sometimes pushes geysers of pressurized chemicals up the pipes of abandoned wells. Many are so old that their ownership is unknown. Small operators simply ran out of money and fled, leaving it to the state to fix the problem. State crews have the funds to plug up twelve orphan wells each year; around two hundred thousand are scattered across the hills and valleys of western Pennsylvania, and more than a million nationwide. Whenever the price of oil dips, more companies fold; in the coronavirus-stricken spring of 2020, at a low of $20 a barrel, one state official said he was bracing for a "mass abandonment." Somehow, after a century and a half, there's still more to lose.

This is only one story of power, which made western Pennsylvania the fateful origin place of an extraction regime that spread throughout the world, changing the structure of human society. Other power sources, namely gas obtained through hydraulic fracturing, or fracking, have a much bigger impact on Petrolia today. Yet the fracking industry's language of salvation, promising "generational economic and environmental opportunities," simply picks up where oil left off. Moreover, as historian Christopher Jones writes, investments in power infrastructure have a self-reinforcing momentum. The system of pipelines, power plants, and distribution built for oil whetted an insatiable appetite for any and every fuel, in whatever form was cheap and bountiful. At first, the supply of energy outstripped any demand for it. Only as these "routes of power" meshed into homes and workplaces did they become indispensable for tasks that used to be manual. "The more energy we use, the less we seem to notice," Jones reflects. This magical force allowed the inhabitants of industrialized nations to imagine limitless growth without worrying about where its profits went.

This story of power began with the appropriation of Native land and Native voices, and it may seem as if Native people have vanished from the plot. This was certainly the dominant narrative crafted by oil's promoters and consumed by the public. As oil became a routine rather than a miraculous boon, its association with Indigenous traditions, real and imagined, faded. Oil and gas logos featured Indian mascots in feathered headdresses well into the 1960s, but few people today would recognize that *Seneca oil* once meant petroleum. Erasure is never an accident or simple negligence. Involved from the first inklings of extraction and exposed to its myriad consequences, Native nations continue to play a central role in oil politics. Protests against pipelines, the arteries of that American "lifeblood," assert that Native sovereignty and survival are prior to such demands. They are an often-unwelcome reminder that, as Nick Estes writes, "U.S. history is a branch that grows from the tree of Indigenous history, not the other way around. U.S. history is the covetous branch that thinks it's the tree."

Many counternarratives exist to the petroleum ideology, seeded by Spiritualist entrepreneurs and entrenched by evangelical free-market fundamentalists, which took oil as a limitless bounty bestowed by God upon a righteous nation. Conservationists, consumers, and oil workers challenged the industry's assertion that it was accountable to no one but the Almighty and its shareholders—yet in response to democratic demands, companies successfully argued there was no public interest beyond the right of each individual to seek their share of the American treasure. Critics such as Upton Sinclair warned that the treasure itself was cursed. Perhaps the spirits, or the malevolent world-soul of oil, laid a trap ingenious in its simplicity: we could get free whenever we wanted if we put the treasure down. This Manichaean view, that oil must be either divine or satanic, equates the material substance with the ruthless extraction system, as though one inevitably spawned the other.

This was not historically the case in North American Indigenous worldviews, where oil had other meanings and relations. Co-opting these "wiser" Indigenous meanings will not help US society escape the trap. Alternative frameworks exist for non-Native people, without claiming Indigenous ones. Rather, the story of oil as a commodity unfolds within a larger story of dispossession, in which varied Native philosophies were forcibly overwritten. Respecting and giving ground to those philosophies is an acknowledgment that the curse of oil is not natural or inevitable, and an accounting of how it came to feel that way. Today's Native nations live in complex relations to resources, but for many activists who live on the front lines of climate change, a future in which the world survives oil is one in which they take their land and knowledge back.

Looking back to the tale of "The Black Gondolier," where oil is an animate force possessing its victims, the story's horror is based on the threat of any nonhuman thing having thought, agency, and desires. This is horrifying in a tradition that asserts dominion over nature: both God and reason set man apart and above the material world. The notion that oil, instead of being the material of power, could itself wield power, drives poor Daloway to madness. Horror represents a tear in the veil of Enlightenment, a hidden reality where humans aren't all that matters. Given the tremendous violence used to suppress this reality over the centuries, it returns with violence. Like Daloway, we imagine that anything with power must be striving for domination.

In contrast, Vanessa Watts, a member of the Bear Clan from Mohawk and Anishinaabe Nations, writes that, going back to their origins, Indigenous societies were built by human and nonhuman members. In Haudenosaunee history told by John Mohawk, Sky Woman fell down through the clouds, and birds helped to break her fall, carrying her to the back of Turtle. Turtle helped her form the first land on the surface of the water. That the earth is formed from the bodies of Sky Woman and Turtle, and all those who helped them, Watts writes, means that "land is alive and thinking." Land, mineral, plant, and animal worlds are "full of thought, desire, contemplation and will." Society is made up of mutual good relations among these worlds. In this cosmology, it's not surprising or terrifying for oil to think and act. Rather, the horror lies in how Western people have conducted their relations with it.

Métis/Otipemisiwak anthropologist Zoe Todd speaks of oil as a "paradoxical kind of kin—the bones of dinosaurs and the traces of flora and fauna from millions of years ago." It is a teacher, "reminding us of the life that once teemed here." Nothing about it is inherently "violent or dangerous"—only the capitalist drive to extract and commodify petroleum "weaponises these fossil-kin, these long-dead beings, and transforms them into threats to our very existence." If colonization warps all relations into domination and possession, leaving oil in the ground becomes a mode of resistance. Both complex systems of knowledge and historical struggles over resources have shaped the powerful counternarratives of Indigenous environmental protection. The violent totality of capitalism often placed Native communities in a double bind: they had to exploit the land to survive—to become economically "developed"— yet this survival risked lasting damage to land-based communities.

Located near the epicenter of the first oil rush, the Seneca Nation had to seek its share of the profits or see that resource stolen by settlers. Seneca leaders, long used to dealing with manipulative railroad and timber companies, signed the first lease for drilling on their land in December of 1859, only four months after the Drake Well strike. They obtained a healthy one-third royalty for the Nation, and a requirement that the company "educate and instruct in the art and business of salt and oil, any Indian of the Nation which said Nation might designate" as an apprentice. None other than Jonathan Watson, Petrolia's first millionaire, soon took over that lease and drilled twenty-five test wells on the Allegany and Oil Spring territories. It's unclear whether he trained any Seneca apprentice in the oil business, though he paid $1000 to the Indian Orphan Asylum for children who had lost parents to epidemic disease. Watson was already laboring under his personal curse, and the wells were all dry. The promised royalties to the Seneca never materialized.

Speculators gave up on the area entirely until a fresh oil frenzy took hold in the 1890s. The "deep oil" found in the Bradford and Chipmunk fields inspired new drilling in western New York. Another white-run Seneca Oil Company formed in 1897, securing a lease under disputed circumstances for four thousand acres of the Allegany Territory. Seneca historian Randy A. John traces prolonged struggles between the Nation's elected president, who had close ties with white oilmen, and critics such as Andrew John Jr., who opposed leasing "the most valuable lands, upon which the Seneca Indian people are now living and peaceably enjoying the products of the soil." Within the year, the Seneca Oil Company had drilled eleven wells yielding a hundred barrels a day.

The principal players in the new Seneca Oil were connected to a ring of powerful businessmen and politicians who did not intend to continue leasing from Indians—they planned to relieve the Seneca of their land entirely. Their scheme involved a congressman, Republican Party bosses, and an oil millionaire named Albert T. Fancher, who was closely associated with Rockefeller's Standard Oil. They persuaded New York governor Theodore Roosevelt that the Seneca Nation should be broken up, assimilated into US society, and each family given a private parcel of land. Everything left over would be for sale at discount prices to Fancher, Rockefeller, and their friends. This policy, called allotment, might sound familiar—it's the same one that would-be Indian advocate James Peebles supported in the 1860s. Congress had forced allotment on most Native nations through the passage of the 1887 Dawes Act. The Seneca were able to resist the Dawes Act because they held legal title to their land, but now a powerful cabal had determined to simply take it from them anyway.

"Oil fever was out in the open," writes historian Laurence M. Hauptman of the shameless land grab, which culminated in a high-stakes struggle, from 1902 to 1906, in the US House of Representatives. Seneca Nation president William C. Hoag and his fierce critic Andrew John Jr. united to fight the scheme, rallying citizens and representatives from allied Haudenosaunee nations. They found a strategic partner in Pennsylvania senator Matthew Quay, known for using his considerable power as a Republican Party boss to defend Native rights. Quay pushed for the Seneca's demands in the backrooms of Congress, especially remarkable given that he took enormous bribes from Standard Oil. In the midst of this struggle, Ida Tarbell's exposé of the Standard hit the presses, stoking public anger against Rockefeller as a greedy monopolist. For once, white people were persuaded to support Native land rights—the corrupt oil industry was a common enemy, before the public relations revolution made it synonymous with white, middle-class prosperity. The allotment bills failed.

The Seneca Nation was intact, for the moment. Drilling by white companies continued on leased Seneca land, with a fraction of revenues going to the tribe. Bad oil leases were hotly disputed in Seneca politics. Along with these deals came the risk of fires, oil spills, and all the dangers endemic to Petrolia. Unlike the "floating and unsettled" people of Pithole, who came and went in less than a year, the Seneca had no other land, no illusion of a next frontier. There were different and sometimes conflicting views as to how the land should be used, but it was theirs in perpetuity.

Throughout the twentieth century, Native communities across the United States have tried to gain needed income from an inadequate land base, and they have also lived with the fallout on their land, water, and food. Scholar and journalist Dina Gilio-Whitaker (Colville Confederated Tribes) writes that, though Indigenous communities consistently "view the Earth as a living relative to be honored, not harmed," energy development was often seen as empowering, as it was in many white communities. For almost fifty years, the Navajo Nation hosted the West's largest coal-burning power plant, a source of middle-class jobs and affordable electricity, which rained pollution on their homes. This corresponded with rising rates of cancer and asthma. The aging plant shut down in 2019, despite pleas from the Navajo government, leaving economic devastation in its wake. Though the pattern of capitalism burning through a region and moving on is familiar, the Navajo are not free to move on from their ancestral land. Indigenous people were ghosted from the dominant narrative of fossil-fueled perpetual growth because they were both the hidden source of its power and the evidence that it could not be sustained.

In 2016, more than ten thousand activists from around the world answered a call from the Standing Rock Sioux Tribe in present-day North Dakota to fight the construction of the Dakota Access Pipeline, or DAPL, which would route oil through the burial grounds and waterways of the Oceti Sakowin, or Great Sioux Nation—another land grab like that of the Fancher ring in 1890s New York. Groups of Seneca Nation leaders and activists made the cross-country journey to the protest site. Jason Corwin, a filmmaker, environmental educator, and former director of the Media and Communications Center for the Seneca Nation, worked with collaborator Tami Watt to document this coming together of Indigenous people, a moment of resurgence in a centuries-long struggle for the land. "The whole set of laws put into place since the 1920s as it pertains to governance of Native nations," he explains, "were made specifically to facilitate resource extraction." The Standing Rock Sioux Tribe's only official recourse came from the slow workings of this stacked legal system. Meanwhile, police and private security forces attacked those gathered to protect the land, using water cannons and dogs.

Corwin and Watt's film connects the struggle against DAPL

to the Seneca Nation's battles with energy developers. Corwin sees why his nation once struck deals with these companies: "to an impoverished community, it was something," even when they were shortchanged. As in Petrolia, old wells are a curse on the present-day population. "We've been dealing with that legacy for years," Corwin notes, "finding these abandoned wells that are leaking and trying to remedy them." While fracking companies claim to revitalize the region, Corwin counters, "Nobody here is benefiting from any oil or gas development taking place around our territory. We bear the impacts of the pollution."

When the Seneca activists came home from protesting the DAPL, they learned that the aptly named Empire Pipeline company, a subsidiary of National Fuel, was planning a Northern Access Pipeline—NAPL—through their land. Another fight began, and Corwin kept filming. The dynamics of such conflict have changed since the nineteenth century. By now, many non-Native people in the region are also skeptical about the oil-and-gas industry, fighting against it as a threat to their health. Major environmental groups provide legal and financial support. Still, these constant struggles for the right to control what happens on Native land drain tribal resources. As Corwin emphasized, the law favors corporations. Every new pipeline, well, or waste dump spawns expensive court cases and appeals. Victory can be fleeting—months after activists defeated the NAPL in one case, Empire Pipeline got the best of them in another.

Despite this burden, the Seneca, like many Indigenous and non-Indigenous communities, are working toward what's often called energy independence. "The Seneca Nation has watched their resources be exploited for hundreds of years with little economic benefit," writes Anthony Giacobbe, director of the Seneca Nation's energy projects, "and in turn have inherited a legacy of environmental and safety hazards." He frames the promise of renewable energy in terms of sovereignty, the right of Native people to full self-determination over their lands and lives. To bring their wind and solar online, the nation formed its own power company, Seneca Energy. This is a pointed counternarrative. In 1859, the firm that sent Edwin Drake to drill for petroleum was called Seneca Oil, named for Indians who it supposed had vanished. In 1900, another Seneca Oil Company knew that Indians were still there and tried to steal their land. The simple act of a nation claiming its own name is also one of claiming power.

Media and environmental groups still indulge the trope of the "ecological Indian" who will save the earth from climate change, justifying Indigenous sovereignty as a means for the greater good, but perhaps also constraining it to actions, such as the DAPL protest, seen as noble but nonthreatening. Diné geographer Andrew Curley urges us to understand these movements as "struggles for territorial independence," such that the US government can no longer overrule tribal governments for the supposed "greater good" of American interests and pipelines. The legal category of "domestic dependent nations," invented to limit Indigenous sovereignty in this way, affords certain political and economic rights while denying the tools for true accountability. The many nations that converged at Standing Rock in 2016 continued a movement of global pan-Indigenous solidarity that began in the 1970s, when activists proposed a United Nations Declaration on the Rights of Indigenous Peoples that only passed in 2007. The United States, Canada, and New Zealand voted against the resolution, which, though completely non-binding, called on them to return those hundreds of millions of acres.

Sovereign peoples define who they are, what they value, and what they need to live. To that end, Curley writes, some groups "happily engage in the worst forms of extractive industries, yet maintain our rights to the lands that we've relied upon for thousands of years." Self-determination is not conditional, and it currently operates in the grim context of capitalism and colonization. Still, Gilio-Whitaker asserts that "long-term environmental health and spiritual balance" are central to Indigenous politics, and many Indigenous activists describe the end of capitalism and imperialism as part of their struggles for land and environmental justice. Among them, Diné legal scholar Michelle L. Cook envisions "self-determined, sui generis economic systems that are not premised on fossil fuels, global bank involvement, or colonial economic modalities and mediums of exchange."

The return of Indigenous land requires something more than a cordial talk between sovereign nations. One of those nations, the "militarized white supremacist empire," as Sisseton-Wahpeton Oyate scholar Kim TallBear puts it, would have to undergo a political and spiritual transfiguration. It would have to relinquish not just Indian mascots and Columbus Day, but an immense amount of wealth and power—the foundational claim that US conquest was a "just war" through which God's chosen nation realized its destiny. The United States is also not a monolith, despite centuries of manufactured consent built on myths such as those of Drake and James, with the money of Pew and Rockefeller.

Many people saw through the mirage of "God's gold," from socialists such as Upton Sinclair to the radicals who embraced Spiritualism, communalism, and visions of a stateless society. Dissent often grew from profound religious faith and questioning of power; the Reverend Martin Luther King Jr., recast after his assassination as a moderate, demanded in 1967 "a better distribution of wealth within this country for all God's children." "You begin to ask the question 'Who owns the oil?'" he intoned, pointing, as Sinclair had, at the profits made from basic human needs. While Cold War conservatives and liberals alike extolled the United States as a benevolent Christian nation, King insisted on the need "to x-ray our history." "Our nation was born in genocide" against Native peoples, he wrote. "Moreover, we elevated that tragic experience into a noble crusade." Though painting in broad strokes, King looked to Indigenous struggles to understand how people outgunned by the strongest police and military force in the world can fight back against the logics of wealth extraction and white supremacy.

In that way, Indigenous sovereignty is tied to the possibilities of mass politics, of the shared struggle proclaimed at Standing Rock where non-Native activists joined as Water Protectors under Native leadership. Solidarity is not merely supporting a popular cause such as #NoDAPL, but resisting the structures that oppress and extract from all of us with different intensities. TallBear suggests that beyond the sovereignty of nations lies a kind of kinship, establishing shared life and obligations. Rather than negotiating between rigidly opposed interests, "making kin is to make people into familiars in order to relate," she writes. For TallBear it is a "discomforting idea" given the betrayal of kinship at the foundation of the settler state—Henry Schoolcraft's betrayal of Jane Johnston, the white refusal of "a world where many worlds fit." It's understandable that Native people would not want to go down that road again; yet, as US citizens feel their own isolation and precariousness more harshly, they may also find that kinship as a "diplomatic strategy" can be a powerful thing.

The idea of giving back land, or leaving oil behind, always triggers cries of ruination: jobs and revenues gone, entire towns of hardworking Americans vaporized. Yet the economic process of ruining has always been plain to see as it traverses US communities, leaving behind everything from collapsing steel mills to abandoned big-box stores. The oil chronicler McLaurin imagined that a foreign traveler would "gaze upon the deserted oil-wells of Venango county a thousand years hence," but one could have that experience gazing at Pithole in 1865. John D. Rockefeller didn't mourn Pithole and wouldn't mourn Oil City either. Nostalgia keeps people in small towns and large ones from imagining something different; they must only ask for more of what's killing them. TallBear has no regret about "the quieting of these rural settler towns that were made possible by the elimination of Native peoples . . . these small towns and their 'American' mythological stories." Often any sense of relation seems choked by American mythological stories. TallBear describes, from her vantage, a benevolence of ruin rather like the grace of vanished Pithole.

In 1873, the geologist and Spiritualist William Denton celebrated how God reveals the hidden secrets of the earth and the power locked within ancient deposits of oil. His wife and daughter were mediums who journeyed psychically, as Abraham James had, through the subterranean realm. "All the past is really ours," he proclaimed ecstatically, "and may be used for our benefit." Nothing more simply conveys the American conception of history as a material resource to be extracted, refined, and utilized for power, perhaps with the guidance of Indians and women. Denton prophesied a future "greater, better, more beautiful and perfect, than we ever dared to dream." An exclusive group of people, for a brief moment in the twentieth century, enjoyed something like that dream under the benediction of oil, and they may never wake from this violent enchantment. Imagine burning the past to fuel its own erasure, an engine of perpetual forgetting. Yet unlike oil, memory persists and reemerges. Those with Denton's sympathies may distill history to pure triumphalism, pure profit, but its suppressed, volatile elements are always, in new ways, coalescing.

PART 3

POWER ON
THE SUSQUEHANNA

Assets from the rock

What were they thinking? Late in the summer of 1926, a crew of dynamiters scrambled over a gigantic rock face in the middle of the Susquehanna River, setting charges and running for cover as explosions opened up cracks in the surface. The artwork on those rocks may have been created four thousand years ago, among the oldest Indigenous landmarks on the East Coast of North America. It had long stood in the heart of the Susquehannock people's territory, later under the influence of the Haudenosaunee Confederacy to the north, a living part of the cultural practices that brought different Native communities to the river's shore. From a distance, the island-sized boulder appeared draped with dusty lace. Close up, dense clusters of shapes and figures danced across its surfaces. Europeans from William Penn onward had marveled at the carvings and speculated on their meaning, but only recently had archaeologists begun to regard them with scientific curiosity. Just in time to be too late.

The rock art survived in pieces, which the dynamiters dredged from the river below. For a century these petroglyphs would struggle to express meaning without their context; they told an Indigenous history of the land, which to white scientists appeared as a mystery. Removed from relations to living Native people, to the river, and to the cosmos, petroglyphs couldn't perform their purpose and wouldn't tell archaeologists much about that purpose. White observers took apparent silence as an invitation to project desires, fantasies, and earnest inferences. Those deafening explosions in the summer air produced another silenced object, like the plundered mounds and appropriated "Indian legends" of the previous chapters, that for a time served settlers' somewhat confused purposes. Actually, the explosions created more than ninety silent objects that circulated around the state of Maryland for the next century, from the halls of science in the heart of Baltimore City, to tidy small-town squares, to a neglected rubble heap in a public park.

Though collectors had stolen bits and pieces of the petroglyphs before the 1920s, the professional dynamiting was, ironically, a preservation effort, a last resort to save some of the artwork from oblivion beneath the reservoir of a hydroelectric dam. The Conowingo Dam in northeastern Maryland, then the second-largest hydroelectric project in the United States, rose from the riverbed in the morning of the electrical age, when half of America still burned kerosene for light. The grid that eventually connected sites of energy production with outlets in every house was a new kind of flow, instantly moving power across vast distances. Importantly, the grid was not unified, but owned by many competing private interests trying to deliver the most cheaply produced power—from water, coal, or oil—to the highest-paying market. Elements of the landscape decomposed into a portable commodity, echoing the transformation of the petroglyphs from vital landmarks to valuable artifacts. Despite weighing hundreds of pounds each, the petroglyphs were caught up in an economy of dislocation.

The company that built the dam spoke of bringing cheap electricity to small towns and farmhouses. In the end, they ran their wires north to capture a more profitable Philadelphia market, scoffing at demands from Maryland's socialists and labor unions that the dam should be a public utility. Denied their claim to one natural resource, Marylanders hoped to capitalize on another: the ancient past. Just as the dam produced power by spinning the poles of a magnet around a copper coil, the petroglyphs' power came from rapid oscillation in meaning. They were Indian and non-Indian, primitive and civilized, mundane and exalted, all at once. Investigators would refer to them as "chicken-scratch" Indian rocks and, in the next beat, attribute them to refugees from the lost city of Atlantis. The mystery of the petroglyphs may seem like a small, cobwebbed local mystery, but these are monumental artworks. That they were rendered into fragments is another of American empire's vanishing acts. Despite the deadly force of those acts, they did not sever the Indigenous past and future. Landmarks are constantly made and remade–the demand for a fixed, literal meaning in stone inscriptions, like the control of water behind massive dams, did not account for unexpected transformations. Indigenous groups throughout North America, eventually supported by environmentalists and archaeologists, would challenge the permanence of dams and the supposed silence of ancient objects.

People educated in the United States absorb a treasured set of myths about where power comes from: innovative discoveries, scientific progress, a divine and inevitable plan. These stories are stratagems that arise from and conceal power's uncertain processes. It takes a lot of work to transform a wild river into electricity, and to make Indigenous rock art into a symbol of American identity. Though the dam's turbines provide renewable energy, it helped to create an ever-growing hunger for voltage that drove development of coal, oil, and gas. Though the petroglyphs seemed like a marketable piece of heritage, they never yielded up the answers that white Americans craved. Their meaning couldn't be extracted from a specific place, despite entrepreneurial efforts to disperse it like current down a wire.

Dynamiting the petroglyphs to save them from the dam seemed like a good cause to concerned citizens, local history buffs, and archaeologists at the time. Perhaps white residents felt a degree of guilt over how much of the Indigenous past they'd already erased, but that feeling was wrapped in a view of the petroglyphs as *their* cultural asset. Newspapers called them the wellspring of a heritage "as richly filled with human achievement as the ancient civilization of Egypt and Rome." Editorials painted a picture of fallen greatness waiting for Americans to reclaim it—coded language alluding to the nineteenth-century theory of a "lost race." This ubiquitous trope, that America once belonged to a white "forgotten civilization," reared its head again in the sleepy water-faring towns of the lower Susquehanna. Despite the promise of a return to past glory, these towns would decline as the dam decimated their fishing industries.

Wealth, people, and commodities at this time were concentrating in cities such as Baltimore, which made it a more suitable heir to the "forgotten civilization's" assets. The dean of the Maryland

Academy of Sciences, a retired mining geologist named Francis C. Nicholas, would mastermind the petroglyphs' removal and deliver them to the Academy of Sciences' downtown Baltimore headquarters. To pay for this undertaking, he courted the city's business elite, promising that the rock art specimens would be "worth at least $25,000 a year to Baltimore as long as Baltimore exists." Where he got that astronomical number is a mystery; the Academy of Sciences did not charge admission, and the idea of a city relying on the "tourist economy" for income was not a glimmer in anyone's eye at the height of industrial production.

Rather than accruing value, the petroglyphs quickly became a flock of heavy albatrosses. Nicholas was a charismatic figure whose colleagues at the academy described his reign as "dictatorial"; he often strode around town in a black cape, the costume of a lifelong fortune-seeker in foreign lands. As an "economic geologist," his business was scouting for gold, silver, gems, and oil and persuading investors to get the treasure out of the ground. In this capacity he

Petroglyphs at Conowingo pictured in an 1893 Smithsonian report.

hyped mineral enterprises with great bravado, including a scheme for oil drilling in southern Maryland that sold many shares but produced no crude. He used a swindler's pitch to sell the petroglyphs, appealing to bankers and executives who expected even their charity to produce dividends.

There's something else strange about this pitch from one of Baltimore's leading scientific gentlemen: the proviso, for "as long as Baltimore exists." Here Nicholas prefigured the demise of the city at a time when American progress seemed to have no limit. Such visions of cataclysmic rupture are familiar from the nineteenth century, when settlers contemplated Indigenous earthworks as emblems for the transit of empire. "A long, and a gloomy night of gothic darkness will set in upon mankind," mused one historian, and eventually "the wide-spread ruins of our cloud-capp'd towers, of our solemn temples, and of our magnificent cities, will, like the works of which we have treated, become the subject of curious research and elaborate investigation." The petroglyphs would survive the next apocalypse as they'd survived previous ones, perhaps lying in the rubble of Nicholas's museum for future archaeologists to discover. Very old objects have this danger. They reveal the precariousness of the present.

The Susquehanna River was a disappointment to early European colonists, who wanted a commercial shipping highway and found instead a series of rocky waterfalls and rapids. When erstwhile British mercenary John Smith explored the Susquehanna in 1608, his party slogged ten miles upriver before turning back at an impassable point, which he named Smith Falls. He never reached the islands etched with petroglyphs that stood above the falls. These ancient images marked a site used by Native people, stretching back unknown generations. Smith met with leaders of a local group that his Algonquian guide called the Susquehannock. No one recorded what they called themselves. Colonists did record the Susquehannock name *Conowingo*, "at the rapids," for the narrow place where it was safest to cross the river, where a hydroelectric dam would one day arrest the water's descent.

Power's processes make the difference between naming, being named, and namelessness. Native place names didn't just dwindle into legend; a struggle for power, and for knowledge, is stamped on our maps. At the beginning of colonization, white survival depended on Indigenous sciences—geography, navigation, ecology, meteorology—whose theoretical foundations were alien and therefore dismissed by Europeans, though they gladly made use of the practical results. The trope of the "Indian guide," a generous emissary handing over the keys to the kingdom, erases the political function of knowledge exchanges as Native people sought to build respectful alliances with whites and were betrayed. Indian names are only the surface traces of a deep knowledge system that, because it operated on its own terms, threatened European domination.

European renaming inscribed ownership and familiarity. Settlers on the Susquehanna called the largest petroglyph site Bald Friar Island because its polished dome reminded them of jolly Catholic mendicants. Places such as Pilot Town, Port Deposit, and Safe Harbor implied smooth sailing, but the river still foiled the colonial desire for efficient long-distance shipping. It was a raging torrent in spring, when all the snow of central New York and Pennsylvania drained down to the Chesapeake Bay. A few months later it dried to a trickle, shallow enough to walk across—a "noble but freakish stream," in the words of one local columnist eager to see it dammed.

Because the lower Susquehanna region belonged to the Susquehannock nation during the modern period, settlers often named them as the creators of the petroglyphs, not accounting for the history of Native people's migrations and political conflicts over many centuries. This gave the petroglyphs a tragic aura as remnants of a once-mighty enemy. English descriptions of the Susquehannock cast them as the quintessential savage warriors, emphasizing their gigantic stature and fearsome appearance. These tales covered over the Susquehannock's strategic prowess in navigating the warfare and economic upheaval brought on by colonization. In the early 1600s, they refused fixed alliance with a single European nation. Instead, they seized control of the fur trade between the Native interior and the occupied coast, becoming a powerful intermediary. Colonists often fled rather than fight what they believed to be supernatural foes.

Archaeologists centuries later bought into the early narrative of the Susquehannock as especially hostile and violent, supporting this belief with an elaborate reading of patterns on broken pottery. They seemed eager to construct a story about a tribe that deserved to be exterminated. Refuting these claims, archaeologist Jay F. Custer called them "idle speculations that most likely can never be tested in any meaningful way." More concrete sources reflect that the Susquehannock, in the seventeenth century, became a fearsome force as they sought the upper hand in a world thrown out of balance. By the 1680s, though, they were so badly weakened by war and epidemic smallpox that they made peace with their relatives the Haudenosaunee, who belonged to the same linguistic family, and accepted an offer to join together for survival. Many Susquehannock moved north to live in Haudenosaunee communities, while others took refuge with the nearby Lenape. Some, adopting the name Conestoga, settled near Lancaster, Pennsylvania, under the protection of the Quaker governor William Penn.

The last fourteen Conestoga seeking shelter in Lancaster became the target of a murderous rampage in 1763. Quaker leaders had locked them in the town workhouse, promising protection, when an armed mob of Scots-Irish settlers broke in and attacked elders, women, and children. Local officials offered no defense against the brutal slaughter. The anonymous murderers, seeking land and vengeance for previous violence in the French and Indian War, were known as the Paxton Boys. This English-sounding name came from their hometown of Paxtang, originally Peshtank, established by Shawnee and Lenape people. In an outraged pamphlet, Benjamin Franklin denounced the "*Christian white savages* of Peckstang" for their rampage. In this way names are twisted back on themselves, conscripted in a deranged crusade to exterminate their own origins. This act of ethnic cleansing decimated the Conestoga, but the Susquehannock as a whole did not vanish, as popular books and articles continue to report—many had already been adopted into the Haudenosaunee, and their descendants belong to the Seneca, Onandaga, and Seneca-Cayuga Nations today. Especially on the East Coast, such narratives of extinction obscured the complex pathways of Native survival.

The widespread belief that the Susquehannock were gone imbued the petroglyphs with romance as the last trace of a vanished people. Europeans became the rightful inheritors of the ancient rock art. The white settlers who claimed the Susquehanna's banks in some ways followed the same livelihoods as the Native peoples they dispossessed, fishing, hunting waterfowl, and farming, yet they had very different means and ends. Scotch Irish and German farmers on the upper Susquehanna Valley, among them descendants of the vigilante Paxton Boys, toiled to produce surplus crops and pay their debts for the land that colonial rulers had sold them. Despite many failed attempts at digging canals, the problem of "too many rocks and not enough water" prevented inland farmers from shipping their wares out to the Chesapeake Bay. Moving south, the river emptied into the bay as it always had, but now, all along the shore, tens of thousands of enslaved Africans labored on tobacco plantations. In the early nineteenth century other rivers became engines of the Industrial Revolution, driving textile mills and early manufacturing, but it was hardly worthwhile to build a factory on the erratic Susquehanna. The river had failed to serve American progress, and for a time it was left to this uneasy peace.

Power is a long game, though. Quietly, as early as the 1880s, strangers began buying up land around Conowingo under inconspicuous business names. This was delicate speculation; the agents worked for rival companies fighting to lock down the entire riverfront before locals caught on and raised their prices. Inspired by the massive power plant at Niagara Falls, these companies envisioned damming the Susquehanna for hydroelectricity. The investors, bankers and industrialists from New York and Philadelphia, were enticed by hydropower as a practically free source of profit—that is, if you didn't factor in the cost of building a dam, which engineers estimated at $45 million (well over a billion in today's dollars). The tremendous price tag led to numerous false starts; the project stalled for so long that a rival dam was completed twenty miles upstream in 1910. Yet the Holtwood Dam, rather than quashing the dream, proved that the demand for electricity would only grow with greater supply. Finally, on March 8, 1925, the Philadelphia Electric Company (PECO) began pouring the Conowingo Dam's foundations.

Years earlier, PECO engineers had surveyed the river and picked the narrows at Conowingo as the optimal site. Measuring the drop and the rate of flow, they calculated that the dam could generate 1.15 billion kilowatt hours of electricity per year under optimal conditions. This was more than twenty times the annual consumption of a midsize city at the time. A supply of electricity so enormous didn't yet have a market, but the dam's investors were confident they could create one.

When the Conowingo Dam was sketched on paper, most Americans burned kerosene for light. Over the previous half century, they'd adopted coal and oil for stoves and steam engines, but muscle power still served for much of the labor of everyday life. Three decades after Edison patented the light bulb, only 16 percent of homes were wired for electricity, a reflection of how expensive or unnecessary this amenity seemed to ordinary people. Nevertheless, a long energy transition was underway, with the mid-Atlantic states as its ground zero—from the oil fields of Titusville to the mouth of the Susquehanna. Historian Christopher F. Jones explains that energy transitions—the development of a whole new power infrastructure—are not an inevitable outcome of scientific progress. Speculative investments in wells, pipelines, and dams created what Jones calls "landscapes of intensification," where the energy surplus piped in from distant sources drove "the dramatic growth of manufacturing enterprises, urban populations, and leisure patterns based on consuming energy." The men who built the network of plants and wires that crosshatched the land were not passive gamblers. They were the most powerful men in the United States, and they intended to get their return on investment.

In 1910s Baltimore, downtown shoppers flocked to the glowing window of the House Electric. The flashy showroom was illuminated until midnight, turning darkness into day with lamps that needed no oil or matches. The store's benevolent aim to "properly educate the public" about the wonders of electricity was a thin premise for salesmanship: the steep up-front cost of getting one's home wired was merely the price of admission to the modern, luxurious life that new appliances promised. Comfortable furniture invited people to linger, ladies were offered tea, and the cash register was at the back, forcing customers through a maze of alluring cut-glass chandeliers. Naturally, the shop was owned by the local utility company. An industry journal explained, "The sale of electrical equipment by the central station plays an important part toward increasing the connected load." It's not that electrification was sinister—countless people died in fires started by kerosene lamps—but rather that getting people to change their energy source and to use more of it than they had before took a lot of money and effort.

The House Electric had many imitators, as power companies used showrooms, radio and newspaper advertising, and door-to-door salesmen to enroll customers. The Philadelphia Electric Company became the second-largest appliance retailer in the country in the crucial years before the Conowingo Dam went online—all those irons, washing machines, vacuum cleaners, and refrigerators meant a guaranteed market for its power. Refrigeration in particular had many doubters; PECO warned holdouts, "Domestic refrigeration is here to stay!" Another market was in the rapid growth of electric trolley systems. Major industries switched from steam to electric power, and entire factories were built just to capture the round-the-clock flow from hydroelectricity. Unlike a coal-burning power plant, the dam's fuel was free, and not to use it seemed to waste it. But the Susquehanna did not offer unconditional bounty. Even the huge lakes created behind the Conowingo and Holtwood Dams were not enough to keep power flowing during dry seasons. Jones points out that dams on the Susquehanna only made sense as part of a larger, integrated power grid that mainly used coal and oil. With everything running on electricity, customers would not accept an August drought shutting off the lights.

Though advertisements proclaimed that every American was

entitled to modern electrical convenience, utility companies had no such populist agenda. They needed to sell more of their product while keeping down costs. Dense cities were ideal markets because delivery was so efficient; rural America, which often provided the raw materials, was left behind. By definition, the energy transition succeeded when electricity became essential to everyday life, but this created a new kind of deprivation for people who couldn't pay the bill, or who didn't matter enough to be connected to the grid. When PECO faced local opposition to damming the Susquehanna, it countered with generous promises of local benefit. In 1923, reports claimed that the dam would "stimulate agriculture and manufacturing" in small riverside towns. "The public will get much more than it will give," assured a bullish local newspaperman. He did not foresee which public would give and which would get—in this case, his readers in the hinterlands gave so that a distant city and its business elite could enjoy what he trumpeted as "this great source of wealth." Because of the forty-year construction delay, many people stopped paying attention to technical details, not noticing that the power from the dam was bound for Philadelphia.

Only after trucks began pouring concrete into the riverbed did locals recognize the bait and switch. When the limelight turned on Conowingo in 1926, everyone from fishermen to socialists attacked the Philadelphia Electric Company for stealing Maryland's waterpower. The spirit of the waning Progressive Era, with its ire against corporate greed and political corruption, rekindled briefly. The town of Havre de Grace sued the power company for cutting off its fish supply. The Federation of Labor accused Maryland governor Albert Ritchie of taking bribes from PECO, and members of Ritchie's own Democratic Party agreed, crowning him the "Prince of Conowingo" for his ill-gotten gains. Many groups believed that the governor "sold out the rights" of the people of Maryland, as Ritchie's gubernatorial rival put it in a vitriolic campaign. Labor leaders demanded a publicly owned dam providing affordable energy to all citizens. The Socialist Party agreed, comparing PECO to an enemy "occupation."

The dam site had been "occupied" almost since 1608, when John

The spillway of the completed Conowingo Dam.

Smith reached the falls below Conowingo. White Americans rarely reflected on the Indigenous population dispossessed for white economic gain—they preferred to see that as progress. In an age of growing inequality, though, working-class whites felt themselves steamrolled in the name of someone else's progress. Despite all the protections and benefits of their race, they were in turn exploited by powerful interests that held down wages while raising the cost of food, shelter, light, and heat.

The cry for a public power supply was not far-fetched: many states already had public utilities and cooperatives. Progressive reformers were pushing a national "Giant Power" plan that would centralize the grid to serve the "needs of humanity." The status quo, where rival companies built their own private lines and then engaged in cutthroat rate hikes, reeked of waste and inefficiency to rationalizers such as Pennsylvania governor Gifford Pinchot, whose state, bookended by oil and hydropower and bursting in the middle with coal, was an epicenter of the industry. Though he opposed public ownership as too socialistic, Pinchot argued that regulators must impose an integrated, highly efficient system on utilities—if the electric monopoly was an elephant, the public interest should ride atop, rather than cower "on the ground helpless under its knees."

The elephant, however, was not so easily tamed. The National Electric Light Association (NELA), which represented five hundred private utility companies, launched a comprehensive assault on Giant Power that set the gold standard for later misinformation campaigns—for instance, the effort of fossil fuel companies to sow doubt about global warming. The NELA poured money into advertising, bought its way into university and public-school classrooms, and deployed experts to undermine the basic fact that regulation and municipal utilities produced cheaper rates. All this convinced politicians and voters that Pinchot's Giant Power plan, despite its embrace of private enterprise, was a socialist scourge. Echoing the arguments of the power companies, Maryland's Governor Ritchie called public utilities "unthinkable," emphasizing the "inherent unsoundness and usual inefficiency" of the state that he ran. Finally, because of balanced-budget laws, Maryland couldn't take on debt without raising taxes. It was simply impossible to build a dam and wait for the return on investment. Better to let rich men build it and buy the power back from them at whatever price they asked.

People along the river began to look at the rock art above Conowingo and see not just the romance of vanished Indians, but also a warning about their own future. They knew that they never had a real chance at stopping the dam, whether to save a local fishing economy or a set of ancient petroglyphs. America craved cheap electricity; protests targeted the "Power Trust" that drove up prices and denied service to rural areas. However, amid such worldly strife, the ancient carvings were a variation on the memento mori. Rather than the inevitability of death, they stood for the inevitability of progress. While death was a great equalizer, progress demanded constant struggle: climb to the top of an ever-shifting modern economy or be left underwater. White people who couldn't keep up fancied, in their grievance, that they might "go the way of the Indians," as though the problem with Indians was mechanical obsolescence.

The deluge

The Conowingo Dam, quickly surpassed in size and power by the monumental Works Progress Administration dams of the 1930s, still teeters at the limit of human control over nature. The story of how it was built, for whom, and what it splintered apart may seem unexceptional, but that's the thing about power: one is not supposed to think about it, it's not supposed to have a particular history. The flow of power across vast distances into a housewife's vacuum cleaner was a clarion call of freedom for much of the twentieth century. Yet as workers poured millions of tons of concrete into the bed of the Susquehanna and other rivers around the country, our possibilities began to narrow and our choices became ever more perilous. Joan Didion referred to the Hoover Dam as "a monument to a faith since misplaced . . . the notion that mankind's brightest promise lay in American engineering." The future now seems embodied in that dark, deep reservoir full of amorphous catastrophe.

I often drive the narrow two-lane road across the spine of the dam, where the high water sloshes against its inward curve and the spray from the turbines arcs a hundred feet down the other side. Cranes mounted on rails crouch over the structure, the words CONOWINGO DAM in art deco neon on a scaffold high above. Most people today find such infrastructure unremarkable; the river is simply held back by a dam, which generates electricity. Yet we sacrifice human lives to build these improbable things—on the same day in 1927, workers Stephen Collins, twenty-eight, and O. P. Shelton, thirty-two, fell from the crest of the dam to the rocks below.

Visiting any large dam is always to imagine it breaking. This was rather common around the turn of the twentieth century: Austin's "Great Granite Dam," the St. Francis Dam in California, most fatally the South Fork Dam in Johnstown, Pennsylvania, all victims

The Johnstown Flood of 1889, caused by the catastrophic failure of the South Fork Dam, killed more than twenty-two hundred people.

The Johnstown Flood of 1977, when six dams in the region overtopped after heavy rains, killed eighty-four.

of bad engineering. Another rash of failures occurred in the 1960s and '70s as early twentieth-century dams aged—Johnstown, Pennsylvania, flooded again in 1977, inundated with 128 million gallons of water during heavy rains. Today, the aura of decay that hangs about our neglected infrastructure, and the increasingly tumultuous weather, whisper of more failures to come. In the action-movie fantasy of escape from such a disaster, our hero outruns the flood or fire that swallows the world. Viewers are supposed to identify with him and the adorable child he rescues, to identify as clever and strong survivors, rather than recognize themselves among the millions dying in a CGI conflagration. In reality, there will be no high-speed getaway. In reality, disasters breed traffic jams. In a photograph of the gridlock on I-10 out of New Orleans as Hurricane Katrina blew in, people have left their cars and chat while leaning against the highway median.

Avid nature photographers know that Conowingo's spillways attract hundreds of bald eagles, mascots of American greatness, every fall in their southward migration. The eagles gather to eat stunned fish shooting out of the turbines. In this scene they are glorified scavengers. Walking down the boat ramp toward the river during eagle season, one notices a constant, rapid-fire clicking sound. Phalanxes of photographers station themselves below the dam to bag the prizewinning shot of our national bird, talons bared, swooping down on a pulverized shad. Among these eagle appreciators, mostly men in camouflage gear hunched behind barrel-shaped zoom lenses, a reverent silence prevails except for the automatic firing of camera shutters.

Wealthy Americans used to hunt big game for sport, exterminating the buffalo, nearly wiping out bears and moose, mountain lions and eagles. Bagging these trophies was an affront to Indigenous societies in which nonhuman creatures were regarded as kin and invested with important spiritual roles; it also had the effect of decimating their food supplies. Patrician New Yorkers Theodore Roosevelt and Madison Grant promoted hunting as the key to restoring the masculinity of pampered rich men such as themselves, through a sort of blood ritual in which they absorbed the potency of their mighty prey. Only when they realized that they'd nearly wiped out the good animals did this crew start talking conservation.

Wildlife photography developed as a way to protect animals, and it has a generally peaceful devotional quality. It seems accessible to people from many walks of life. Still, the rapid firing of cameras during eagle season at Conowingo bears uncanny echoes of the past. It whispers of a longing that can be dangerous in larger proportions. Nature has something people want—something real and permanent, fearless, and, not to eagle-wash the point, free. Cameras allow us to capture our object of desire without killing it, which is surely a great innovation. They also reveal the phantasmal quality of desire, its receding horizon: neither a photograph nor a taxidermied pelt are the actual thing. The actual thing is embedded in motion and time from which we can't extract it. Confronted with the unresolvable contradictions of our own metered lives, what can we do besides go out and shoot more.

The Conowingo petroglyphs would lie abandoned in a rubble heap by the 1950s. Why, then, was it a foregone conclusion that they had to be "rescued" from the reservoir in the first place? Why is it so unbearable for something to lie hidden below the surface? The saviors of the petroglyphs discussed this in terms of profit and loss—Americans believed that these objects, like the falling waters of the Susquehanna, held mysterious value locked inside them. Whoever captured their meaning would reap great profit, even beyond the $25,000-per-year boon promised by Academy of Sciences dean Francis Nicholas. To lose them was to lose some latent possibility for making sense of American history. Photographs wouldn't do; the thing itself was needed.

The key to unlocking the petroglyphs' value lay in the hands of archaeologists. Many communities such as the one around Conowingo wanted to preserve the past and wring some benefit from it, but lacked the skills, knowledge, and funds. For help, they often wrote to the Smithsonian Institution or the Bureau of American Ethnology (BAE), the country's major centers of professional archaeology. However, these experts had lost interest in the domesticated landscape of the East Coast; by 1900, they believed they'd learned all they needed to know. Their apathy was based on the theory of a "flat past," which came to dominate the field around this time. As part of debunking the Mound Builders myth, archaeologists declared (correctly) that prehistoric North Americans were ancestors of modern Indians, but they claimed that this prehistory only extended back about eight thousand years. The evidence for their theory was limited; its aim was to put a stop to epic tales of the lost race while not giving Native nations credit for anything in the way of civilization. The BAE asserted that Indian prehistory was "flat"—Native people had migrated from Asia, spread out, and lived since then in roughly the same places where John Smith found them in 1608, with few changes until the violent relocations of the modern era. Thus, archaeologists turned west in search of new material, chasing the frontier of empire.

When residents of small Eastern hamlets wrote in about Indian antiquities, the busy staff of the Smithsonian and BAE often urged them to take matters into their own hands. Alice Ferguson, an artist who discovered a prehistoric village on her Maryland farm, was told that "nobody wanted it" and taught herself how to document and preserve the site. In a more disastrous case, a Maryland sewing-machine repairman wrote to the Smithsonian about a Native burial ground and was encouraged to conduct his own excavation. He haphazardly dug up more than seventy bodies, cracking bones with his garden shovel, and sold the human remains to collectors. Amateur archaeologists could be highly skilled and well-informed— they produced almost all the research on the East Coast from 1900 until the 1960s—but the absence of professional training, money, and accountability clearly left sites such as the Conowingo petroglyphs in great danger.

Public pleas to save the petroglyphs at least provoked a visit from the Smithsonian's curator of American archaeology, John L. Baer, who arrived in the autumn of 1923 to photograph and make plaster casts. Newspapers speculated that Baer would move the petroglyphs to Washington, but over the next few years, he backed away from that expensive project, while plans for dam construction marched forward. The Smithsonian's failure to act heightened the looming threat, and local outcry over the "famous Indian rock" surged.

Bel Air resident George L. Hopper declared himself "deeply perturbed" by the impending loss and to raise awareness published a nostalgic account of the petroglyphs. His desire to save the site may or may not have been related to his legal battle with the Philadelphia Electric Company, which condemned his land to build the dam. Hopper certainly expressed powerful empathy for others who had lost their land in the name of progress. He presented a unique theory about the petroglyphs: that they were maps of Susquehannock Indian territory, representing the tribe's "ownership or claim" to valuable flint quarries. These maps proved that white men "robbed the Indian of all his worldly possessions . . . feloniously and unjustly," Hopper wrote. In a thundering moral condemnation of colonialism, he concluded that the theft of Susquehannock land would "ever remain and be to our state an inheritance of eternal dishonor and shame." He presented the petroglyphs as documentary evidence of crimes against Indigenous people.

Hopper had reasons to identify with the Susquehannock in their struggle against the greed of profit-driven invaders, overlooking the glaring difference between his position as a white businessman and that of Native nations facing genocide. As he saw it, the electric company "feloniously and unjustly" condemned his land, which he had purchased to mine the same flint quarries that he imagined the Susquehannock once claimed. It's as though he projected his own beloved property maps onto the ancient carvings. His interpretation, tangled in his personal grievances, was almost certainly wrong from an archaeologist's perspective. Yet he broadcast a truth about history and power that few Americans wanted to take seriously.

Hopper was one of many area residents who published their personal theories about the mysterious Conowingo inscriptions, along with precise instructions on how to reach the site. While official rescue efforts sputtered out, private collectors seized their opportunity to plunder. A *Baltimore Sun* reporter described the

Smithsonian archaeologists as "hunting ancient relics along the Susquehanna," and why should interlopers from Washington monopolize the bounty? "It seems to be the open season for ancient races," the reporter added. Relics and races: eliding artifacts with their human creators. This bit of metonymy is especially grisly given the legacy of white gangs such as the Paxton Boys hunting actual Native people.

Into the relic hunt stepped the caped Dr. Francis Nicholas, of the Maryland Academy of Sciences, who made his first visit to Conowingo in June 1926. He found many petroglyphs already chiseled off by "curio hunters and vandals." "Most of the good pieces have been taken," he complained, threatening to call off the academy's salvage effort. He seems almost sulky about the poor sportsmanship of the amateurs. The pervasiveness of hunting metaphors reveals how Americans thought of artifacts, like wild game, as theirs to pursue for pleasure and profit. No one knows how many pieces were removed and sold on the collectors' market; in 2001, archaeologist Edward J. Lenik located ten petroglyphs from Conowingo decorating the garden of a suburban home.

By October 1926, Dr. Nicholas recovered from his disappointment and returned to the scene of the crime with boats, dynamite, and a crew of quarry workers. He'd finally raised the money for a great and heroic rescue. Nicholas and the workers rowed across the rapids to the islands, where they chiseled and blasted the hundredfoot boulder known as Bald Friar or Indian Rock. Though they couldn't remove every petroglyph, their firepower allowed them to take large specimens, albeit in small pieces. At their peril, they gathered the fragments out of the turbulent river. From the top of Bald Friar they had a clear view of the Conowingo Dam scaffolding a quarter mile below; as the dam went up, the rocks came down.

Back at the Academy of Sciences' Baltimore headquarters, Nicholas spent the next few months reconstructing the fragments from memory and gluing them together with a special Italian cement. The academy counted "about ninety" petroglyphs in its possession. The best ones were mounted outdoors along the walkway to the academy building. William B. Marye, a respected amateur archaeologist who had studied the original site, called these displays "somewhat sorry and depressing."

Nicholas celebrated the petroglyphs' arrival in Baltimore as the beginning of a major scientific project: it was time for archaeologists to determine their meaning. They'd become a high-profile historical mystery, and he imagined his academy as a pilgrimage site where researchers would gather to solve it. However, neither Dr. Francis Nicholas nor anyone else, amateur or professional, had any real clues. The inability of science to crack open the surface and access a buried meaning is part of what made the petroglyphs such an albatross. Scientists knew that they mattered but had no authoritative story about why. They had already decided that modern Indians were not participants in this quest. Instead, the petroglyphs served as a sort of Rorschach test illuminating the mind of the beholder. Stories about them reflect changing European assessments of Native culture, including the persistent urge to write Native people out of the picture altogether.

Before the removal, local antiquarians (some of whom had snatched pieces for themselves) described the images as "grotesque figures" of "Indian sign language," or as primitive "hieroglyphics." They spotted fish, turtles, turkeys, and trees, which supported their assertion that the "Indian mind" was limited to depicting concrete objects—never mind that European artists also painted representations of commonly seen things in the genre known as still life. Perhaps the inferiority of the work lay in its style rather than content. Francis Nicholas noted the "crude, raggedly executed outlines . . . lacking in detail." However, the modernist avant-garde was, at that very moment, dethroning realism with abstraction. Apparently not a fan of this trend, Nicholas claimed that an unnamed curator "in charge of the Morgan and Frick art collections" had judged the petroglyphs to have "more artistic merit than many modern canvasses which brought high prices." With appropriated motifs from "primitive" cultures all the rage among painters such as Picasso and Gauguin, Nicholas could claim the genuine article.

Nicholas's statements to the press veered all over the map, suggesting that his primary agenda was to garner interest in the academy's new acquisitions. He had a blank canvas to work with; previous studies were obscure and mostly forgotten by the 1920s, so Nicholas harnessed the drama of snatching the petroglyphs from the dam's rising waters to create a media spectacle. He soon introduced the salacious notion of human sacrifice, suggesting that long grooves running down the rock surface were meant to drain away the blood of victims. Nothing grabs public attention like human sacrifice, but drawing that conclusion from a series of vertical lines requires a vivid imagination. It soon emerged that Nicholas was seeing through the distorted lens of the lost-race theory.

At times he spoke of the rock art as "a monument to the Indians," but the story that he built up over a yearlong press junket diverged from this commonsense premise. The first step toward an alternative history was asserting that modern Indians had no connection with the petroglyphs. Some Susquehannock people had reportedly called them "older than memory" and "of no consequence" when queried by settlers. Here was a fork in the path: Nicholas could simply posit that the Susquehannock did not want to share their views on the petroglyphs or that another Native group lived there before the Susquehannock. Instead, he reached for "the Mound Builders, who may have wandered across Pennsylvania to fish in the Chesapeake Bay [and] marked these rocks." They appear when you least expect them.

The lost-race theory was, he admitted, conjectural. Nevertheless, Nicholas proceeded to connect some far-flung dots: the Conowingo petroglyphs resembled rock art from the Caribbean and Central and South America, he said, which in turn resembled Egyptian imagery, which revealed the ultimate origin, "a common stock of refugees from the lost continent of Atlantis, some of whom went to Egypt and some to America," becoming the Mound Builders. Nicholas spun this theory to a journalist who ran it as a feature story in the *Baltimore Sun*.

Evoking the Mound Builders was still, in 1927, a surefire way to stir curiosity in white audiences. Moreover, the idea of Atlantis as the racially superior source of all civilizations, first conjured in the 1880s, was having a renaissance with the sensational work of psychic healer Edgar Cayce and folklorist Lewis Spence, author of *Atlantis in America*. Perhaps Nicholas wagered that popular fascination with Mound Builders from Atlantis would rub off on his collection of rock art; perhaps he believed the bogus theory. Because he spoke through the newspapers rather than obscure journals, he became the easiest source for future researchers to find. The seductive lost-race idea had attached itself like a parasite to the petroglyphs.

Despite the theory's appeal, it branded Nicholas as part of an older generation of antiquarians who were increasingly on the fringes of science. Professionals and up-to-date amateurs believed in the flat past, that North America had been populated only by Indians, and not for long. Their dispute was whether Iroquoian or Algonquian tribes created the art found near Conowingo (the group they labeled Iroquoian includes the Haudenosaunee and the Susquehannock). Archaeologists Donald Cadzow and William Marye proposed that diamond-shaped figures on the rocks were snake heads, representing the "great serpent" of Algonquian myth. Others, looking at the same figures, saw the ceremonial face masks of the Iroquois, each group reasoning based on what they knew about recent Native cultures, and estimating the petroglyphs' age at a few hundred years.

Only in the 1930s, after the sensational discoveries of spear points embedded in Ice Age bison at the Folsom and Clovis sites in New Mexico, did leading archaeologists finally accept the existence of an Indigenous "deep past" in North America, with human habitation extending back more than eleven thousand and possibly more than a hundred thousand years. Although the petroglyphs likely don't belong to that early period, the expanded time horizon opens space for a vast Indigenous history of which they are a part. Archaeologists today believe that the Conowingo rock art belongs to the Archaic period, as early as 2000 BCE, thousands of years older than previous estimates.

Many features of this distant past—religious beliefs, social forms, cultural histories—can't be reconstructed in the framework of Euro-American science. Native scholars and activists, from writer LeAnne Howe to archaeologist Sonya Atalay and many more, argue that this past belongs in the framework of their own Indigenous knowledge and relationship to the land. Chadwick Allen cites the "continuous genealogies" of Indigenous people who "redreamed, rebuilt, and repurposed . . . studied, contemplated, and discussed" ancient sites during the centuries before colonization, as they consciously shaped their forms of social and political life. The Susquehannock, and the Haudenosaunee people whom they joined, lived with and related to the petroglyphs, which were likely created by an earlier Algonquin group. While settlers read the rock art as a cipher of lost people, members of the Haudenosaunee interpreted and continue to interpret them as a vital source of knowledge. Since colonization, Western science has built up and torn down a series of imagined North American antiquities, each shaped by the desire to elevate civilized over savage races, yet claiming to represent a universal truth that subordinated all others.

Human-made stuff compels us to think about what it means and how it fits into our story. Who is the "us" of our story, though? The race science of the nineteenth century had arranged humanity into various grades, with white Western Europeans at the apex. Only the Nazi genocide of the 1930s and '40s forced the official rejection of race science (which nevertheless persisted under different names). In the wake of World War II, the idea of one human family, with its newly discovered basis in the genetic record, became a rallying cry of liberal tolerance. In 1950, the United Nations issued an official statement on race that declared, "Scientists have reached general agreements in recognizing that mankind is one. . . . The likenesses among men are far greater than their differences." Colonizing nations adopted a framework of universal rights that Third World liberation movements used to declare independence from their former oppressors. Yet two desires were at play: apologetic Western countries, still unwilling to cede their hegemony, wanted "one human family" defined by the liberal values of technological progress and capitalist economic development; Third World and Indigenous nations wanted sovereignty, not only in their territories and their politics, but sovereignty of the mind. Especially among

Indigenous thinkers, this meant reasserting the validity of world-views that did not align with those of Western science, the systems of knowledge and relations that underpinned their existence as nations. Protecting the whole fabric of being upon which Indigenous life depends would take more than individual rights. That all humans are equally human does not mean that there is a universal human story.

When non-Native scientists excavate graves and sequence genes in a quest to complete the story of humanity, Indigenous communities often answer that they know their stories already. As much could certainly be said to the archaeologists of the 1940s who "discovered" North America's deep past. Western science has long been used to justify land theft and subjugation, attempting to overwrite what Indigenous people knew. Kim TallBear points out that the non-Native urge to "reconcile" different worldviews into a master narrative is misguided; at times "we may need to agree to disagree."

Did the people of the lower Susquehanna chart the passage of stars, planets, and seasons in stone? Did they worship serpents, or the sun? All this is possible, and numerous possibilities can exist at the same time. As we track changing archaeological theories, they too express the dreams, purposes, and logics of the research cultures from which they emerged. Edward J. Lenik, a leading authority on North American rock art, takes the ecological view that archaeologists should limit themselves to evidence from the material environment. He believes that most of the carvings from Conowingo are representations of fish. People went there to catch fish, which sustained their way of life, and they covered the rocks with pictures of fish from many inventive angles. The idea that everything is fish offers a mundane counterpoint to Francis Nicholas's lurid idea of human sacrifice. Yet this logic of decoding says little about the cumulative meaning of petroglyphs as monuments that pass on many facets of history to future generations.

It's apt that Francis Nicholas compared the Conowingo rock art to avant-garde paintings, though the cranky antiquarian meant it as an insult. Abstraction as a modern aesthetic was influenced by Europeans' obsession with Indigenous art, which they collected, admired, and imitated but often lacked the context to understand. What made their art modern was this global dislocation, a break in the chain of meaning elevated by its perpetrators to an aesthetics of pure form. Even appropriations, though, become part of history.

Dislocated objects are never truly cut off from the past, but in new, unimagined settings, they say new things—they can be heard speaking the story, and the story about the story, depending on who listens and how. In the setting of the air-conditioned state archaeology warehouse, or the courthouse square of a small town, they might show Americans a future where our great cities don't exist, as Francis Nicholas foreshadowed, where our works are fated to become cryptic signs with no signification. That's a white story of guilt and cosmic retribution, a particular neurosis of empire. It wrongly assumes that what's past is gone—that the attempt at obliteration was successful.

Indigenous creation, invasion and death, survival and rebirth, are embedded within petroglyphs as parts of a living landscape. Sonya Atalay, an Anishinaabe-Ojibwe archeologist who works on the repatriation of Native American remains and objects, writes about *ezhibiigaadek asin*, "the place where knowledge is written on stone," a large group of petroglyphs on the traditional terri-tory of the Saginaw Chippewa Indian Tribe of Michigan. Central to the site is an image of an archer holding a drawn bow; Atalay explains, "This archer depicts our ancestors shooting knowledge into the future to benefit later generations. These images were re-corded on stone because our ancestors knew a time would come when our language, traditions, and practices would be threatened." A good future requires a living connection with the past, which the Saginaw Chippewa Indian Tribe maintains by holding a sum-mer solstice ceremony at the site, bathing the stone in water and sweeping it with cedar boughs, and retelling the histories it con-tains, traditions handed down with "strict methodological rigor." Through ceremonies, the people actively care for the knowledge of the petroglyphs, which is land-based knowledge woven into the history of the place.

In 1881, a catastrophic forest fire burned the area and exposed the *ezhibiigaadek asin* to settlers, who "discovered" and named it the Sanilac petroglyph site. Much like at Conowingo, archaeologists dated the images to approximately a thousand years ago and bemoaned how little about their origins and meaning could be reconstructed from academic forms of evidence such as carbon dating. The creeping evil of lost-race theory reached a tendril into this void, with some hobbyists attributing the Sanilac petroglyphs to Vikings. Yet there was no mystery. "There are accurate and knowable interpretations of those petroglyphs," Atalay writes. "Conventional archaeology has failed to obtain such knowledge," at first refusing to recognize Anishinaabe teachings. She describes the challenge, as a Native archaeologist, of "braiding knowledge," using Western science as a tool to enrich Indigenous reality. Her story of the *ezhibiigaadek asin* doesn't begin with, or even include, the 1881 "discovery" and investigation. The idea of a broken timeline, of a void between prehistory and the present, is not consistent with the teaching of the petroglyphs themselves, whose spirals show the "unbroken continuum of the past with the present and future."

Lake Perfidy

The effort to make the Native past extinct, to break the flow of knowledge and conscript its artifacts into imperial museums, had a design like damming a river: it captured power and transmuted that power into a commodity; it took a specific flow, carefully tended over countless generations, and rendered it into universal materials of science, or the electric grid. If this metaphor seems like a stretch, consider the history of Native Americans and dams. As the writer Thomas King puts it, "You might be surprised to discover how many excellent dam sites just happen to have been found on Indian land."

In place after place, throughout the nineteenth and twentieth centuries, dams went up and Native communities had to flee the rising waters. Nick Estes, a scholar, activist, and citizen of the Lower Brule Sioux Tribe, whose river basin lands were flooded in 1963, describes the building boom as "a destroyer of nations." This destruction, of course, served a second creation which began with what one federal report calls a "new class of western sharecroppers" enticed into buying, renting, or squatting on semi-arid land. Government and business elites bargained on migration to funnel the volatile working classes into a rigorous and isolated life on the frontier. Massive water projects were supposed to engineer human populations, both white and Native, into the ideal form of small family homesteads: "everyone for himself," as a Wyoming official put it. He confessed that would-be farmers faced "deplorable conditions . . . it is a wonder that any succeed." Most failed, and the real profits flowed to landlords, speculators, and industrial-scale agriculture.

When choosing dam sites, state and private developers used the utilitarian logic of "the greatest good for the greatest number," arguing that reservations were sparsely populated and seizing land

A gigantic "dummy homesteader," like a Trojan horse, unleashes land grafters, timber grafters, and "power monopolists" in this cartoon criticizing the corrupt giveaway of "public lands" under the guise of helping small farmers.

by eminent domain. Yet authorities also argued that it was "for the Indians' good" to assimilate them into the majority culture. Dam building is a cruelly specific way of pursuing this end, since the fertile bottomlands around rivers were often the areas that Native groups had fought to preserve during treaty negotiations. Especially in the semi-arid west, water was the lifeline that sustained farming, fishing, and access to traditional plants. In this way, Native people could meet at least some of their needs despite losing much of their land base. Of course, such low-lying areas are the first to flood when a river is dammed.

As investors in the Conowingo Dam learned, these projects are astronomically expensive. Private corporations could venture the money on the East Coast, where they had a guaranteed market for electricity. In western states, where the free market failed to bring amenities to a sparse population, property owners demanded that the government overhaul the landscape. Eager to see capitalism thrive on the frontier, Congress bankrolled immense public works so that private industries could be "self-sufficient." Between 1882 and 1910, the Army Corps of Engineers built the first major dams on the upper Mississippi, on the same Ojibwe lands that Henry Rowe Schoolcraft had surveyed in his quest for the origin of the great river. The dams flooded Ojibwe towns, gardens, rice and cranberry marshes, and ancient effigy mounds. This began before hydroelectricity; the aim was to control water levels on the river so that shipping could run year-round.

This dawn of aggressive dam building coincided with renewed government efforts to end treaty relations with Native nations and sell off their land. The 1887 Dawes Act mandated that most reservations be broken up into individual "allotments"; the "extra" land not allotted to documented tribal members would be taken by settlers. Through decades of legal wrangling, many Native groups were able to regain their federally recognized status, but they lost about ninety million acres, two-thirds of their previous land base. The Army Corps of Engineers further dispersed Native communities under the premise of economic development, a cleaner, more modern version of sending in the cavalry.

In 1902, Congress created a new federal agency, the Reclamation Service, dedicated to "reclaiming" the waters that "annually go to waste" in the free flow of rivers. This idea that water flowing down a river was "wasted" became a constant refrain. Reclaiming also applied to the "waste places," where settlers, "in their eagerness for lands, have pushed on . . . in the hope that either a wise Providence or a dutiful Congress, or both, would eventually rescue them from the dangers of drought." Farmers had been sold the promise of a western Eden; they faced the reality of the dry climate with increasing desperation and entitlement. To deny their demands, thundered North Dakota senator Henry Clay Hansbrough, "is to admit that national progress has reached the end and that we are henceforth doomed to slow decay." In water management, too, the only alternative to endless growth was ruin.

Indigenous farming methods were adapted to local landscapes; Pueblo and Navajo people grew fruit orchards in what looked, to settlers, like desert, while the Ojibwe harvested rice from marshes. As the Reclamation Service overhauled waterways to meet the needs of industrial farming, real estate, mining, and manufacturing followed in its wake, all demanding cheap electricity and protection from seasonal floods. Pressure mounted on the government to fix the problems created by reckless development. In 1920, Congress passed the Federal Water Power Act, which allowed officials to authorize dams on Indigenous land without consent. Eager businessmen and engineers chose the sacrifice zones that would be flooded to provide water and electricity for the "rapidly increasing population." Roosevelt's New Deal gave needed cash infusions to these enormous projects, celebrated as a triumph of the American workingman. The firm that built the Hoover Dam ensured that the "American workingman" was white and not allowed to form a union; attempts at negotiating fair pay were rapidly crushed with scab labor pulled from the endless ranks of the unemployed.

The incredible scale of these Depression-era dams stirred the patriotic spirit of distant observers and visitors, who saw a nation rising triumphant from its time of trial. President Roosevelt's trip to the construction site of the Grand Coulee Dam on the Columbia River led him to endorse an unprecedented 550-foot "high dam" design, which would make it the country's largest hydroelectric plant. He envisioned a "planned promised land" of irrigated small farms for Dust Bowl refugees, who had already burned through the once-fertile soil of the Midwestern prairies. When completed, the Grand Coulee Dam submerged eighteen thousand acres belonging to the twelve Confederated Tribes of the Colville Reservation and wiped out the salmon fisheries that were the basis of their way of life for thousands of years. Many farms were never connected to the promised flow of water from the Columbia River. The dam's boosters claimed validation when it helped to power aluminum and plutonium production during World War II; President Truman declared, "It would have been almost impossible to win this war" without hydroelectricity. This would prove a fateful association—not just progress, but democracy itself depended on harnessing the flow of the nation's rivers. The oil industry had already equated American values with fuel in the nineteenth century. Manifest Destiny was quickly expanding its global scope.

In the postwar period, money flowed into infrastructure projects with an eye toward outdoing the Soviet Union. The dramatic display of man's control over nature became its own rationale for dam building, instilling resistance to communism through a spectacle of power and growth. The US sent hydraulic engineers and planners overseas to "turn back the tide of communism" in the Third World, while the Soviet Union pursued similar hydraulic diplomacy. Many historians feel that, at this juncture, dams were built for their own sake, even when they had little chance of accomplishing the stated goals of flood control, river navigability, and hydropower. The moderate power generated by midsize dams could have been captured with less grandiose designs. "Recreational use" was another common justification, essentially that white people boating in a reservoir took precedence over Native land rights and a panoply of downstream damages. "Water development itself is a kind of religion," asserted environmentalist Marc Reisner, with controlling every drop as its highest commandment. Historian Richard White concludes that damming rivers became "a veritable crusade, urged on moral, patriotic, religious, economic, and scientific grounds." Bruce Babbitt, interior secretary in the Clinton administration, admitted in 1998, "We overdid it"; every major river in the continental United States had been dammed, except for the Yellowstone.

Also in the 1950s, and with the same Cold War paranoia, the federal government again moved to abolish Native nations and force their members to accept US citizenship. Called termination, this set of policies revoked the limited advances of Franklin D. Roosevelt's "Indian New Deal," which had restored tribal sovereignty after the ravages of the Dawes Act. The backlash reached critical mass in 1953 with House Concurrent Resolution 108, which dissolved dozens of tribes, liquidated their treaty rights, and declared them US citizens. Congress felt that the collective land ownership and community structure of Indigenous peoples was opposed to the American ideal of individualism and private property. Their presence as "nations within a nation" represented a vulnerability to creeping communism. The termination acts pointedly used the language of liberty: Indians would be "freed from Federal supervision and control, and from all the disabilities and limitations" of reservation life. Their land, still seen as "wasted," would be freed to serve the mission of democracy through economic growth.

There was always a justification for dam building as a way of shaping society and shoring up wealth: while a "planned promised land" of small family farms proved untenable, dams created booming desert metropolises like Los Angeles, Phoenix, and Las Vegas, complete with green suburban lawns. In specific local struggles, and in a bird's-eye view of thousands of dams across the nation, it's clear that these were political projects with political benefits for their instigators. They also provoked new waves of Indigenous resistance that mounted in the 1950s and '60s. Indigenous people consciously shaped the agenda for an emerging US environmental movement which they saw as a potential ally, asserting ecological authority based on their traditional land ethics.

As dam proposals rolled out in New York State, some leaders of the Haudenosaunee, or Iroquois Six Nations, began appealing to the UN for their sovereign rights and demanding the "democratic self-determination" that the US promoted overseas. In the early 1950s, the New York State Power Authority claimed fifteen hundred acres of the Tuscarora Nation's land for an expansion of the Niagara Falls hydroelectric complex and was met by activists who blocked roads, shot out nighttime surveying lights, and confronted heavily armed state troopers. The reservoir was reduced to 550 acres, still inflicting what Chief Clinton Rickard called "scars that will never heal." Ninety miles south, a longstanding "conspiracy of interests" among businessmen and politicians laid the groundwork for the Kinzua Dam, which submerged nearly ten thousand acres of the Seneca Nation's Allegany Territory, as well as the Cornplanter tract, in 1965. The Army Corps of Engineers and Eisenhower administration presented the Kinzua Dam as a flood-control project for cities along the Allegheny River, but this destructive approach was a product of racist federal policies combined with state incentives for tourism and economic development.

New York had sought that land for a long time, and if they couldn't have the land, they'd have a lake to boat in.

The Seneca Nation hired their own engineer and developed an alternative flood-control plan that relocated a smaller number of white residents. The US government rejected this plan and broke its 1794 treaty with the Haudenosaunee, appropriating Seneca farmland, homes, graveyards, and the Cold Spring Longhouse, a center of the traditional religion of Handsome Lake. Amid growing public protest from celebrities, politicians, and religious groups, Johnny Cash penned a popular ballad, "As Long as the Grass Shall Grow," condemning the legacy of broken treaties. Cash quoted Seneca leader Melvin Patterson, who named the reservoir behind the dam "The Lake of Perfidy." While a private company leased Kinzua from the government and made millions in profits, the United States "significantly harmed the Seneca Nation's treaty rights, including its reserved water rights, to the pecuniary benefit of downstream interests," as a Seneca Nation newsletter describes it.

During the same decades that the Seneca and Tuscarora fought reservoirs on their land, they also fought against legal termination, holding out until the cresting wave of Native activism drove President Richard Nixon to advance a series of reforms culminating in the 1975 Indian Self-Determination and Education Assistance Act. The Seneca had kept their nation together through the traumatic relocation, building new homes for hundreds of people in the months before the water rose. Congress offered a onetime financial settlement of more than $15 million; the power generated by the dam is worth about $13 million each year. The river's altered flow causes fish kills and algae blooms; the recreational lake is filled in summer but lowered in the winter, leaving exposed mud flats that quickly erode. Seneca environmental monitors work to counteract these forces, building artificial marine habitats, rescuing landlocked fish, and fighting other sources of water pollution such as fracking. The flooding of these lands and communities remains, according to curators Rebecca Bowen and Dana Reijerkirk, a source of irreparable trauma even amid "a legacy of resilience."

Reclaiming the flow of waterways has been central to Indigenous activism in many places, with Native nations fighting to control dams that have operated for decades without regard for their way of life. After a dramatic takeover of the Winter Dam in 1971, the Lac Courte Oreilles band of Ojibwe eventually won an agreement to cooperatively manage the dam and build their own hydropower station. Since 2000, large-scale dam removals in the Pacific Northwest have restored salmon runs and Indigenous fishing-based traditions. The arduous, uncertain process of reclaiming water is also part of connecting the past with the present and future. The petroglyphs of *ezhibiigaadek asin*, on the land of the Saginaw Chippewa Indian Tribe of Michigan, are an intentional message from the past, meant to guide future generations through struggle to renewal. The Kinzua Dam, the Winter Dam, and so many others interrupt the message, but even these interruptions become part of the story. What was lost is not forgotten, and memory is also a form of power in ongoing assertions of sovereignty.

We live in a time of power flows, when no one denies that light and heat are part of a reasonable quality of life. The socialists of the 1920s, and ecosocialists today, see these as rights that we can provide for everyone in a world of unprecedented wealth. Given the need for a rapid transition away from fossil fuels, hydroelectric dams are not the obvious public enemy of the moment. John McPhee mocked rigid environmentalists who see dams as "metaphysically sinister . . . the absolute epicenter of Hell on earth." While promoted as a source of clean energy, only 3 percent of the country's more than fifty thousand dams produce electricity. Many have outlived whatever usefulness they might have claimed; decaying and neglected, in the hands of companies that defer maintenance, they threaten the public with calamities like the 2020 failure of the Edenville Dam in Michigan, which regulators warned of for more than a decade.

The models of hydraulic engineers who argued that the benefits outweighed the costs failed to predict how dams altered erosion, salinity, temperature, and ultimately contribute to the destabilizing effects of climate change. Historian Varsha Venkatasubramanian warns that dams built for flood control "might actually make these new floods worse as they reduce the capacity of upstream watersheds to control and absorb the sudden impact of an extreme storm." There's no profit in decommissioning dams, yet many need to go. For Venkatasubramanian and other advocates of public control, the larger question is to whom energy belongs and who pays the costs not measured in kilowatt hours. Given what we know about these externalized costs, which take the form of environmental destruction and human suffering, the struggle ahead requires unseating the entrenched dealers in power, who, as Andreas Malm writes, "are constitutionally incapable of responding to the catastrophe in any other way than by expediting it."

Indigenous communities are hardly alone in envisioning collective ownership and control over resources as an alternative to extraction and profit. Cooperative and public power companies serve almost 30 percent of US residents; they have their roots in unfinished New Deal efforts to empower workers and consumers. In past decades co-ops favored coal, but a wave of member activism has led to the overthrow of boards and demands for renewable energy. Activists from Maine to California are pushing to create publicly-owned utilities that can lower rates and build green infrastructure, to "take back the grid," as Boston's campaign demands. Delivering electricity to the poor is as much a concern now as it was for the socialists who sought public ownership of the Conowingo Dam in the 1920s, but today's advocates of a Green New Deal see economic justice as inseparable from environmental and racial justice. The unjust legacies of Progressive planning, which segregated and steamrolled communities of color, must be redressed as those same communities struggle to protect themselves from the dangers of climate change. No neighborhood or nation by itself can stave off what is coming; much depends on changing the essential character of energy from a buried treasure to a thing cultivated in common.

It's not possible to slot these transformations into corporate sustainable-development plans. Nick Estes asserts that "Indigenous ways of relating to human and other-than-human life exist in opposition to capitalism" and they can only work in concert with others who seek revolutionary transformation and an end to empire. The notion that market competition will green the economy has, so far, provided electric trucks but nowhere to charge them, and certainly not public transportation. Indigenous revolutionary socialist group the Red Nation, framing its Red Deal in response to calls for a Green New Deal, concludes that "Native liberation therefore cannot emerge from forms of economic or institutional development," but requires "an entirely new system premised on peace, cooperation, and justice." Sid Jamieson, a citizen of the Cayuga Nation who advocates for historic and environmental preservation on the Susquehanna, noted that, in his understanding, these values have long been the basis of the Haudenosaunee Confederacy and other forms of Indigenous political organization. Dams, taken for granted in the usually seamless infrastructure of power flows, expose engineering and planning as inherently political, and the need for mass movements to redefine the public of new public works across class, race, and national borders.

Rock flows

The Conowingo petroglyphs did not produce $25,000 a year for the city of Baltimore, which in today's dollars would add a much-needed $300 million revenue stream. They definitely didn't win prestige for the Academy of Sciences, which had to sell its headquarters in 1944 and move to the top floor of the public library. No one took notice when it shipped the petroglyphs to Druid Hill Park, a vast green space northwest of the city's center. The crumbling boulders fit perfectly in the park's romantic landscape of pavilions and statuary that evoked earlier times and exotic places. What was supposed to be temporary storage turned into fifty years of oblivion. Not total oblivion—people periodically rediscovered them, but only for long enough to remove a few for their own use before the curtain, a thick coat of vines, dropped again.

In a photograph from 1950, a woman perches atop a heap of rocks that looks like construction refuse or a collapsed temple. Light falling from the upper left catches lines, circles, and "serpent heads" grooved into the surfaces. The scene artfully juxtaposes an old and battered ruin with the fresh, feminine face of youth. The woman is as much a prop as the petroglyphs are in this image of mysterious things safely domesticated. She was strolling in Druid Hill Park with Raymond Thompson, a writer for the *Baltimore Sun*, when they found the unusual rocks by an old carriage house. Thompson took her picture and published it above a story about this forgotten curiosity.

Rummaging in the *Sun*'s morgue, he found Dr. Francis Nicholas's articles from the 1920s. Thompson's account of the petroglyphs is filtered through the carefree confidence of white America in the post–World War II boom years. Whereas Nicholas always inserted the caveat that no one could know for sure what the petroglyphs meant, Thompson gave direct "translations" from unspecified "experts." Nothing lay beyond the grasp of science after the atomic bomb. Thompson breezily explained that the petroglyphs were "traffic signs" for ancient travelers on the Susquehanna River. Maryland's first inhabitants boating along their watery thoroughfare were much like modern citizens cruising the newly built highway system. Eisenhower's national highways, like his dams, served as battlefronts of the Cold War, steamrolling communities in the name of security—to evacuate cities after nuclear attack, but mainly to evacuate the white middle class to the suburbs. Thompson made a careful racial distinction between the Algonquian Indians and the "unknown race," possibly giants, who carved these traffic signals "centuries before the Algonkian occupation." This piece effortlessly evoked the lost-race myth, painting a picture of a non-Native prehistory without ever having to say it. The story was headlined "Signs of Civilization." Beneath his breezy tone, perhaps Thompson, who joined the air force that same year, hinted at the old anxiety of civilizational succession. Soaring at ten thousand feet, pondering nuclear doomsday, one could imagine touching down in a future

Raymond Thompson photographed the Conowingo petroglyphs abandoned in Baltimore's Druid Hill Park.

world where the highway is empty, the meaning of its weathered signs a matter for speculation.

When you don't know what to look for, seeing signs is difficult. The etched lines of petroglyphs are easy to miss, especially in black-and-white photographs. To make them visible, researchers used to trace them with white chalk. Local assistant Martin Kurtz did this for an archaeological expedition in 1916, climbing over jagged boulders in the middle of the Susquehanna. At twenty-eight, he was young and fit, proving his usefulness to Warren K. Moorehead, the famous archaeologist in charge. Tracing is a physical gesture, repeating past actions, and also a way of finding out where things come from—seeking a point of origin.

Usually no one photographed the tracing process; it ruined the illusion of a natural phenomenon. In 1960, however, the *Baltimore Sun* captured Martin Kurtz at age seventy-two crouched behind a petroglyph, once again rubbing chalk dust into its outlines. Kurtz glances to one side, but the rock carving, shaped like a human eye, stares insistently up at him. Is this a moment of judgment? Kurtz

Martin Kurtz dusts a petroglyph with chalk in front of the Elkton Library.

has been a good citizen, running his family's funeral home in the quiet town that he never left despite his youthful flirtation with science. The ancient boulders that he climbed when his life was still unformed are shattered, while he remains whole. Yet even in his capacity as undertaker, he can't close the uncanny eye, which has seen millennia pass before it.

This reunion occurred outside the public library in the small town of Elkton, where the local archaeological society had "rescued some specimens from complete oblivion at the Druid Hill Park graveyard." The contrived scene illuminates like a flashbulb the brief arc of one twentieth-century life. It also alludes to an absent other, the people beyond the reach of memory who first drew the pattern. Does their meaning survive in these gestures, or is repetition now merely technical? Kurtz belongs to a series of white men re-chalking the outlines, photographing, and then illustrating them as diagrams for scientific journals, disembodied figures displayed in a grid. One can appreciate a kind of humility in this devotion to tracing the shape of what they didn't know.

Given the general neglect of the petroglyphs, it's remarkable that people in small towns continued to seek them out, showing up in Baltimore with front-end loaders to claim their piece of history. Harford County, Maryland, celebrated its two hundredth birthday in 1973. Volunteers led the party planning. Some of them were old enough to remember the strange carved boulders that once stood in the Susquehanna River near their childhood homes. For the county bicentennial, they wanted the petroglyphs back. Hazel Numsen, a local flower arranger, led the charge, arguing that the petroglyphs belonged to the county and were part of its heritage. Obviously there's no right of repatriation that allows white communities to claim Native artifacts. However, the Academy of Sciences didn't have much of a case for keeping the pieces, which were still exposed to weather and vandalism in a city park. Hazel Numsen got all the rocks she could afford to move—eight pieces of the Conowingo petroglyphs, "her prizes," were trucked forty miles to the town of Bel Air and displayed amid country music, a beauty contest, and a pageant de-

Hazel Numsen
with her petroglyph
prize at the county
bicentennial
celebration.

picting "pioneer life." Smiling for a photograph, Hazel knelt beside a
bull's-eye carving with one hand gracefully pointing to its center, like
an archer showing where she'd hit her mark. The "mysterious Indian
petroglyphs" are still at the county historical society today.

Then all was silence for almost thirty years, until Charles Hall
got a job as Maryland's state archaeologist in 2001. "When I arrived,
I was told to find these stones and do something about them," he
recalls. The intervening decades had seen a major transformation
in archaeology: post–World War II university funding produced a
bumper crop of professional archaeologists, and the National Historic Preservation Act of 1966 gave them jobs. The act required
professional surveys of every government-funded development
site—most significantly, thousands of miles of federal highways—
like an advance guard for suburban sprawl. Preservation once again
rang with a certain irony, as Native nations actively fought against
roads that bit huge chunks out of their lands.

Under a new ethos of stewardship for what they were displacing, states created agencies to manage sites and artifacts. Archaeologists, for the most part, no longer hunted buried treasure, human

skulls, or evidence of superior races. They sifted and documented every minuscule fragment of anything—a process-bound discipline rather than a swashbuckling adventure. Amid the highway building boom, there was little time or money to recuperate those pieces of the past that had languished in collectors' attics and defunct museums. The Conowingo petroglyphs were nearly mythical. Archaeologists knew they had been removed from the river but had no idea where they went.

Charles Hall learned from old newspapers that the petroglyphs were somewhere in Druid Hill Park, which covers 745 acres. He called the head of Parks and Recreation; they'd never heard of any petroglyphs. Finally, he tracked down a retired Parks and Rec employee who agreed to lead him to a gravel lot where maintenance workers parked their cars. There, deep in the undergrowth, was a large part of the Indigenous rock art that had towered over the roaring Susquehanna River for four millennia.

The engineers who designed the Conowingo Dam weren't worried about tiny bits of sediment carried along in river water. They meant the dam to stand for hundreds of years, but perhaps didn't realize how this detritus would accumulate. Or, less innocently, they didn't consider it the company's problem. Maryland's environmental agency notes that "no efforts have been undertaken over the life of the Project, such as routine dredging, to maintain any trapping function." A century later, the sediment—a sludge of agricultural chemicals, suburban runoff, and sewer overflow—has piled up behind the dam, almost two hundred million tons of it, and the reservoir can't hold much more. Every powerful storm churns the sediment and sends it over the floodgates. Rushing downriver, it chokes aquatic plants and animals. Putrid, toxic algae bloom in what's essentially a fertilizer bath.

Unforeseen consequences were a hallmark of the mid-twentieth-century dam-building frenzy. Further west, grand irrigation schemes went sour when fields became encrusted under thick deposits of alkali salts, along with selenium, boron, arsenic, and mercury carried in the water. High concentrations of these minerals made swathes of the Bureau of Reclamation's "planned promised land" unworkable. These are among the reasons that, as John McPhee expressed sardonically, environmentalists "mysteriously go insane at even the thought of a dam."

Environmentalists who spent decades cleaning up the Chesapeake Bay are, indeed, irate about the toxic sediment problem and the lack of accountability. PECO, the Philadelphia company that built the dam, is now a subsidiary of Exelon, the nation's largest electric utility with multibillion-dollar operations in forty-eight states. Waterkeeper groups see dredging the reservoir, which has a $300 million price tag, as the best option, and they want Exelon's operating license revoked unless it agrees to this measure. Exelon maintains that sediment is not and has never been its responsibility. Water just passes through the turbines; the dam itself doesn't pollute. Antagonists have revived the original 1920s protests: Conowingo harnessed a natural resource for private profit and left the public to bear the consequences. Now, after making money from free water for a hundred years, the company should take responsibility. If it expects the taxpayers to fix the mess, maybe the taxpayers should also get the dam.

The Onondaga Nation of New York joined the fight over the dam's management in 2013, acting as the Firekeeper of the Haudenosaunee Confederacy. "The Nation," they asserted in a legal filing, "is culturally affiliated with the Susquehannock Indians," whose traditional territory the dam occupies. Because the Susquehannock were incorporated into the Haudenosaunee, the Haudenosaunee have a "deep and abiding" responsibility for the waterway. While maintaining their political sovereignty from the United States, they add that their involvement "is also in the public interest." Their expanded definition of the public, as all human and nonhuman life and land, contrasts sharply with the racial and economic "greater good" that justified building huge dams to begin with.

Conowingo is at one end of a 444-mile-long river, the longest in the Eastern United States. Sid Jamieson explains that the Susquehanna was a central route of Indigenous travel, trade, and diplomacy for thousands of years and also the path by which

Haudenosaunee democratic principles were communicated to Europeans, who would take great interest in these ideas. To preserve this history, environmental groups and Indigenous leaders, including Jamieson, have planned a restored foot trail along the Susquehanna from Cooperstown, New York, in the north down to the Chesapeake Bay. The Haudenosaunee Environmental Task Force, Jamieson notes, is "committed to conserve, protect, and restore our environmental, natural, and cultural resources as our Creator instructed us to do."

The Haudenosaunee have also supported the return of the Conowingo petroglyphs to the banks of the Susquehanna. During centuries of separation, Haudenosaunee people have "known all about the petroglyphs in a certain sense, known that they are in pieces," Jamieson says. He describes the rock art's removal as an act of destruction rather than salvation. "Why would you blow something like that apart? We believe that everything has a purpose, everything has a being, everything has a place." He sees simultaneous loss and possibilities in the petroglyphs. They are "written, historical stories," yet after centuries of disruption, "that story is going to be undetermined now, forever. We're not a part of that time." Still, he suggests that Haudenosaunee people today can interpret the petroglyphs with their language and symbolism and read in them the changing history of the region. Certainty "is not the important part, I don't think," Jamieson concludes. As with any work of art, we can't know definitively all that was in the maker's mind.

In 2016, an environmental group called the Chesapeake Conservancy, for which Jamieson acts as an adviser, raised funds to build a small exhibit for five of the petroglyphs inside an old mill near their original location. Jamieson, like archaeologist Sonya Atalay and Indigenous studies scholar Chadwick Allen, describes the rock art as the written memory of Indigenous people, a message from the past for the future. Its meaning is not a great mystery, but inheres in its relation to land. "The important thing is that it's still there. . . . There doesn't need to be an ending, if you will—it doesn't need to be 'this is what it says' or 'this is what it means.'" Neither

Jamieson nor Charles Hall, the state archaeologist, see the return of the petroglyphs as complete, though the money to house more of them on-site is lacking. "It would be nice if we could gather them all up and put them in one place again," Jamieson remarked at the opening of the exhibit. Inside the dusty mill, it's possible to hear the sound of the river, but not to see the sun.

The Conowingo Dam is an entrenched part of the power system. Many people might wish the dam had never been built, but they can't wish that it vanish. Ten miles up the Susquehanna is the Peach Bottom Atomic Power Station, a nuclear plant that depends on the reservoir's waters to cool its radioactive core. Both the dam and the nuclear plant are classified as renewable energy, in that they do not burn fossil fuels. They also provided a cover for the massive growth of fossil fuel emissions in recent decades, an increase of more than 60 percent between 1995 and 2018, while energy conglomerates boast the availability of green alternatives for those who choose them. The vision of simply replacing oil, gas, and coal with such alternatives—or some yet-to-be-invented technology that unleashes a utopian age of even more abundant power—takes as inevitable the need for new, profitable frontiers of growth. To question this necessity "is to admit," as the doomsaying senator from North Dakota put it in 1902, "that national progress has reached the end." The senator's version of "national progress" is increasingly unsurvivable.

The dam's conundrums have no marketable solution, and are likely to be addressed retroactively in the form of disaster management. Every flow of power from the periphery to the center of capital has this counterflow, the unwanted remnants, contaminated, biohazardous, radioactive. What was once tucked out of sight can travel long distances, bearing strange and unexpected dangers; all it takes is one big storm to bring it to the surface.

Buried under the contentious sediment in the Conowingo reservoir are the rest of the petroglyphs. Seven islands in the river were inscribed with rock art, and Francis Nicholas, on a limited budget for dynamite, only harvested one, leaving the rest to the flood.

As environmentalists and Indigenous groups become increasingly vocal about wanting rivers restored to their free-flowing state, what would it mean for those petroglyphs to see daylight again? "If that dam ever goes away," Sid Jamieson reflected, "there could be a better understanding of their story. There's still more to come, there's a day when the sun may shine on them. The story's not over because they're still out there." It's only been a hundred years, just a blink of that stone eye. The stars and sun are still the same. People are wondering what convulsions await our turbulent world—for "as long as Baltimore exists" has become a more certain "until the oceans rise." A potent and dangerous fear of loss is in the air. Petroglyphs show us the paths across time that knowledge can take. Change does not have to mean destruction and loss, sacrifice and salvage; it can be the halting process of building a more complete world.

PART 4

TRACE ELEMENTS

A tale which must
never be told

" . . . a tale which must never be told, and yet which
everyone knows."

—George Herriman

A black cat named Krazy appeared in the comics section of newspapers across the United States in 1913. She or he, depending
on the day, headed a trio of animals—Krazy, the devious mouse
Ignatz, whom she loves, and a clumsy canine cop—caught in an
eternal cycle of desire, violence, and shifting identities. The mouse is
the aggressor, hurling bricks at Krazy's head; the cat cherishes this
abuse, mistaking it for affection. Officer Pupp throws Ignatz in jail
and woos Krazy, but the next day Ignatz is free and the cycle repeats. Their antics unfold across a sculptural, ever-shifting dreams-
cape modeled on the American Southwest. Mesas and adobe houses
tell us that we are in a strange, elastic version of northern Arizona,
where George Herriman, the comic's author, often vacationed.

Krazy Kat was strange for a newspaper comic strip, and editors
complained that it didn't fit in with their usual fare. It survived
for decades because publishing tycoon William Randolph Hearst
saw Herriman as a modern artist, like Picasso or James Joyce, who
brought high culture to the funny pages. Herriman's fans, among
them T. S. Eliot and William Burroughs, agreed, obsessing over
Krazy Kat and trying to divine its meanings. Critical praise caught
Herriman by surprise; he claimed that his inspiration came not
from the modernist movement in art, but from the landscape and
mythology of the Southwest.

Readers may have assumed that the carefree Krazy Kat, often seated on a log strumming a banjo, was a caricature of African Americans, given the racist tropes that pervaded newspaper comics in the early twentieth century. But the star of the strip has such integrity that it's hard to see Krazy as an object of derision. Since a birth certificate listing Herriman as "colored" surfaced in the 1970s, comics fans have tried to detect the significance of race in the work of a man who lived as white his whole adult life—whose curly dark hair led his colleagues to call him "the Greek."

Concealing and revealing color is a constant theme of the strip: Krazy drinks a jug of milk and becomes white, then drinks a jug of ink and becomes black again, invisible against a black background. The central tragedy of Krazy's life is her steadfast love for the Ignatz, who responds by throwing bricks at her head. One could venture into armchair psychology and read this as a metaphor for Black people who sought the acceptance of white America and received relentless violence in return. Krazy's favorite song begins,

Original watercolor of Herriman's characters sent to a fan, c. 1925.

"There is a heppy land fur fur away," both a cat joke and a reference to slave spirituals.

One thing that puzzles many readers is the comic's Southwestern setting—perhaps the characters enact racial politics, maybe they're just funny animals throwing bricks, but why are they in the desert? The geometric patterns of Navajo art appear on rocks, hillsides, and in the sky. Instead of growing in the ground, trees and cacti sprout from Native pottery, giving Ignatz the perches from which to drop his brick onto Krazy's noggin. Herriman's landscape is saturated with Indigenous motifs, which he absorbed through extended stays in Navajo villages and white trading posts—the people he called Navajo call themselves Diné, and their homeland Diné Bikéyah, while their official territory and government are known as the Navajo Nation. By all accounts, Herriman was sincerely devoted to learning about Diné culture and sought in Indian Country an alternative to the master narrative of white America, one that he felt was truer and more enduring. His friend Gilbert Seldes recalled that Herriman hoped to die there, "lying down on a cactus leaf until he was shriveled up and blown away by the wind."

The patterns, rugs, and pottery in the background of *Krazy Kat* are a clue not just to the author's travels, but to his method of disorienting readers. Herriman did not draw Diné characters in his published work, declining to offer them up to newspaper audiences, just as he kept Krazy's race and gender unspecified. Krazy goes by *he* and *she*, *Miss*, *Mrs.*, and *Mr.*, "any one which you like"; a convention emerged to refer to Krazy as female, though writer Gabrielle Bellot describes the character aptly as gender-fluid. Other animals call Krazy "a lady" when wearing a dress, male when driving a car, and male or female when declaring love for Ignatz, projecting their own expectations about gender roles. Perhaps the root of the comic's surreal strangeness is that Krazy and her friends are living in someone else's world, acting out a slapstick pageant of race, gender, and class amid a persistently alive Indigenous landscape that seems to toy with them. As Krazy and Ignatz discourse on the nature of language or time, geological forms flicker and morph behind them, rivers become trackless desert, there's a vague anxiety: How will they ever get home? Where would home even be? They are caught in a trickster's dream—and the trickster is Herriman, a mixed-race man playing a white man seeing his reflection in Indians.

Though *Krazy Kat*'s origins were in many ways deeply personal, the comic fed a growing popular fascination in the early 1900s for all things Southwestern. At first, artists, writers, and adventure seekers flocked to this region as a last frontier, a reservoir of wild lands and authentic cultures. Herriman's friend and fellow cartoonist Jimmy Swinnerton was part of a bohemian circle that frequented a ranch in Kayenta, Arizona, and this seems to be how Herriman first came to visit sometime in the 1910s. Many guests, such as Swinnerton, traveled West on a doctor's prescription to recover from tuberculosis, neurasthenia, and other ailments; they found their spiritual as well as physical vigor renewed by the experience. These pilgrims' notion of the "Southwest" as a remote region, a frontier or borderland of exotic encounters, presumes that the world's spatial coordinates center on a map of the United States. As archaeologist Joseph Aguilar explains, this is "part of the national project of replacing Indigenous societies with settler colonial ones." Pueblo people do not live "in the Southwest of the American world, but at the center of the Pueblo world," and the case is similar for other Native peoples whose worlds were invaded.

Celebrated artists, among them Ansel Adams, Georgia O'Keeffe, and D. H. Lawrence, congregated in Santa Fe and Taos, New Mexico. Residents of these "art colonies" eagerly engaged with Pueblo and Navajo crafts, hoping to reinvigorate American art by incorporating Native ideas. The novelist Willa Cather was a frequent visitor, and her 1915 book, *The Song of the Lark*, includes a striking scene of a white artist's rejuvenation. Cather sends her exhausted opera-singer protagonist to the desert, where a wealthy patron "has a big worthless ranch . . . near a Navajo reservation." The value of the "worthless" land was only apparent to the spiritually refined.

At the ranch, the singer spends long days exploring Indian ruins, where the ground is littered with broken pottery. "The atmosphere of the canyon was ritualistic," a sacred retreat from the enervating pace of modernity. She falls into a trance and has a vision of the Pueblo women who created the ancient water jars. "What was any art," she realizes, "but an effort to make a sheath, a mould in which to imprison for a moment the shining, elusive element which is life itself?" While "the Indian women had held it in their jars," the singer is inspired to use her lungs as vessels for the same life force. "One ought to do one's best," she realizes, "and help to fulfill some desire of the dust that slept there.... In their own way, those people had felt the beginnings of what was to come." This passing of the torch from ghostly Indians transforms her voice into a uniquely American product; suddenly, she outshines her European rivals on the stage.

The white inheritance of Native vitality depicted in so many works from this period marks a new permutation of the old manifest destiny. These artists didn't assert that a superior white civilization was commanded by God to commit genocide. Rather, they saw an imperative for white Americans to absorb the best of Indian nature—before it was, tragically, too late. Philip Deloria points to the 1890 massacre of nearly three hundred Lakota people at Wounded Knee, the shameful close of the "Indian Wars," as a moment when fear of Native violence diminished and US popular culture embraced the "antimodern romantic primitivism" often on display in the Southwest.

The need for lost-race theories faded in this context. Archaeological debates persisted about the migrations of different Puebloan groups from the ancient sites of Mesa Verde and Chaco Canyon across the Southwest in the thirteenth century. Sometimes these Mesa Verde people were said to have "vanished," and archaeologists disbelieved modern Pueblo histories of a migration from that area. Promotions for Mesa Verde evoked the melancholy sentiments of ruin-gazing, the "glamour and mystery ... of a lost race of humans." This hook quickly gave way to an acknowledgment of undeniable continuities: "There is not a shadow of a doubt that they were Indians." The economy of Southwestern authenticity depended on Native people being the original occupants of the land, though it denied them control over that land.

As this cultural economy developed in the early 1900s, painters such as Joseph Henry Sharp and E. Irving Couse could gain fame and fortune depicting Native people in traditional settings. Native artists pursued their own creative visions, experimenting in new media and techniques, but white viewers and buyers of their work expected it to reveal, in one critic's words, "the primitive manner of their ancestors." Their work was often categorized as "craft," with large cuts of sales going to the white dealers who "scouted" Native talent.

Representations of the Southwest produced by white artists, along with the Native crafts coveted by collectors, kindled a trend that soon swept mainstream America. Homemakers set up "Indian corners" in their living rooms to display Native handicrafts, or imitations purchased from catalogs. *Krazy Kat* was not a prized status symbol like those pots and rugs, but rather a disposable medium that wound up in gutters and outhouses. Herriman showed no interest in commerce or art-world trends, insisting that his job was to draw talking animals. Nevertheless, his passion for the landscape of northern Arizona influenced audiences both high and low: e e cummings papered his college dorm with *Krazy Kat* strips, and the desert across which Wile E. Coyote chases the Road Runner is indebted to Herriman. *Krazy Kat*'s freewheeling backdrops partook in a broader longing for place and identity, for tradition and exoticism, that drove Americans of all classes and backgrounds to look toward the Southwest.

Many white travelers went there in search of a vanishing way of life and turned what they found into a commodity. The textiles and pottery that circulated, first among elite collectors and then among middle-class homemakers, were a kind of symbolic resource connecting the buyer, by way of the Indian hands that had (supposedly) crafted them, to an unbroken ancient tradition. In reality, Native art was never static. The white marketplace created a new set of demands to which artists responded. As Santa Clara Pueblo artist and activist Marian Naranjo explains, the making of rugs and pots became a means of economic survival when old ways of living on the land were outlawed. What white consumers saw as authentically Indian was in part their own hungry shadow cast across Indian Country.

In this way, the rush for handicrafts anticipated another rush that would soon engulf the Southwest. When the first nuclear test shot was fired at White Sands, New Mexico, in 1945, the atomic age dawned with the desert as its ground zero. J. Robert Oppenheimer, remembered as the scientific mastermind of the Manhattan Project, suggested the location for this top-secret effort to beat the Nazis in building an atomic bomb. Long before the war, when Oppenheimer was a sickly teenager, doctors sent him out West to restore his health. Near Los Alamos, New Mexico, he rode horses and attended Pueblo dances. Like so many others who took the "West cure," Oppenheimer felt spiritually transformed by his encounter. He's often quoted declaring, "My two great loves are physics and New Mexico." Yet his was a Romantic passion that consumed its object. A hundred nuclear bombs would be detonated over the Southwest between 1945 and 1962.

The fuel for these bombs at first came from colonial uranium mines in the Belgian Congo, but soon prospectors located more convenient uranium deposits on the Colorado Plateau that ran beneath the land of the Navajo, Pueblo, Ute, Hopi, and Apache Nations. Fallout dispersed over a vast range that encompassed Native communities as well as Hispanic and white towns. The nuclear economy altered the future of land-based Indigenous people, leaving a million-year radioactive legacy that contaminates homes, water, livestock, and sacred sites.

Throughout the Cold War, waste from Los Alamos National Laboratory flowed through Pueblo lands to the Rio Grande. The worst nuclear disaster in US history was not the partial meltdown at Three Mile Island, but the uranium-mill dam breach on the Rio Puerco, which released ninety-five million gallons of radioactive slurry into a Diné farming community. Reckless handling of nuclear material occurred throughout the country, even in the heart of cities such as Chicago and St. Louis; the most egregious, long-term, and preventable contamination fell disproportionately on communities of color and the poor denied information about what was happening, who had to fight bitterly to defend their land and health. The nuclear program, framed as so essential to America's survival, was paid for by foisting untold risks onto its disenfranchised.

There were two American Southwests, one a source of natural and cultural riches, the other an absorber of radiation, from slag to fallout. Yet the two Southwests were twined together in the everyday lives of residents, a dangerous pairing that came to seem unexceptional. The careers of two nuclear scientists exemplify this entanglement. The first, Francis Harlow, was a Los Alamos physicist who studied Pueblo pottery in his spare time, becoming a national authority on it. With a meticulous eye, Harlow established the history of specific styles and artists, rendering the Pueblo past legible for experts and defining it as a global commodity. He belongs to a lineage of Los Alamos scientists who became fascinated with Pueblo culture, and of white collectors in unequal relationships with Native artists. In this world, the desire to possess particular pots expresses the larger metaphor of the Southwest as a spiritual resource.

The second person is Floy Agnes Naranjo Lee, also a researcher at Los Alamos. Lee devoted her career to studying the health effects of radiation, which were poorly understood at the beginning of the Manhattan Project. Specifically, scientists knew little about the impact of low-level radiation—the kind that comes from living or working near contaminated sites—over long periods. Hers is a story about risk, and how difficult it is to comprehend and dwell in a landscape of risk. In the urgency of World War II and the Cold War, US officials chose again and again to impose undisclosed risks on communities throughout the Southwest. With one face, the nuclear program claimed to protect America, and with another, hidden face, it harmed its most vulnerable people. Lee had a unique perspective on the two faces of government policy: her family came from the Pueblo of Santa Clara, and she was one of the few Native people working in technical jobs at Los Alamos. Her family knew all too well the kind of hypocrisy that was possible in the pursuit of power. Yet the only way for Lee to learn what was at stake in radiation exposure was to work in laboratories that also built bombs, under leaders who argued for the harmlessness of nuclear testing.

These two people and their life projects are strange and complicated mirrors of each other. Harlow, who fit the storybook image of a "self-made" American rising in the world through his own ingenuity, was a seeker on the frontier like so many before him. With violent conquest safely in the past, he found fulfillment in his encounter with Indigenous traditions. As an individual, he cared deeply about Pueblo art, but each individual is part of larger currents—in his case, a current of settlers who transformed the region into a landscape for white consumption. In contrast, Floy Agnes Naranjo Lee was raised by her Native father and white mother at the Albuquerque Indian School where they taught, often visiting relatives at the Santa Clara Pueblo. The imperatives of government-sponsored assimilation, educational achievement, and cultural survival existed side by side in her everyday life. For all her hard work and ingenuity, Lee did not frame her story in the satisfied terms of American "self-making"—in her later years she was not afraid to express unease. She had traveled deep into Cold War America's nuclear culture, riding the current of risk, that invisible, almost mystical force that has come to define modern life.

Though Lee hoped that her research could protect the public from danger, science left enough uncertainty that it was used by both sides in the nuclear debates that raged from the 1950s through the 1990s. US policy was to concentrate risk in the "uninhabited desert" of the Southwest and at other sites devalued because of who lived there and how they lived. Environmentalists warned that risk is ultimately borne on the air, entering white suburban homes in cartons of milk laced with radioactive strontium 90. Before the era of climate change, many saw nuclear apocalypse as the great leveler: if the entire nation was a potential "sacrifice zone," then the interests of the people and the capitalist-imperialist state would seem to diverge in a fundamental way.

Activists from disparate backgrounds tried to come together in one struggle for human survival. Yet those from marginalized groups asserted that risk falls unevenly; just as with climate change today, the worst impacts of the bomb would hit those with the least power. The work of white supremacy and class domination built this arrangement and continues to nurture fantasies of a well-stocked bunker in the ruins for the deserving few. The victories and failures of the antinuclear movement feel familiar today, as once again we reckon with the strategic timescale of power: How long before difference is leveled by catastrophe? What if no catastrophe could do that work for us?

In a *Krazy Kat* strip from 1935, Krazy gazes longingly into a shop window at a majestic Pueblo pot decorated with an image of the sun. Pottery displays were common enough in Santa Fe, Albuquerque, and even small towns such as Kayenta and Alamogordo, where the tourist trade was brisk. Since larger pieces are more likely to shatter in the kiln, they're high stakes to build and expensive. In his memoir, the physicist and collector Francis Harlow describes half of the Santo Domingo Pueblo turning out to see a twenty-three-inch-tall storage jar fired. He estimates its value at a few thousand

Krazy pining after a piece of pottery.

dollars in today's money. In the comic, Krazy can only admire such a pot, "bein' witout funs," but she has an eye for craftsmanship unusual among cartoon animals.

Krazy's predicament echoes that of tourists to the Southwest in the early twentieth century, who might admire high-art pottery but ultimately went home with more affordable trinkets. Many were drawn to the region by the evocative prose of travel writers who made expeditions across this "last frontier," seized from Mexico under the Treaty of Guadalupe Hidalgo in 1848. Excavations in the 1870s revealed the great antiquity of what archaeologists then termed Pueblo ruins, and mainstream America had once again discovered a lost romantic past—more exotic than the familiar mounds of the Mississippi Valley, though undeniably Indian.

Famed archaeologist Adolph Bandelier wrote a novel, *The Delight Makers*, dramatizing prehistoric Pueblo life for popular audiences. Like Henry Rowe Schoolcraft, Bandelier used storytelling to diagnose the ills of "the Indian mind"—superstition, "communistic socialism," and too-liberal sexuality among them. Bandelier's book, though accurate in its descriptions of material culture, suggested with a heavy hand that Native people would have to develop an individualistic mindset to become civilized. Yet, for white readers, it provided a tantalizing glimpse into the strange beliefs and customs of a supposedly vanishing past.

The first railroad line to Santa Fe opened in 1880, and Santa Clara Pueblo historian Tessie Naranjo traces a transformation of her community's artistic traditions to this date. Curators from the Smithsonian and other museums swept through first, buying up all the old pottery they could find—heirlooms that, on top of their emotional significance, had served as a "reference library" for potters. Paying poor people for their ancestral objects was seen as part of a modernizing effort to convert them to the cash economy. Potters developed new forms such as ashtrays, candlesticks, and cream pitchers catering to middle-class tourists, who wanted a simple memento of their once-in-a-lifetime trip. Figurines described as "rain gods" sold by the barrelful. Wealthier visitors looked upon such mementos with scorn and demanded a product imbued with "real" Indigenous meaning.

The pottery market was a contradictory drama of entitlement: a white public wanted to encounter and draw from the reservoir of ancient forces that the Southwest symbolized. Yet the wellspring of these forces, the Native population, was also living evidence of certain genocidal crimes. Thus, "discoverers" of Southwest art framed Indians as relics of a vanishing past that white people were called upon to salvage. Unlike Bandelier, who thought that the Pueblo were gradually progressing, art connoisseurs thought they had "degenerated" in modern times, falling prey to evils of civilization such as the need to earn a living by selling mass-produced tchotchkes. A well-funded crowd of artists and intellectuals who came to the Southwest seeking authentic encounters became self-appointed gatekeepers of authenticity. They sought Pueblo potters who could replicate the designs found on ancient pottery, establishing training schools and an Indian Arts Fund to promote their preferred styles. Historian Margaret Jacobs calls them "uplifters"—elites who aimed to improve Indians both culturally and economically by asserting their power as patrons and connoisseurs.

Art buyers have wielded their influence in many times and places; artists' visions intersect, in a market economy, with the need to sell their work, while judging lesser people's labor is the connoisseur's version of a productive activity. The tastes of uplifters, and collaborations with archaeologists, encouraged Pueblo potters to revisit ancient designs while also experimenting with new modes, such as the famous black-on-black style of Maria and Julian Martinez. Native artists regarded these changes with both pride and unease. For centuries, settlers had devalued Native cultures and tried hard to wipe them out. Tessie Naranjo writes that the revival of old ways was empowering, even if collectors also favored it. Collectors' demands led to a shift from communal production to individual artistry—she notes that potters began adding signatures to their work and competing for prizes. A traditional potter as well as a historian, Naranjo asserts that Pueblo pottery was meant for everyday use, not the decorative perfection of museums. As collectors who prided themselves on visiting the Pueblos often realized, many hands were involved in creating a pot that bore one famous name.

The warehouse of A. H. Fidel, Wholesale Acoma Pottery,
San Fidel, New Mexico, 1934.

The nature of connoisseurship is to enforce its tastes on others, and uplifters of the new Native arts market wrote books and articles, gave talks and hosted teas, to promote appreciation for authentic pottery. Whether readers owned a signed piece by the renowned Maria Martinez or an anonymous ashtray, they should know where they stood in the hierarchy of cultural assets. Once enlightened with this knowledge, even people of moderate means would want to own a real piece of the American past embodied in the hands of Pueblo craftspeople. Novelist Willa Cather phrased this desire as an obligation—"these potsherds were like fetters that bound one to a long chain of human endeavor." Perhaps white Americans needed a stylish fetter to make them feel that they belonged. In the 1910s, when the Ford Model T hit the market, the hunt for Southwestern art extended beyond tourist traps and into Native communities.

It's not a coincidence that the turn to a tourist economy overlapped with a series of government policies that drove Native people around the Southwest into poverty. The distinctive challenges faced by each of the nineteen New Mexico Pueblos, Diné (Navajo), Hopi, Apache, and other nations had common roots in the systematic assault on their diverse and sophisticated strategies for thriving in their homelands. The Diné homeland, Diné Bikéyah, lies between four sacred mountains in the current US states of Arizona, New Mexico, Colorado, and Utah. Diné communities had long cultivated peach orchards and cornfields, which the invading US Army slashed in 1864. After four years of brutal internment in Fort Sumter, the Diné secured a treaty to return to a portion of their land in 1868. Though they built up their territory through federal grants and purchases, they still faced economic hardship. When droughts struck in the 1930s, Diné shepherds couldn't adapt by spreading out their flocks, and sheep overgrazed. Government scientists seized upon overgrazing and the soil erosion that followed as a justification for slaughtering hundreds of thousands of Diné sheep. As with the slashing of peach trees, officials hoped this would force many Diné to abandon their land-based way of life and simply leave the reservation, opening up coal, oil, and other mineral treasures to white prospectors.

Pueblo ancestors had lived in present-day New Mexico, Arizona, Utah, and Colorado for thousands of years, and the Pueblos of the Rio Grande Valley faced a similar assault in the 1920s, when an act of Congress threatened to turn over much of their land and water rights to settlers. Pueblo leaders were joined in their protests by the circle of white artists in Taos and Santa Fe who had embraced Southwest culture as a source of "primitive" inspiration. While these artists promoted romantic views of Pueblo people, they also worked zealously with the nineteen governors of the All Indian Pueblo Council to fight the notorious Bursum Bill. A campaign in newspapers and magazines mobilized mass support among the white public. Pueblo representatives, including Floy Agnes Naranjo Lee's great-grandfather, Santa Clara Governor Santiago Naranjo, brought their protest to Washington, where the bill was struck down.

The groundswell of public support for Pueblo land rights in the 1920s was a moment of possibility, when the desire for spiritual fulfillment and authentic culture that brought white visitors to the

Southwest led them to back Native demands for justice, in a limited way. One of these advocates, John Collier, dedicated his career to work that he saw as promoting Native land and cultural preservation, helping to restore nations dissolved by the 1887 Dawes Act. However, as the US Commissioner of Indian Affairs in the 1930s, he persisted in a romantic view of Native ways as an antidote to the ills of modernity. Expecting every Native nation to embody the same ideals that he identified with the Pueblo, he outraged many—the devastating Navajo stock reduction program of the 1930s was a Collier initiative, which failed to relieve Diné poverty or turn semiarid terrain into an agrarian Eden.

Once Collier and other Progressives were deposed in a backlash against the New Deal's perceived socialism, the imperative to modernize Native nations out of existence and wring profit from their lands returned in full force. Officials described the Southwest as an unredeemable, barren desert, hostile to human enterprise—yet they also colluded with railroads, ranchers, and mining companies to secure it for private ownership. There had already been promising discoveries of copper, coal, and oil; prospectors were searching for the mother lode, a way to make the conquest of the Southwest pay off. Environmental historian Traci Brynne Voyles calls this wastelanding—a self-fulfilling process whereby a region is declared unfit for habitation and then exploited until it really is dangerously polluted.

The wastelanding of the Southwest might seem contradictory, since it was a site of such compelling natural and cultural encounters. But tourists passing through Monument Valley and the Painted Desert were encouraged to see them as empty spaces. The national parks created "natural" landscapes by once again pushing Indigenous presence out of the frame, except for a few picturesque photo opportunities. With specimens of nature preserved, the rest of the desert was due for development. Part of the region's allure was that great wealth was believed to lie below its barren surface. The other part of the allure, for the engineers of the Manhattan Project, was the barren surface itself.

In 1917, an entrepreneur named Ashley Pond built a boys

school on the former Los Alamos Ranch, high on New Mexico's Pajarito Plateau. The school was another place for sickly city dwellers to restore their health through outdoor exercise, near where the teenaged Robert Oppenheimer went for his own rejuvenation. In 1942, Oppenheimer and Lieutenant General Leslie Groves chose the school as the location of the Manhattan Project's Site Y, the unit responsible for building and testing the atomic bomb. Peggy Pond Church, daughter of the Los Alamos School's founder, vividly remembered when the government seized her family's land, along with that of dozens of Pueblo and Hispanic subsistence farmers. What she saw as a meditative frontier life, growing up in "a curious timelessness" amid the mesas and arroyos and searching for arrowheads in Indian ruins, ended with the violent influx of scientists and soldiers to Los Alamos.

Not only did Peggy Pond Church mourn her dispossession from her beloved desert landscape, she also felt the new society of Los Alamos as an affront to her spiritual and political beliefs. "It became a study in the use of power," she reflected in her journal. Now, Niels Bohr or Robert Oppenheimer might show up for tea at the house of her close friend Edith Warner. While Warner received them warmly, Church described them as emissaries of destruction and contrasted the violence of the atomic bomb with the peaceful holism of the Pueblo people whose land it scarred. Amid her impassioned defenses of Native ways, Church seemed unable to face her own role as a settler who helped clear the path for such development. Her three sons grew up to be engineers at Los Alamos and Sandia National Laboratories.

Church belonged to the generation of white intellectuals, connected through the Taos and Santa Fe artists' colonies, who considered themselves respectful students and proponents of Indian spirituality. Church's Pueblo neighbors chose to share with her certain traditions, which she rendered through her own poetic prism as a belief in "the wordless power that surrounds one in rock and stream and sky ... the energy of heat, of light, of motion, and finally of life itself." Against this, she contrasted the unnatural activities of Los Alamos: "Atomic energy, knowledge without love. The symbolic relationship to life, the ecological. That is what the Indian has that the white man lacks." Church was correct that American empire lacked an ethical relationship to the land. She had identified that lack and tried to fill it with Pueblo cosmology, while the question of how white citizens who cared for land and life could change the imperatives of their nation remained unanswered. This feeling of lack, though unspoken, was quite ubiquitous—it brought many artists from the cities to the desert and sent countless Pueblo pots on the reverse journey. Indeed, the Los Alamos scientists whom Church scorned felt it too, and they sought the same remedy.

Thousands of Los Alamos personnel from all corners of the world were sequestered for years in this isolated place. In oral histories, they invariably recall that attending Indian dances, exploring Indian ruins, and collecting pottery were among their few leisure activities. Los Alamos officials warned against looting artifacts from the mesas, but this was not a strong deterrent. During the war, in a secretive atmosphere of round-the-clock work, the nearby Pueblos were an exotic retreat. From the Manhattan Project days onward, scientists seemed to seek relief from the knowledge of what they were doing by stepping "out of time" into an imagined Indigenous timelessness.

Of course, Pueblo people were very much on the clock, traveling long distances each day to work in housekeeping, child care, construction, and maintenance at the laboratory, alongside many from nearby Hispanic communities. At other Manhattan Project sites, the Black service workers who made the operation run were treated as invisible, but Indians held a special status as "objects of romance," in the words of historian Peter Bacon Hales. The site's reliance on Pueblo maids and nannies made white women tourists in their own homes. "I'm sure she'll be worth her wages in entertainment value alone," wrote one woman of her maid. "She is sweet and picturesque, and I love to watch her." Seeking more ethnographic intimacy, white families finagled invitations to dinner in the homes of their Pueblo domestic workers, which they later reported among the interesting experiences of their time in New Mexico. In the act

In December 1945, a party celebrating the war's end brought together San Ildefonso Pueblo dancers and square dancers from Los Alamos National Laboratory. Both groups took pride in the Allied victory to which they had contributed, yet the prominent US flag is also a reminder of ongoing colonization of Native lands.

of displacing an Indigenous world, they longed to learn about and connect with it. While they engineered death and destruction, they saw its opposite in ancient traditions honoring the sacredness of the land. Their acquisitive curiosity looks, in retrospect, rather like the desire of the guilty to possess innocence. Los Alamos scientists and their families were supposed to be ambassadors of the American promise: an ascendant young nation turned toward the future with a clean conscience and an open mind.

Collecting Los Alamos

Francis H. Harlow made it to Los Alamos through the postwar opportunity that lifted so many of the "greatest generation" up from humble beginnings. His mother died when he was young, and he moved in with an aunt while his father put in long hours at a variety of odd jobs. Harlow, a gangly, uncoordinated "social misfit," had few friends and spent his time working at a local drugstore or wandering in the woods. A bright point in his rather gray childhood was the annual engineering fair at the University of Washington, which guided him toward science. As soon as he graduated high school in 1945, Harlow enlisted in the army and wound up, unglamorously, as a dental hygienist on a Texas military base. Upon discharge, the GI Bill provided him with "$75 per month, plus tuition, books, and supplies" to get a bachelor's of science degree, while teaching, laboratory jobs, and the newly created National Science Foundation got him through graduate school.

Though not a prodigy, Harlow was meticulous, systematic, and practical. Even his way of expressing himself is disarmingly precise: in graduate school he recognized that a career in quantum mechanics was "outside the scope of my anticipated conceptual abilities." After finishing his physics PhD in 1953, he found a match in the field of fluid dynamics. He was especially intrigued by turbulence—the chaotic interplay of forces in a tornado, a bursting dam, or the detonation of a nuclear bomb.

Less than a year after defending his dissertation, Harlow stood on the deck of a navy command ship in the South Pacific, watching through dark goggles while a bomb five hundred times as powerful as the one dropped on Hiroshima exploded over Bikini Atoll. It was the policy at Los Alamos that new personnel had to witness a test shot firsthand. During the first days of his working vacation,

Harlow went scuba diving among the doomed flora and fauna of the coral reefs, which he thought must be "the most beautiful and exciting" in the world. He gazed with the same hyperacute eye as the bomb "transformed a peaceful island to a raging column of infinite complexity." The mushroom cloud, symbol of man's capacity for apocalyptic destruction, was to Harlow an "incredible intricacy of material behaviors." The Operation Castle thermonuclear explosions of 1954 were unexpectedly powerful; Castle Bravo, the largest of the six bombs, pulverized ten million tons of coral reef, which rose in a radioactive fireball and rained down upon nearby inhabited islands. "The whole experience had a tremendous effect on my emotions," Harlow wrote. He returned to Los Alamos inspired to develop new techniques for modeling such events mathematically.

Harlow's obscure memoir, *Adventures in Physics and Pueblo Pottery*, would seem to promise an explanation of what links the subjects in its title: how Harlow and many others at Los Alamos understood their love of Native art in relation to the work of Cold War science. But Harlow saw no substantive link, just the happy geographical coincidence that living in New Mexico led him to study pottery. Physics and Pueblo pottery were simply the two passions that engaged his prodigious analytical abilities in complementary ways. Sorting potsherds was less "scientific" than his day job, but still involved reconstructing the relationship between parts and wholes using minute details, the "incredible intricacy of material behaviors" that he admired in the mushroom cloud.

Other clues to the relation between the nuclear laboratory and the Indigenous world were perhaps too mundane for Harlow's probing attention. Anthropologist Joseph Masco points out that many streets in the town of Los Alamos have Indian names: Zuni, Yuma, Apache, Navajo, Tewa. To Masco, the reference point is ambiguous. They could commemorate Native nations, in the long US tradition of memorializing people who never went away. Or, considering that a number of streets in Los Alamos are named after weapons, they could commemorate a series of bombs detonated in the South Pacific in 1956 that were, in turn, named for Indians as imperial mascots. The idea of ingesting the defeated enemy's "warrior ethos" into US military culture—just as white artists ingested Native aesthetics—was also the basis for the army's official policy of naming helicopters for "American Indian tribes and chiefs."

Meanwhile, in the Pueblo homeland, in view of ancestral sites, Los Alamos scientists built experimental stations dubbed kivas after the underground chambers where Pueblo communities conduct their most important ceremonies. After a couple of fatal mishaps, all Los Alamos criticality experiments took place in these remote stations. The nuclear kiva claimed continuity with the past—the "mysterious religious rituals" of the Pueblo had given way to the new secrets of the atom. In a fundamental misrecognition, it equated what Tewa anthropologist Alfonso Ortiz called a spiritual tradition of "seeking life" with the scientists' mission to build weapons of mass death. Yet the Pueblo were not gone and did not need any heirs or memorials; they were only on the other side of a security fence, seeking access to several thousand shrines enclosed within the laboratory's classified domain. The term "Indian ruins," applied by archaeologists, collectors, and day-trippers to the Southwestern sites they plundered, is not accurate, as Pueblo people still use those living places today—if they can get in.

During his early years at Los Alamos, Francis Harlow spent his spare time studying fossils and geology, but he soon shifted his attention to the Pueblo artifacts so abundant in the region. None of his hobbies were casual. He found large quantities of "spare time," aided by Patricia Harlow, his wife, who managed their household and growing family. To fully comprehend the field, he spent weekends bending his lanky frame over boxes of potsherds in a subbasement at the Laboratory of Anthropology in Santa Fe, sometimes with his children napping in the corner. This other laboratory was established by John D. Rockefeller Jr. in 1927 to bring order to the chaotic world of plundered Native antiquities. Its curators set Harlow to work reassembling shattered ceramics. Just as nuclear scientists had to set off bombs to study how bombs worked, the broken pieces of pottery were a "revelation of the materials used in constructing a vessel."

Harlow rebuilt pots with prodigious efficiency, noting their style, time period, and place of origin, to the great joy of the Laboratory of Anthropology's staff. He was by no means naive about the history of violence that had led to the Pueblo becoming a subject of white investigation. The period that interested him most was the Spanish reconquest of the 1690s, a traumatic upheaval in Pueblo history.

Dynamic Indigenous societies practicing irrigation-based agriculture had developed in present-day New Mexico over thousands of years. At the time of the Spanish invasion, they lived in ninety-eight interconnected city-states with distinct languages and traditions that the Spanish lumped together under the name Pueblos. The Spanish began seizing Pueblo land in the 1540s, declaring it the province of Santa Fe de Nuevo México; they imposed a system of forced labor and tried, with limited success, to convert the Pueblo to Catholicism. In 1680, Pueblo leaders united in a carefully planned revolt. After more than a century of Spanish rule, they drove out the occupying army and initiated a cultural revival, bringing back forbidden traditions.

Twelve years later, though, the rearmed Spanish marched back and demanded a peace treaty, which soon turned into a bloody reconquest. Many Pueblo resistors in the lowlands left their towns and retreated to fortified sites such as Tunyo, or Black Mesa, a sacred geological formation rising more than six thousand feet at its highest point. Finally, in 1694, Spanish general Diego de Vargas laid siege to Black Mesa for nine months, until its Tewa Pueblo defenders came down from the heights and negotiated a surrender.

Francis Harlow became somewhat obsessed with tracing the collision of diverse styles and forms in the pottery of the revolt and reconquest. Part of his fascination came from the heroic resistance that produced these artifacts. "Every time I drive by Black Mesa in my comfortable car," he wrote, "I am filled with wonder at what the Indians endured in this tragic period." Perhaps he viewed the turbulence of nuclear explosions with the same pathos and precision as the potsherds left on the mesa. His role was simply to study the material transformations that resulted from world-historical events that were, themselves, beyond his control.

The market for Pueblo pottery continued to heat up in the

1960s and '70s, so Harlow's skills were soon in high demand. With prices rising, counterfeits appeared, and it became important to authenticate each piece, whether ancient, historical, or modern. He befriended white collectors and dealers, archaeologists, and Pueblo potters, who sold their work to his Los Alamos colleagues out of his garage. In his diary, he recorded regular visits to Maria Martinez of San Ildefonso Pueblo, a leader of the revival in artistic pottery whose black-on-black designs won worldwide acclaim. The problem was that many older pots were unsigned, leaving their value in question. When people asked Martinez if she had made a particular pot, she generally said yes.

Just as white tourists in the 1910s worried that they were being sold fake rain gods, collectors worried that Martinez was tricking them. Tessie Naranjo argues that the idea of individual artistry, though important as a source of income for modern potters, was not at the heart of the tradition they had inherited. Martinez openly explained that her husband, family, and friends took part in building and painting her pieces. She may not have shared the collectors' urgent desire for provenance, however, she did have encyclopedic knowledge of the region's potters and their styles. When Harlow approached her with his highly technical questions about glazes and the patterns on jar rims, she told him what was what. He considered her a friend, but still felt the need to test her identifications by presenting her with the same pot on different visits, as though conducting an experiment. Through him she shaped the authoritative texts that secured the value of her community's work.

Though he knew plenty of dealers who made good money from Pueblo pottery, Harlow donated his valuable collection to the Museum of New Mexico. His salary as a senior Los Alamos scientist enabled him to simply enjoy "observing the forms, designs, and colors of beautiful things." In a way, he continued the work of the early twentieth-century uplifters, who wanted to make Pueblo pottery an artistic and archaeological field rather than a trade. Yet Harlow, drawn to technical minutia, took little apparent interest in paternalistic social control. Indeed, he seemed only to revel in the challenge posed by the change over time of particles or traditions

Harlow and Maria Martinez in 1973. The pitcher on the floor was commissioned from Maria Martinez by the Los Alamos School in the 1910s, and bears the school's logo as interpreted by Julian Martinez. Photo by Adam Martinez.

in motion. In his memoir, Harlow called the region's non-Native people settlers and included himself. Like most of the scientists around him, he simply preferred to focus on the kind of problems that he felt best suited to solve.

For Francis Harlow, physics and Pueblo pottery were ways of making an American identity for himself. Through physics, he joined an exclusive scientific community and secured a more-than-middle-class life for his family, fulfilling the dream of upward mobility. Through the study of Pueblo pottery, he grounded himself in the material history of the place he called home. His love of New Mexico echoes the feelings that drew so many artists and seekers to that region to reinvent themselves. His house was filled to the brim with symbols of the Southwestern identity he'd assembled— not just pottery, but Navajo rugs, paintings of local life, and the motorcycle that he rode to work across the desert. These symbols were available to anyone who wanted to belong somewhere in an increasingly homogenized and anonymous world.

During the first few decades of his tenure, Los Alamos National Laboratory (LANL) dumped radioactive waste into the landscape and communities that Harlow loved so much. To some extent, the laboratory's strict classification kept employees such as Harlow from knowing what it wasn't their job to know. Initiated into a culture of secrecy, many scientists chose to trust rather than question leadership's reassurances. Other workers, especially in maintenance and production, knew that they were exposed to dangerous materials on the job. "We had worked ourselves into a box that we couldn't walk away from," technician Phil Schofield explained to a local historian. "We had families, we had to pay bills." Rashes, lesions, and cancers were common, yet Schofield described lost radiation badges, evasive doctors, medical records that vanished.

Not until the fall of the Berlin Wall did the veil of silence around LANL begin to lift. For the first time, local residents could use laws such as the Clean Air and Water Acts to demand information about nuclear waste. Yet they didn't trust the answers that LANL officials produced after decades of misinformation. The early 1990s saw a ramping up of environmental activism in the area—antinuclear crusaders connected with Pueblo governments, white environmentalists, Chicano groups, and the descendants of Spanish settlers known as Hispanos, all pressuring the Department of Energy, which controls the lab, for transparency and remediation. When LANL told the San Ildefonso Pueblo that their land was completely free of health risks, the Eight Northern Pueblos Office of Environmental Protection produced its own study showing "alarmingly high levels of radiation." In the 1970s, Harlow's research group had created models for harvesting geothermal energy from deep underground—seemingly a clean source of power. By 1992, the lab was ready to test it out by detonating six tons of TNT below the Jemez Mountains, but Pueblo governments were fed up with experiments on their land. The explosions were "culturally disruptive," they argued, threatening their relations with sensitive natural forces. For the first time, they stopped a Los Alamos project in its tracks.

It's not that Harlow was especially hypocritical or naive to look the other way from the threat that his laboratory posed to the land that he so closely identified with. The hypocrisy was a larger one— the way that a symbolic desire for identity and place was so easily fulfilled for white settlers, while Indigenous people faced a continued battle to hold on to their actual land and traditions. After centuries of explicit persecution, the threat of the twentieth century was invisible and slow. It took the form of risk and uncertainty. Marian Naranjo, a Santa Clara Pueblo activist and organizer of the women-led environmental group Las Mujeres Hablan, emphasizes that the beginning of the nuclear project marked a new chapter in colonial violence against land-based people. "This culture of violence was forcibly incorporated into our story," she writes. "The rocks recorded it. The land and water recorded it. Our DNA recorded it to be forever held by our children." Yet Naranjo and her collaborators "have been told there is not enough evidence" to prove any harm. Indeed, the harm caused by radiation is a matter of probability and is almost impossible to prove. Reconstructing the path of a specific fallout cloud on a specific day in the 1950s would be a task for the precise, dogged mind of Frank Harlow, but he only studied explosions, not their consequences.

"And the other face
was terrible"

Floy Agnes Naranjo Lee was one of the few Native American laboratory technicians at Los Alamos during the war years. While day laborers were bused in from the Pueblos each morning, she lived in the bubble of secrecy that was the Manhattan Project, prevented from visiting her father and grandparents in Santa Clara Pueblo a dozen miles away. Trained on the job as a hematologist, Lee carefully monitored the blood of scientists for abnormalities, though no one could tell her what materials they were working with, or what kind of problems an exposure might cause. Even her superiors lacked basic information about the effects of radiation on the human body, besides that it was bad.

Lee's blood draws were so routine that she became friends with her patients, whom she knew only by number due to the lab's security protocols. She often played tennis with a man who later revealed himself as Enrico Fermi, the famous Italian physicist who engineered the first nuclear chain reaction. After the bombings of Hiroshima and Nagasaki in August of 1945, this and other secrets became public. Lee, along with the rest of the nation, read about the catastrophic energy released by breaking the bonds of uranium and plutonium atoms. Though the bomb's explosive power was widely celebrated, the US government continued to suppress information about what, exactly, radiation was. Word of an "atomic plague" afflicting the Japanese survivors leaked out, but with few details; John Hersey's graphic *Hiroshima* wasn't published until a year later, and scientific censorship persisted long after that. People struggled with the concept of an invisible, lingering force that killed slowly. Even the leaders of the Manhattan Project disagreed about the long-term risks of handling fissile materials, an abstract worry compared to the urgency of winning the war. They had only read about the acute radiation poisoning that afflicted Japanese survivors of the bomb. Soon, Lee and her colleagues saw it for themselves.

On May 21, 1946, she was called to the Los Alamos Engineer's Hospital to draw blood from a regular patient, the physicist Louis Slotin; that afternoon, he had been exposed to 2,100 rem of radiation, more than four times the fatal dose, when his hand slipped in the midst of a delicate experiment. Physicists called it "tickling the dragon's tail"—bringing a plutonium core to the brink of criticality. This core went supercritical for a tenth of a second before Slotin threw off the tamper. As the days passed and Slotin's body swelled with internal radiation burns, Lee counted what was left of his white blood cells until there was nothing to count.

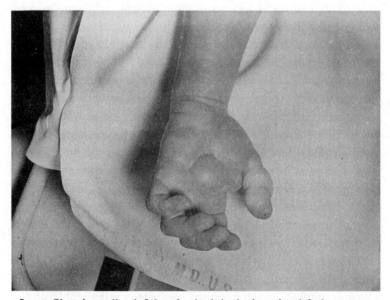

Louis Slotin's swollen left hand, which he had used to lift the tamper from the overheating core. For scientific purposes the laboratory's Photographic Group carefully documented the progression of his radiation burns.

She also monitored Alvin Graves, who had stood behind Slotin in the lab, peering over his shoulder at the plutonium sphere that became known as the demon core. Slotin had shielded half of Graves's body from the radiation. Graves "went around with a normal face, and the other face was terrible," Lee recalled. "His white blood cells were so low that they didn't even understand why he was still living . . . and then it started to come up a little, and a little and a little more. My God, everybody was so happy." Graves, thirty-six at the time of the accident, seemed to recover completely. He died suddenly at age fifty-five; his former laboratory director emphasized that Graves suffered a heart attack, and that heart disease ran in the family.

Hiroshima and Nagasaki changed everything for some of the scientists who had labored on the Manhattan Project for years. They felt, reported physicist Edward Teller, "profoundly disturbed by the questionable morality of dropping the bomb" without first giving the Japanese a chance to surrender—though this might seem a naive thing to expect after such immense military investment in a new superweapon. Some participants claimed they hadn't believed that the weapon would be used on civilians or, as President Truman put it, "all those kids." Teller, for his part, embraced nuclear war and made light of his colleagues' remorse: "No amount of protesting or fiddling with politics will save our souls." For Lee, who wasn't privy to reports of the true horror in Japan, it may have been the criticality accident with Slotin and Graves that changed everything. She had seen what radiation could do and wanted to understand how. She would study its effects for the rest of her career. Distilling a great amount of technical detail, she remarked toward the end of her life, "Radiation is bad."

Returning to the accident of May 1946, when all of Los Alamos was watching Floy Agnes Naranjo Lee watching the leukocyte counts of the exposed scientists. Returning to the two faces of Al Graves, the burnt face and the shielded face, one face "normal" and the other "terrible." The beholder knows that the faces aren't separate at all—they look different but belong to the same body, and inside that body, even as it survives, unseen processes have been set in motion. These are the two faces of the nuclear Southwest, and the two faces of American freedom: one that is sacrificed and one that gains, the illusion that they are somehow separate, that the damage can be contained.

Al Graves's divided face brings to mind the two-faced gods of many religions, such as the Roman god Janus, who looks simultaneously to the past and the future, presides over doorways, bridges, and borders, beginnings and endings. His divine functions don't clearly point to the common use of *two-faced* to mean "duplicitous." Perhaps this connotation lies in Janus's liminal role, his mysterious ability to be in two times or places at once—he sees what is coming but doesn't warn us. Said to be the inventor of money, the god was emblazoned on early Roman coins. Now we're closer: a coin, also, has two faces on one body. For one face to show, the other must be hidden. We say "two sides of the same coin" and mean that supposedly distinct phenomena are in fact contingent on each other: like profit and poverty, a zero-sum game. The expression conveys cynicism. "You mean you didn't know that one person's gain is another's loss?"

The idea that the hidden face requires special insight to uncover seems inconsistent with the nature of coins, which are constantly in motion, like Janus, on a million mercantile journeys around the empire. They are a basic tool for the teaching of probability, in which scenario we think of the coin as spinning in the air, governed not by gods but by chance. A coin flip is treated as a binary decision point—heads or tails—which guides events down one path while voiding the path not taken. It conveys the grim necessity of choice. Indeed, the resort to flipping a coin is a startling confession that there are no rational criteria for who gets what and the outcomes are empty of meaning. Yet we can't linger at the crossroads, can't have it both ways, and certainly can't have or be two things at once.

Many philosophers argue that, were it not for the binary structure of language and values that dominates modern European thought, the notion of two or more things in one would be common sense. It emerges from everyday experiences of transforming, melding, and recombining and underlies numerous cosmologies ancient and modern. It's not a difficult thought experiment to move beyond the mark on the coin and consider the entire coin as an object whose faces have faces, as a plated piece of metal that will liquefy at around a thousand degrees. But this is not a melting pot or a manifesto for cyborgs—merely knowing that binaries are artificial has not diminished their power. Pretending that we've transcended such superficial markers as race, class, gender, or ability, hides the enduring way the American coin is weighted. The face of misfortune rarely turns on men like Slotin and Graves, who designed the mold in which a particularly fatal coin was cast.

Physics does offer empirical validation, for those who desire it, of the simultaneity once ascribed to two-faced gods. Einstein's realization that matter and energy, time and space, are two sides of the same coin made possible many quasi-spiritual insights about the nature of reality. The transformation of chemical bonds into free energy fueled the chain reaction that burned half of Alvin Graves. The results of splitting an atom can only be predicted probabilistically; it's more like splashing a bucket of paint than taking apart building blocks. But the people who dwell in this exalted realm, closest to what science supposes to be the great and final truth of our universe, are no more free for their knowledge. They often refuse to recognize the hidden face of what they do. Concerned scientists such as Einstein, Oppenheimer, and many others, who feel a moral responsibility for the uses of their work, find that political power follows different laws. While initiated into the dark alchemy of nuclear fission, "we have not learned," bemoaned journalist Walter Lippmann, "how to release hitherto inaccessible intellectual and moral energies."

Over her long scientific career, Floy Agnes Naranjo Lee published under different married names. Names that are fixed for life are easily recorded by history. The work of women scientists is harder to track when their identities shift with the social demands of marriage and motherhood. Her daughter, Patricia, describes her "incredible drive and discipline in her work. . . . She often felt at a great disadvantage, being a woman in a traditionally male environment, but she was proud to be a trailblazer." Later in her life Lee received numerous honors as a female Native American scientist, though they rarely went into great detail about her research, which is dispersed across myriad academic databases and government reports. Like the pots that Maria Martinez made with her family and neighbors, scientific knowledge is a collective process to which historians often attach a famous name and story. For women researchers, who are so often erased in the writing of history, it is important to get names and stories on the record.

The daughter of a Tewa tailor from the Santa Clara Pueblo and a white teacher from Indiana, Lee was born at a crossing of worlds. Her father's family, the Naranjos, were leaders in Santa Clara politics. He met her mother while they both taught at the government-run Indian boarding school in Santa Fe; the couple then moved to the Indian school in Albuquerque. Among her mother's students were painters who became known for the Santa Fe Style so coveted by collectors of Southwestern art. Lee grew up on the school grounds among pupils separated from their families in the name of government-enforced assimilation. The New Mexico boarding schools were less brutal than others due to the unique ability of nearby parents to shape school policies, but they still enlisted students in hard labor on farms or as domestic help in white homes.

Since Lee had no need for such "retraining" she went to the local Catholic school, where nuns spoke of Indians as savages. "That really got to me," Lee recalled. "But I finally realized the reason for some of the prejudice. People just didn't know, and they still don't know. They don't know about New Mexico." She didn't explain what "knowing about New Mexico" meant to her—perhaps, as Laguna Pueblo writer Paula Gunn Allen expresses it, New Mexico meant living in "a confluence of cultures," hybrid forms and identities. As Tewa scholar Jennifer Marley points out, such knowing also speaks of suppressed historical truths. The state's tourism agencies promote a glossy image of diversity and multiculturalism, as though Native, Hispanic, and Anglo communities all showed up at the same time. For the original inhabitants, "confluence" brought centuries of violence, including public celebrations of the Spanish reconquest that persisted until 2018.

The summer after Lee graduated from the University of New Mexico with a degree in biology, a professor recruited her into the Manhattan Project. The need for staff was so pressing that she would be trained on the job. When she boarded an army bus to an undisclosed destination on the Pajarito Plateau, Lee also got in on the ground floor of a growing biomedical field. Building the bomb involved working with new radioactive isotopes whose health effects were unknown. A few years earlier, the chemists who processed fissile materials had begun to demand medical research and monitoring. "Fear ran deep in the ranks," according to Atomic Energy Commission historian Barton Hacker. Chemists realized that their insurance only covered them for ninety days after an accident, while cancer from radiation might not appear for decades.

When they demanded safety studies on new substances such as plutonium and polonium, unnerving information emerged: ingested plutonium lodged near the bone marrow, a clear leukemia risk. Safe exposure levels were previously calculated on paper, based on the theoretical properties of elements; these levels had to be slashed in the wake of lab results, as far as the military would allow, lest it impede progress on the bomb. Geiger counters and other radiation-monitoring equipment were scarce, making it impossible to enforce these limits at every worksite. Meanwhile, contaminated air and water flushed out of buildings was dispersed freely across canyons and mesas. Los Alamos workers dubbed one radioactive drainage stream Acid Canyon. Its real name was Pueblo Canyon, and it flowed through the San Ildefonso Pueblo into the Rio Grande.

In her new job, Lee reported to Louis Hempelmann, a physician with the Sisyphean task of enforcing radiation safety through the Health Division of the secret laboratory. All employees exposed to radioactive materials were supposed to wear a badge that tracked their daily dosage; Lee's job was to draw their blood and count their white blood cells, in the hope of detecting overexposure. Hempelmann faced pressure on both sides, from generals who wanted the work sped up, and from senior researchers concerned about their staff. Robert Oppenheimer diverted half the military's supply of plutonium from bomb making so that Hempelmann could administer it to lab rats and, later, to eighteen hospital patients who never consented to the procedure. The Health Division justified these infamous human experiments, which were never disclosed to their subjects, on the grounds that they helped researchers develop blood and urine tests for plutonium. An ethics review decades later found the method sloppy—the patients were supposed to be "terminal," but one African-American subject had only broken his arm and leg—and the deception gratuitous, as members of the public were ready and willing to volunteer for wartime medical research.

The Health Division's work at Los Alamos was chaotic, with scientists dispersed across different test sites and a rapidly changing research program. Lee often had to track down her subjects in distant canyons, or at their homes, to get a blood sample. The popular narrative of Los Alamos during this time is one of a frantic effort to produce the bomb no matter what the cost. The story's other face is that people were endangered without knowing of or consenting to the risks. Laboratory leaders routinely underestimated workers' exposure levels. In retrospect, even Lee's diligent blood tests "provided no basis for early warning" due to wide natural variation—only in an extreme case such as Slotin's would the leukocyte count tell the tale. No one measured the exposure of civilians living near the site, of cattle and sheep, or of water and crops. Instead, an elaborate procedure of denial and silencing was adopted that remained in place for much of the Cold War, extending the Manhattan Project's "state of emergency" around radiation for decades. For someone in Lee's unique position, part of the lab yet not privy to its secrets, it was a double deception: both the workers whose health she monitored and her nearby relatives were at risk.

After Hiroshima, technicians such as Lee were introduced to radiation safety protocols, but assured that the hazard was minimal. It may have come as a surprise, then, when Lee entered Louis Slotin's hospital room in May of 1946 to find him swollen with "three-dimensional" burns and later found Al Graves in the same condition at his home. The samples Lee collected from Slotin and Graves were invaluable, adding to the sparse data from other involuntary human subjects. In 1952, Hempelmann published a study in the *Annals of Internal Medicine* that included the two physicists among nine cases of "acute radiation syndrome." Graves seemed to view the accident pragmatically, recalling that after his hair fell out, he "did not have to shave for a while, which was a byproduct that was useful." On the crucial question of reproducing the race—"Have you had kids since then and are they mutants?"—he assured concerned congressmen that he had fathered two "perfectly normal children."

Surviving radiation poisoning did not inspire empathy for victims of the bomb in Japan or of potential nuclear mishaps at home. Fear of radiation, Graves believed, was "concocted in the minds of weak malingerers." Instead, an apparently recovered Graves acted as a cheerful ambassador from Los Alamos to nearby communities, as well as to towns in Utah and Nevada, insisting that weapons testing over their land was safe. He presided over the notorious Operation Castle in 1954, where Frank Harlow so carefully observed the coral reefs and the mushroom cloud. Graves brushed aside concerns about fallout; by the time the atolls of Rongelap, Utirik, and Ailinginae were evacuated, hundreds of people had been exposed, adding more involuntary participants to the military's health effects research. Residents of Rongelap were returned to their homes two years later, though the land remained radioactive for decades. In a 1957 hearing before the Congressional Joint Committee on Atomic Energy, Graves again argued that low levels of radiation from fallout were undetectable and the public risk was so small as to be impossible to calculate.

When Pennsylvania congressman James Van Zandt asked about Graves's personal experience with radiation, Graves gave his dosage in the accident as about 200 roentgens. The actual dosage, calculated by Louis Hempelmann's Health Division, was nearly twice that, 390 roentgens; at 450 roentgens, the odds of survival are fifty-fifty, a coin flip. Perhaps Graves never read the medical study and continued to believe the falsely reassuring numbers he was told by his Los Alamos doctors. As a former lab director explained, "for psychological reasons," it was unofficial policy "to tell scientists and technicians that they received less radiation than they actually did." In 1979, fourteen years after Graves died, Hempelmann presented another study of nuclear accident survivors in which he concluded that Graves's fatal heart attack "could have been precipitated" by radiation damage.

Picture the two-faced god stamped on that Roman coin. With one face, Al Graves explained to Congress that scientists had no way to calculate the risks of low-level exposure; with the other, he told civilians that there were no risks. But the coin itself has two faces. On the other side is everything that Graves wouldn't let himself see: the shadow of his dead colleague burned onto his body, the shape of the sacrifice that had saved his life, and what he chose to do with that life. It's possible the hidden face did him no personal harm. It's equally possible that he was not, in the end, such a lucky man.

Lee's response to the criticality accident reflects a scientific empathy: the desire to fully understand what had happened, to inspect the coin from all angles. It's not so different from Frank Harlow with his shattered Pueblo pots. The only way for Lee to lay hands on that coin was to travel deeper into the nuclear state apparatus. That, as a technician, she jumped onto the inside track shows her skill in navigating the strange circumstances of the Manhattan Project. At a party marking Enrico Fermi's departure from Los Alamos, a twenty-three-year-old Lee declared to Fermi, her frequent tennis partner, that she wanted "to go and study more about

Sympathy for the atom.

what radiation does to living cells." Fermi invited her join him at the Argonne National Laboratory near Chicago, where the Atomic Energy Commission (AEC) was channeling money into medical research as it drew up plans for a peacetime nuclear industry.

The people who built the atomic bomb had two postwar paths: they could keep making weapons, or they could ride the wave of "swords into plowshares" funding that sought peaceful applications for nuclear technology. A temporary wartime project became a permanent fixture of the US economy, and the secret sites of the Manhattan Project were transformed into national laboratories where both kinds of work would be conducted. Argonne focused on nuclear energy, while Los Alamos would continue to be a center of weapons design and testing. The Argonne Biology Division, where Lee worked, utilized the lab's reactors to study the effects of radiation with unprecedented precision.

Leaving the Southwest for the first time, Lee arrived in Chicago in 1947 and found an apartment in Hyde Park, a short walk from her new job. Her migration paralleled that of thousands of other Native people relocated to Chicago in the postwar period by the Bureau of Indian Affairs (BIA). Unsatisfied with the effectiveness of its boarding schools, the BIA decided to simply move Indians from reservations into major cities, expecting them to assimilate into the urban melting pot. The BIA promised jobs and housing to young families but tried to disperse them geographically so their distinctive national identities would fade away.

Resisting this centrifugal force, Native people built new, intertribal communities throughout the 1950s that would undergird the militant activism of the 1960s. One of these communities formed in Hyde Park, a stone's throw from Lee's front door. Perhaps she noticed the newspaper reports as Chicago's Indians threw off the indifferent stewardship of the BIA and established their own schools, resource centers, and activist groups, but her daughter, Patricia, explains that Lee's "involvement with research was nearly all-consuming." Through the intense camaraderie of the Manhattan Project, Lee had become part of what anthropologist Hugh Gusterson calls the nuclear complex, its own insular culture devoted to grueling high-stakes work and snatches of shared leisure. When Lee visited her family in New Mexico, she also went hiking with Al Graves and his wife, Elizabeth.

At first the Biology Division, where Lee worked, was squeezed into old Manhattan Project quarters, a former brewery near the University of Chicago dubbed Site B, where weapons components were forged. Despite the presence of doctors studying radiation's effects, the site was notorious for lax safety, with visitors reporting "distressingly poor housekeeping" of radioactive materials. The Biology Division's director, cancer researcher Austin Brues, who would later work with Lee on numerous projects, recalled "the massive equipment which rolled, pounded, and thundered away" in the building, "while a bevy of young ladies in a room directly above attempted to see—let alone count—blood cells under the microscope." Lee was one of those "young ladies," walking through the debris and dust of the metal workshop to her lab bench each day. Lee worked at Site B until 1952, while a new facility for Argonne was built outside the city. Women had seized an unprecedented chance to do scientific work during the war years, and some held onto their places despite postwar efforts to drive them back to the domestic sphere. Fine-motor tasks, repetitive calculations, and tending to specimens were seen as gender-appropriate labor; women made significant and often unacknowledged contributions in these highly specialized roles. Lee, for her part, did not intend to stay a technician. She had come from New Mexico not just to work at the lab, but to earn a PhD at the University of Chicago. The field of radiation biology was so new, and technical skills were in such demand, that she would struggle to find time for her doctoral research.

In the University of Chicago Zoology Department, Lee met Clyde Stroud, a student who, like her, had just arrived from New Mexico. Stroud was an air force navigator during the war; when he got home, he devoted himself to scouring the White Sands desert not far from where the first atomic bomb was tested, documenting insects for his master's degree. Stroud's inventory of 451 insect species and subspecies could be taken to refute the idea that the desert was a barren and disposable wasteland. Like Lee's work at the microscope, it was a task of minute precision. They married on September 2, 1949, and soon had a daughter.

The couple made a plan for attaining a stable family life: he would finish his PhD while she worked full-time at the lab, then he would make money while she finished school. Stroud earned his degree in 1951 and joined his wife at Argonne—he easily pivoted from studying insects to studying neutron radiation. If he had lived, he might have worked with the JANUS Reactor, which had two opposite faces that delivered high- and low-intensity neutrons to lab animals. But his days were numbered. Diagnosed with melanoma at age twenty-nine, Stroud only survived another year. He had impressed colleagues as "a very remarkable scientist"; his Chicago office-mate, Robert Sokal, felt that their relationship "really turned me into what I have become." Stroud converted him to biostatistics, a field where Sokal became a leading light. The paper record bears few traces of Stroud beyond these lines of influence, some words of praise in entomology journals. Nor is there a record of what Lee experienced during that last year of their marriage. The terse death notice published in Argonne's 1952 quarterly report only stated that Stroud "endured a painful and crippling illness with great gallantry." Even in a lab that studied cancer, the disease could not be named when it struck among the ranks.

Lee knew that his work on radiation was not the cause of her husband's death—he had only begun to study it around the time of his diagnosis. Was it the sun or sand of the desert, or an accident of nature? Perhaps this drove home the randomness of the risks she sought to control and measure. She'd watched Alvin Graves, with fifty-fifty chances of survival, recover full health. Yet Clyde Stroud, a person at far less risk, met with the other face of probability. In both cases, the most advanced science could not change what had been set in motion.

The best treatment for cancer was radiation, which in turn caused sickness and risk of later cancers—another paradoxical twinning. Lee would again pick up this coin and regard its two faces. What harm did radiation do? Not despite, but because of this power, what could it do to help? She joined the American Association for Cancer Research in 1954. At Argonne, she tested the use of blood plasma infusions to prevent radiation sickness in mice. Alongside Mildred M. Summers, one of the few Black women to work on the Manhattan Project, Lee developed ways to cultivate tumor cells and gauge the effect of different treatments. Radiotherapy promised to give back life, a redemption snatched from the teeth of danger.

Every day, Lee watched under the microscope for changes in the blood chemistry of irradiated mice, counted the cataracts in their milky eyes, and autopsied the livers of the deceased. She was a widowed mother, splitting time between her paying work at Argonne and PhD research that would take fourteen years to complete. She joked that her daughter grew up on a lab bench, and Patricia recalls spending "a fair amount of time in her lab, learning to wash glassware and care for the lab mice and rats." In the early sixties, hoping for funding to finish her PhD—which schools commonly granted to full-time students amid a glut of postwar science

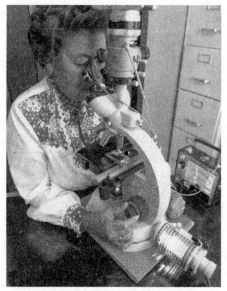

Floy Agnes Naranjo Lee at a microscope in an undated Los Alamos photograph.

funding—Lee visited the Bureau of Indian Affairs in Washington. The superintendent "didn't believe that I was going for a doctor's degree," as Lee remembered it. Despite the BIA's efforts to advance Indian education, she was told, "There is no money allocated for Indians to go on after a bachelor's." She was already a coauthor on numerous publications in medical and scientific journals.

Even before the 1953 debut of Watson and Crick's model of the DNA double-helix, researchers understood that the diffuse symptoms of radiation exposure all stemmed from the destruction of genetic material. Lee took countless photomicrographs of damaged chromosomes and tracked the chemical markers of DNA synthesis in irradiated cell lines. Central to her work were karyotypes, the now-familiar diagram of a cell's chromosomes in sequence. She and the technicians in her group created these manually by printing a photomicrograph, cutting out the best example of each chromosome, and pasting them in order. When digital computers were up to the task in the late 1960s, Lee worked on early karyotyping programs to automatically classify normal and abnormal chromosomes from tissue samples.

Not only could small genetic changes take decades to multiply into cancers, they could also impact future generations. Heredity became another focus of Lee's research group at Argonne—they began to track mutations in the offspring of lab mice. Studies of human heredity depended on "natural experiments" such as Graves's encounter with the demon core and the vast devastation of Hiroshima, which provided endless fodder for American scientists. Operation Castle, where Graves exposed hundreds of Marshall Islanders to high doses of fallout, became another natural experiment. "I was asked to look at chromosomes from some of the survivors on Bikini," Lee recalled. "But the material that they sent me was just impossible to read."

Unlike the race for the atomic bomb, this work was not secret, except to some of its human subjects. By the late 1950s, popular fear of radioactive fallout had swept the United States, but academic and government experts continued to reassure the public. Internally, they argued back and forth without resolution—interpretations of the evidence seemed to depend on other kinds of commitments.

Some scientists, such as Nobel Prize–winning chemist Linus Pauling and cancer expert Sister Rosalie Bertell, embraced the peace movement and raised the alarm about radiation. Pauling, accused of aiding the "Communist peace offensive," was forced to resign as the chair of chemistry at Caltech. He landed comfortably at Stanford and went on to promote state-enforced eugenics for people with heritable disorders such as sickle cell anemia—illuminating an ableist strain in antinuclear concern for genetic purity. People without a Nobel Prize had much further to fall for speaking out.

Others, such as Graves, Teller, and physicist Ernest Lawrence, were professionally and politically invested in weapons development. They saw fear of radiation as an ignorant superstition, yet also believed that less was more when it came to public information. In the late fifties, they promoted the hydrogen bomb as a "clean bomb," "a truly nonradioactive weapon," which would also serve civilians as "a major breakthrough in atomic-power development." Internally, these scientists also used the term *clean* to describe the neutron bomb, developed in the same period as an "enhanced radiation weapon" to kill people without damaging physical property. Soviet leaders insightfully dubbed it the "capitalist bomb."

Lee had worked her way up through government labs, which paid for her degree and initiated her into a world of elite research rarely accessible to women and minorities. She didn't see herself as political, nor did she want to become a public figure. At Argonne, she systematically quantified radiation damage in cells and in animals. Based on laboratory evidence alone, there were no certain answers: test tubes don't translate to real life, where countless variables are uncontrolled. Each study clarified a small piece of a vast picture that seemed to remain always slightly out of focus. Philosopher of science Thomas Kuhn called this "normal science," the work of applying established theories across a broad area, filling out a canon of knowledge. Lee's work was also Big Science, at the heart of a large, complex, and collaborative state apparatus. She served on various research teams that investigated questions deemed important by laboratory leaders and AEC officials. Their findings ran in publicly available journals, but at a level of technical specialization that was impossible for ordinary people to grasp.

However, as the Cold War escalated, Americans did begin demanding information about the bombs exploding over the Southwestern desert, and spreading it through new citizen groups such as the Committee for Nuclear Information. They wanted to hear from activist scientists including Pauling and John Gofman, an AEC whistleblower who refused to "be silent and use the secrecy stamp to keep something from surfacing that I think the public ought to know." To skeptics, the dream of peaceful nuclear energy was also a potential nightmare: "Nobody but God could write the insurance policy we need on nuclear power plants," exclaimed a Pennsylvania insurance commissioner. In the absence of divine intervention, Congress passed the Price-Anderson Nuclear Industries Indemnity Act of 1957, in which the government assumed liability for the catastrophic risks of private companies. It was supposed to be a temporary fix, but the market has never adjusted to solve this problem.

The Atomic Energy Commission felt a strong incentive to show that the atom could give back as much as it took from the commonwealth. The AEC's uranium enrichment would consume more electricity in 1956 "than is produced by the Hoover, Grand Coulee, and Bonneville dams plus the entire original TVA system combined," noted Commissioner Gordon Dean, seeming to admit that intensive dam building had not solved America's energy problems, but only enabled new ones. Pacific Gas & Electric proposed the first commercial nuclear power facility, in California, the following year, but the Bodega Bay plant was never built due to fierce local resistance—a pattern that would repeat across the country. In a series of congressional hearings from 1957 to 1958, experts tried to communicate arcane and nuanced concepts of risk to a public increasingly alarmed at the radioactivity in their midst.

By then, Lee and her colleagues had quantified the damage caused by high radiation doses, but many scientists still held that low levels were harmless. The earth itself gives off background radiation that humans easily tolerate. During the Manhattan Project, regulators had applied a "threshold approach"—unless daily exposure exceeded a set threshold, it could be repeated the next day, and the next, as though the body reset itself overnight. AEC renegade John Gofman and other critics of this standard showed that "only zero dose causes zero damage," and that small radiation-induced changes to cellular machinery accumulate over time. Moreover, they foresaw that honesty and consent would become more important than technical criteria when the public inevitably learned what was happening. As historian Barton Hacker writes, all standards are "politically, rather than scientifically, decided"—how much risk, and for whom, is a political question.

Risk talk has become a mundane part of life for Americans: retirement funds, medical treatments, insurance policies, and much more rest on obscure calculations about which bad things are likely to happen when. Yet thinking about risk remains profoundly difficult, and perceptions of danger or safety are easily exploited. The vanishingly small risk of adverse reaction to the measles-mumps-rubella vaccine, spun into a malevolent conspiracy, has spurred parents around the world to reject vaccination for their children, although measles is far more likely to cause harm than a vaccine. In contrast, high-risk choices feel safe when they're ubiquitous: driving a car is more deadly than skydiving. And we systematically mask structural harms behind the illusion of individual agency. It's legal in many states to fire a cigarette-smoking employee for their risky behavior, while industries that pollute the air bear no responsibility for the illness they cause. We simply see an icon on the weather report warning of a high-asthma-risk day.

Being alive is a risk, which life insurance companies began to quantify in the eighteenth century. Their formulas were based on protocols for insuring cargo in the shipping industry. The word *risk* originally connoted "possibility of damage to merchandise," including crops, manufactured wares, and enslaved people. This was the dawn of actuarial science: bookkeepers developed statistical tools to weigh value against risk, setting the premium that members paid in and the benefits the insurer would pay out. Wealthy Europeans began insuring their lives in the same period that they developed the ruthless metrics of the transatlantic slave trade. Perhaps they found it affirming, rather than dehumanizing, to see their superior value enforced by these calculations—it showed how well the system was serving them. Over the nineteenth century, working-class people had to enter this system too: a wage earner's body was their only asset, and insurance protected their family if that asset was suddenly liquidated.

To make money from the masses, the life insurance industry began collecting data on a large scale to figure out more precisely when its customers might die. They built vast actuarial tables, correlating age, race, occupation, and medical history with life expectancy. African Americans were sorted into a "subprime" risk category and either denied coverage or charged exploitative rates. George Herriman commented on this in a 1944 *Krazy Kat* strip where a brown weasel, considered a "poor risk" by the insurance company, has a beautician bleach his fur; he's "worth a fortune" as a white weasel. Insurers introduced the annual physical exam, promoted as a preventive tool against disease but also useful as a source of such data as weight, blood pressure, kidney function, and lung capacity. The data seemed to justify excluding Black custom-

Mr. W. Weasel goes from brown to white for insurance purposes.

ers, who had a lower life expectancy, though as W. E. B. Du Bois argued in *The Philadelphia Negro*, this statistic was the result of racist policies in housing, education, and labor rather than a biological constant. Separating the statistical individual from social and economic forces obscured the causes of danger, shielding discrimination under a mantle of objectivity. When insurers aggregated thousands of medical records, they could pinpoint each customer within an atomized universe of risk.

Through rituals like the physical exam, individuals became responsible for their own risk management, both to prolong their lives and to make themselves more appealing to the insurance agent and the human resources department. Lifestyle choices such as diet and exercise came to define the gospel of health in the United States. Yet the most accurate predictors of health have always been income and place of residence, things that most people are not free to choose. This repressed tension between individual control and external forces has an uncanny effect on Americans, steeped from the cradle in rugged self-determination. We're afraid of things that threaten the integrity of the body, that contaminate and seep and infiltrate. The experts who advise an anxious public about their "life chances" deny the relevance of forces that act in historical time, preferring the vain, foreshortened timescale of personal achievement.

That the first alarm about radiation exposure in the Manhattan Project was raised by chemists worried about their insurance coverage is significant. They recognized that a new kind of risk had entered the scene—or rather, that risk had materialized in a remarkable new form, plutonium. This substance would enter your bones and emit radiation for thousands of years after you were buried. Whose responsibility was it to deal with the unknown consequences of exposure? The chemists secured a secret commitment from the army to pay out $10,000 each to injured workers or their families. The imperative for secrecy during World War II and then the Cold War created an obvious wrinkle in individuals' ability to manage their own risk: What about people who, unlike the chemists, didn't know that they were being exposed or didn't understand what it meant, and whom no one would believe?

. . .

Popular unease about the new atomic age manifested in a genre of entertainment that we might call radiation camp: Godzilla, an endless B-movie series of rampaging giant insects, and superheroes from Spider-Man to the X-Men imagined unintended consequences of toying with radioisotopes. Heritable mutation became a ubiquitous science fiction trope, and stories such as Poul Anderson's "Tomorrow's Children" suggested that the survivors of a nuclear winter would have to embrace the monstrous offspring of their own folly. As Joseph Masco points out, the omnipresent threat of nuclear ruin became a "powerful new domestic political resource"; the government itself produced myriad images of devastated cities and homes to bind Americans into a Cold War social contract based on fear. In retrospect, mass culture might seem like the only catharsis for a public that never had a choice about whether to accept these risks.

In the early days after Hiroshima, some Manhattan Project veterans thought the choice should lie with them; as Linus Pauling put it, "Scientists should take far more than the normal part in decisions about world affairs." The Atomic Scientists' Movement sought to ban weapons development and testing worldwide, but their logical proposals to avert nuclear war had no traction with political leaders—they were easily marginalized as naive idealists and Communist sympathizers. Edward Teller remarked, derisively, that Oppenheimer wanted to disband Los Alamos National Laboratory and "give it back to the Indians." Instead, a new class of "defense intellectuals," combining weapons science with psychology and cybernetics, emerged to manage the vast strategy game of the Cold War. A former Manhattan Project physicist disparaged them as "the new priesthood," masters of an opaque system with no public accountability. Faith in such experts was the only bulwark against nuclear dread.

In the congressional hearings of 1957, as well as in records declassified in the 1980s, we see that those experts were often flying blind. When questioned about genetic mutation, Berkeley physiologist Hardin B. Jones testified, "In the long run, man may be beneficially affected by good genes yet to be formed, so that increasing radiation exposure . . . may operate to human advantage." In other words, a sort of eugenic experiment to see if radiation produces the superhumans of comic books. However, he then compared this to baking a cake "in half the time at higher oven temperature." Here, one pictures the iconic mushroom cloud. If genetic change happens too fast, we're all dead. Scientists had little data about long-term effects of radiation on human health and admitted as much, yet they also insisted that existing thresholds were the result of objective calculation. AEC critic John Gofman, who had worked with Hardin Jones on radiation studies and considered him "a damn smart guy . . . you could trust him with everything," nevertheless described a very different kind of calculation around safe levels of exposure. "Start to find that low doses are harmful and they're going to fight you every step of the way," Gofman raged. "They're going to fight to preserve the empire."

The American public was not silent on the politics of radiation exposure, even in the early days. While some took consolation in monster movies or backyard bomb shelters, the closer one stood to the margins of society, the less abstract nuclear destruction became. Langston Hughes argued persistently that the bomb was a weapon of whiteness: virulent anti-Asian racism had justified its use on the Japanese. His point held when the United States seriously considered nuking Korea and Vietnam. Hughes thought that Black Americans would be equally dispensable in nuclear war, cordoned off in the "ground zero" of inner cities while white people sheltered safely in the suburbs. Civil rights leaders, and even the Black conservative firebrand George Schuyler, warned that the bomb served "the way of white imperialism . . . small-minded men filled with racial arrogance." However, the calls of atomic scientists, Black leaders, and pacifists for global brotherhood were soon drowned out by the drumbeat of anti-communism. In 1950, W. E. B. Du Bois was arrested for his role in circulating a petition to ban atomic weapons, accused of being a Soviet agent. "The only peace that we can have," insisted Teller, who became a favorite scientific spokesman of the military brass, "is the peace based on force."

"Only justice
can stop a curse"

No mushroom cloud ever appeared over *Krazy Kat*'s hallucinatory desertscape. George Herriman died in his sleep in April 1944; only sixty-three but long in poor health, he was spared knowledge of the atomic age and never saw the Navajo Nation become a uranium hot spot. Perhaps, after the bomb, the kindly artist who spent his wartime ration stamps feeding stray cats and dogs wouldn't have wanted to go on as usual. In a 1988 novel reviving Herriman's characters, Jay Cantor imagines that Krazy quit the comic strip for this reason: "The bomb, she thought, had made the world she couldn't work in anymore." The novel has Krazy witness the Trinity test over the New Mexico desert, where "the earth shuddered like a piece of shook foil, and a tremor ran through her body; both, together, undone." If, as Herriman asserted, Krazy was "a spirit, a pixie," perhaps this revelation of exterminating cruelty was where the Kat and humanity parted ways.

Still, something about the "strictly irrational" yet lawlike violence of *Krazy Kat*, how enemies desire each other and love becomes indistinguishable from hate, seemed to resonate with the calculus of the Cold War. Between 1945 and 1996, the United States detonated 942 atomic weapons within its continental borders. Were they, like Ignatz's bricks, missiles that stoked the affection of their target? They fell not far from Coconino County, mostly at the Nevada Test Site, seventy miles northwest of Las Vegas. "We had long ago written off that terrain as wasteland," boasted Nevada governor Charles Russell, "and today it's blooming with atoms." Locals initially embraced the atomic crop in the name of patriotism and economic growth, but soon found themselves, in a dissenting scientist's colorful terms, "getting clobbered with radioiodine."

Radioactive clouds drifted around the Southwest, spreading "near panic" in rural Nevada and Arizona, Salt Lake City, and as far away as Los Angeles. Geiger counters became household items when the region went crazy for uranium prospecting; residents learned that airborne fallout would also trigger a chorus of eerie clicks. "Geiger Counters Act Haywire," a local paper proposed, as though the devices were to blame. Ranchers reported gruesome sores and cancers in their livestock—a single 1953 detonation was blamed for the deaths of 4,390 horses, cows, and sheep. The *Las Vegas Sun*, originally a booster, reported that citizens were "losing faith" that the Atomic Energy Commission had their best interests at heart. Those exposed to fallout, largely in working class Native, Hispanic, and white communities, would call themselves "downwinders," another contingent in an emerging antinuclear coalition.

While initial opposition to the bomb was motivated by fear of global nuclear war, the domestic testing program stirred a new kind of consciousness about the health effects of pollution. Citizen science became a form of political engagement, as children around the country donated two hundred thousand baby teeth to the Center for Nuclear Information to prove that fallout was contaminating the milk supply. Mothers spread the word about an invisible risk that threatened the security of suburbia. At times, this mostly white middle-class environmentalism made common cause with leftists and people of color who saw the nuclear complex as a tool of political, economic, and racial oppression. More often, this environmentalism appealed to the dominant culture by centering the innocent lives of white mothers and children. The antinuclear movement encompassed diverse and disunified interests from its beginning, drawn together by an urgent sense that humanity's survival was at stake.

To the extent that it's remembered at all, antinuclear protest tends to live in public consciousness as the pastime of tie-dyed peaceniks in the post-Vietnam years—a petering out of the hippie counterculture. "There's still a sizeable number of hippie diehards out there," Rebecca Solnit wrote of her time in the protest camp outside the Nevada Test Site. The clumsy nuclear arsenal has retreated from view behind new tools of empire that equate targeted precision with justice. Nuclear power also faded to the background ambiguously, its spent fuel accumulating in forever-temporary storage while revivalists promote it as a green fossil fuel alternative. Yet in the many strands of the popular antinuclear movement are demands and tensions that continue in today's struggles for environmental and social justice.

Basic social needs were very much connected to fissile material in the minds of mid-twentieth-century activists. Martin Luther King Jr. argued for disarmament as a redistribution of America's wealth away from profit and imperialism and toward human welfare. The diverse coalition that protested the bomb shared King's basic analysis, demanding the right to a collective future. Civil rights, peace, and antinuclear activists developed a common set of tactics in the fifties and early sixties, as historian Vincent Intondi illuminates. The Congress of Racial Equality (CORE) was formed in 1942 by Chicago pacifists, and one of their organizers, Bayard Rustin, was pivotal in making nonviolent resistance and direct action the centerpiece of these movements. In 1950, Rustin proposed that pacifists travel to Los Alamos and lie down before the gates so that no materials could come in or out. His white colleagues rejected this idea as too radical; five years later, Black leaders of the Montgomery bus boycott sought his expertise as they launched a nonviolent struggle that would sweep across the US South. Rustin then cited "the black people of Montgomery" as an example for global antinuclear strategy: "We must use our bodies in direct action, non-cooperation, whatever is required."

Rustin's vision of lying down at the gates of Los Alamos was soon redirected toward the Nevada Test Site. Thirty members of a group he cofounded, the Committee for Non-Violent Action, traveled to Nevada in August of 1957—the military had tactfully scheduled a test shot on the anniversary of the Hiroshima bombing. The protesters held a round-the-clock vigil, culminating in the

The Committee for Non-Violent Action
at the Nevada Test Site on August 6, 1957.

arrest of eleven people who tried to "enter the atomic test ground
and if necessary be atomized," in the words of labor organizer and
anarchist Ammon Hennacy, who had arrived ahead of the main
group to picket the site. During his time in the Southwest, Hennacy
visited with a group of Hopi elders who saw the atomic bomb as
a fulfillment of their apocalyptic prophecies. He eagerly connected
them with his network of peace activists and their warnings gained
an international platform. They utilized white perceptions of Indian
wisdom in pursuit of their goals, reflecting the active role of Indigenous thinkers in the formation of modern environmentalism.

Antinuclear activity reached a crescendo in these years, through
petitions, leaflets, marches, and hunger strikes, and public opinion swung powerfully against the atomic arsenal—between 1956
and 1957 alone, polls showed opposition to weapons testing rise
from 25 to 66 percent of respondents. Many women found this
an entry point to political engagement, using their traditional role
as caretakers and nurturers to make the case against an apocalypse
of male aggression. The group Women Strike for Peace took their
turn picketing the Nevada Test Site in 1962, pushing baby car-

riages labeled EMPTY BECAUSE OF CANCER through the radioactive dust. President Eisenhower placed a moratorium on aboveground nuclear testing in 1958, and in 1963 the Partial Test Ban Treaty with the Soviet Union relieved the American terror of fallout. Rather than a toothless plea, the activism of these years permanently changed the political landscape. Eisenhower feared being "crucified on a cross of atoms" if he didn't secure a test ban.

Bowing to the public will was more a matter of appearances, though, than a rejection of nuclear logic. Tests were moved underground, and both the United States and the Soviets built more bombs than ever, alongside nuclear power plants that would showcase radioisotopes as engines of boundless prosperity. The vision of plentiful, cheap energy won public favor for nuclear plants in the mid-1960s. Only six plants were operating in 1962; a decade later, thirty-seven had come online, with the AEC projecting one thousand by the turn of the twenty-first century.

Along with this boom came increasing scrutiny from antinuclear and environmental groups. Some had believed at first in the "peaceful atom," but by the early 1970s they broadened the slogan No Nukes to include nuclear energy, campaigning against "centralized power that places the rights of corporations and the quest for profits above the rights, health, and well-being of people," in the words of New England activist Cindy Girvani Leerer. On March 28, 1979, their nightmare warnings seemed to come true as the nation was gripped by panic over a partial reactor meltdown at the Three Mile Island plant in Pennsylvania.

The nightmare only deepened with the Soviet invasion of Afghanistan later that year, which reignited Cold War animosity. The public learned of military plans to produce the "enhanced radiation" neutron bomb, designed to "kill man with streams of poisonous radiation, while leaving machines and buildings undamaged." Ronald Reagan took office in 1981 promising a next-generation nuclear arsenal, while cutting $140 billion from social programs. Nuclear opponents from a wide range of backgrounds were ready to mobilize on a mass scale, forming one of the largest social movements in US history. Leerer, a white psychologist and feminist, saw the overwhelming antinuclear response as uniting the struggles against racism, misogyny, and imperialism—a chance to transcend the divide-and-conquer strategy of the capitalist order.

Barbara Smith, the queer Black feminist and socialist thinker who helped define the concept of intersectionality, agreed that this was a moment of possibility. However, she called out "an antinuclear movement that has been notoriously white, homophobic, male-dominated, and class-bound." The sense that they were unwelcome led some African Americans to conclude that nukes were a "white issue" disconnected from the Black freedom struggle—even as environmental justice became a growing concern for Black communities. Citing the legacy of slavery and racial oppression, Alice Walker proposed that "hope for revenge . . . is at the heart of many People of Color's resistance to the present anti-nuclear movement. In any case, this has been my own problem." Nuclear annihilation was seemingly the only force that could hurt those at the top of the racial power structure, finally collapsing, through their own calculating madness, centuries of white supremacy.

Rejecting this vision of ruin, Walker refused to relinquish the world in the name of revenge. "Only justice can stop a curse," she proclaimed at an antinuclear rally in San Francisco. Walker's vision of nuclear technology as a curse animated by white desire resonates with the curse of oil in western Pennsylvania a century before: those whose only dream was profit could not turn away from a fatal source of power. Mainstream American spirituality made racial capitalism into a virtue; for Walker and Smith, it was an age-old evil. "We have been on to the white man and his poisonous capacity for ruin for centuries," Smith wrote.

While the meaning of the curse is clear, what justice means is not always clear. It is not rendered by police and prisons. It can never be singular or complete. As a committed member of the antinuclear movement, Smith demanded space for "female, poor, colored, and queer" leadership—a process of justice that builds new communities and futures, not just another treaty to ease white anxieties. Crucially, as Walker's slogan suggests, this process could not lift the curse in the way angry ghosts are exorcised in horror movies. The curse can be stopped, held at bay, but solidarity means not looking away from what it has done to each of us.

The antinuclear protest of June 12, 1982, in New York City, the largest single demonstration in US history up to that time, included Smith's Necessary Bread Affinity Group, carrying their banner THIRD WORLD AND WHITE LESBIANS UNITE. Smith was surprised to see so many people of color there. Among the million who marched through downtown Manhattan were representatives of the Black United Front, the Asian American Caucus for Disarmament, Hispanics for Survival, the hospital workers union Local 1199, and many others. Behind the scenes, Black and leftist leaders had clashed with white-led peace and environmental groups that wanted a "nuclear freeze" to be the sole objective of the march. They won time on the platform to speak about racial and economic justice. A mainstream movement had managed to accommodate, for a day, the "too radical" vision of the marginalized people who had the most at stake.

A month before the June 12 march, Reagan had already bent to overwhelming popular opinion on nukes, announcing on national radio, "A nuclear war cannot be won and must never be fought." While adopting their rhetoric, he roundly beat back citizen-led initiatives such as the Nuclear Freeze, instead promising to broker new arms deals with the Soviets. As with the 1963 test ban, a symbolic gesture from the White House read as a victory to many moderates who had mobilized—some of whom had no objection to Reagan's other policies. Yet this single-issue victory left behind the marginalized members of the antinuclear coalition, who faced an era of racist neoliberal austerity, which white Americans affirmed in Reagan's landslide 1984 reelection. The Soviet Union's collapse and the end of the Cold War fragmented a movement that had found uneasy common ground in nuclear apocalypse.

For Native and non-Native people in the Southwest, who lived with, rather than awaited, the violence of radiation, the antinuclear and environmental movements became powerful tools to intervene in local struggles. Their fight was only beginning with the Cold

War's close; they would demand transparency and restitution, an end to extraction, and control of their land for Native nations. Organizing often started at the local level to address specific sources of contamination, sometimes supported by groups from outside, at other times neglected by mainstream antinuclear and environmental groups. Protesters from around the world made pilgrimages to the Nevada Test Site, drawn there by its symbolic power as the breathtaking desert terrain where weapons were detonated, and to Mount Taylor, a place sacred to Diné and Pueblo people and threatened by uranium mining. The nuclear landscape encompasses so many sites, from mines to mills, proving grounds to waste pits, that resistance had no single center, but rather reflected the growing internationalism of Indigenous rights and environmental movements. The nuclear timeline goes on, in human terms, forever, and thus resistance also means a permanent process of reclamation.

Both nuclear weaponry and nuclear power traced numerous routes across the United States from the 1950s onward, provoking the nationwide protests discussed above. Their impact remained concentrated on the Southwest, from uranium mining to detonations that scarred traditional Diné, Pueblo, Hopi, Apache, and Western Shoshone lands and left behind a "national sacrifice area" primed for dumping nuclear waste. Native nations were yoked to the million-year half-lives of radioactive isotopes through what Anishinaabe activist Winona LaDuke termed nuclear colonialism: another rush to penetrate and extract value from a land "empty except for Indians."

Uranium had gained a patriotic glow as the agent of US victory over Japan, and it glowed even brighter during the early Cold War, when this "magic ore" signified the nation's ability to defend and power itself—a new, perhaps inexhaustible domestic resource. The Colorado Plateau was branded "a vast treasure chest of raw materials," waiting for "men with ambition, fortitude, and vision" to unearth it. A new frontier revived the national promise after wartime deprivation: "Here in the great West lies opportunity, wealth, happiness for the individuals who conquer her vastness . . . and power for America," boasted a 1955 newspaper promotion. These lines could be about the Hoover Dam in 1936; Titusville, Pennsylvania, in 1866; or Schoolcraft's Michigan Territory in the 1820s.

The hiddenness of uranium called for the same spiritual sensitivity as oil: "the settler will find answers to his dreams" in the desert if he knows how to look. The Indian guide reappeared, still hovering between mythic phantasm and real flesh: in 1952, uranium hunters circulated rumors of a "secret prospecting device" developed by the Atomic Energy Commission. It turned out that "the weapon was a fullblood, keen-eyed Navajo." As Traci Brynne Voyles notes, the instrumental use of Native people and knowledge was baked into the origin story of New Mexico's uranium boom: "Paddy Martinez, a Navajo Indian," discovered the Grants uranium belt in 1950, either by accident while sneaking contraband liquor or on purpose with his excellent "Indian memory," depending on which derisive legend one consults. To verify these Native intuitions, the oil dowsing rod was reborn as the clicking Geiger counter. Few visionaries struck it rich, even fewer than in the wildcat oil days.

Beneath a flurry of speculative leases, the industry was entirely in the hands of mining companies such as Anaconda and Kerr-McGee, which worked directly with the AEC. The fantasy of the divinely guided settler-prospector helped ordinary white people believe that they were the heroes of this drama. The real opportunity that uranium offered to locals, white, Native, and Hispanic, came in the form of mining and milling, jobs which even in 1950 were known to occupational health experts as causes of lung cancer. Rather than disclose or regulate these risks, the AEC chose to study them secretly. The BIA channeled Diné and Pueblo men into uranium work, aiming to enforce the wage economy and the male-dominated nuclear family in place of Native land-based economies and female-headed households. Imposing strict US-style gender roles also effaced the historically important Diné concept of a third or non-binary gender, nádleeh, which was not amenable to assimilation.

The sensational uranium boom, in tandem with western movies filmed in Monument Valley and the attraction of nuclear explosions themselves, brought a renewed rush of tourists to the Southwest. Hundreds watched bombs explode over the Nevada Test Site while drinking atomic-themed cocktails on the roofs of Las Vegas hotels, while others trekked through the desert, and across Diné and Pueblo lands, hoping to stake a claim and work out the details later.

However, a starkly different spiritual image of the Southwest was emerging for those willing to face the sinister realities of the atomic bomb, its fearsome power to obliterate the future in an instant. They came not as tourists, but as antinuclear pilgrims; rather than extracting souvenirs and curios, they aimed in different ways to build power with those who lived and worked in the heart of the nuclear industry. This was Bayard Rustin's vision when he proposed blocking the gates of Los Alamos: the Southwest as a place where evil had been unleashed and had to be confronted.

When the antinuclear movement reemerged to fight the neutron bomb in the late seventies, activists had not targeted the Ne-

The antinuclear movement could claim success in blocking aboveground bomb testing, while the longer struggle against the military-industrial complex and environmental racism has continued to take new forms.

vada Test Site for many years. Sister Rosemary Lynch, a Franciscan nun, learned that the neutron bomb was developed there. In 1977, again on the anniversary of Hiroshima, she gathered a group of nineteen protesters for an early-morning prayer vigil at the Test Site's Mercury Gate. Sister Rosemary described that action as a moment of epiphany: "I saw the sun come up. It was so beautifully illuminating the desert, and it broke my heart to think of what I had learned was happening back there. So it was as though I got another calling in my life."

As nuclear anxieties heightened, the Nevada Test Site (NTS) became a place of pilgrimage for activists from around the world; many, like Sister Rosemary, felt a spiritual awakening as the quiet grandeur of the desert clashed with their grim knowledge of the bomb. By 1986, they had established a permanent Peace Camp across from Mercury Gate, where an array of antinuclear groups gathered, living in tents and cars amid patches of sagebrush. The harsh and exposed desert, to Sister Rosemary and other religious activists, was a place where God had tested the faithful since biblical times.

Indigenous people already had a spiritual geography for this region: the Nevada Test Site occupies the unceded land of the Western Shoshone, Newe Sogobia. "We were created as Newah," wrote organizer Joe Sanchez, "and have always existed in our territory . . . We are responsible for maintaining a healthy relationship with Newah Sogo Bea, since it is the basis of our life." The Western Shoshone National Council (WSNC), calling itself "the most bombed nation on earth," brought to the Peace Camp an emphasis on Indigenous sovereignty, "our right to determine our own future," as Sanchez put it, "on our own terms as a distinct people." Representatives of the American Indian Movement, known for its militancy, visited to deliver their message: "AIM fights cavities on the face of Mother Earth." With the antinuclear group Citizen Alert, Joe Sanchez and his sister Virginia Sanchez helped WSNC leaders Corbin Harney and Bill Rosse coordinate their first "Healing Global Wounds" ceremony at the Peace Camp in 1992, marking five centuries of Indigenous resistance since the start of the

European invasions. By then Joe Sanchez had been diagnosed with leukemia; he died less than a year later, at age thirty-seven.

The rituals of the Peace Camp—at its peak, eighteen hundred people were arrested in one day for crossing a white line onto national security territory—periodically erupted onto the national stage. Celebrities and faith leaders made headlines when they joined the roundups; peace activists arrived from Europe, Japan, the Marshall Islands, and Kazakhstan (where the Soviet Union tested its bombs) to bear witness in the heart of nuclear hegemony. Nuclear hegemony, however, had multiple hearts, and the one that beat five hundred miles away in New Mexico remained less visible in US antinuclear awareness. There, a focus on the health and environmental impacts of radiation was driven by Indigenous organizing.

In Santa Fe and Albuquerque, the birth of the Red Power movement in the 1960s brought a rising generation of Native activists into the fight, led by the National Indian Youth Council and the American Indian Environmental Council (AIEC). They launched an insurgency against the "chicken-hearted" Bureau of Indian Affairs and tribal leaders who had accepted uranium as a source of jobs and royalties. Winona LaDuke traced the lines of convergence that led to the first large antinuclear gathering in New Mexico, in April 1979: a Diné group walked three hundred miles from Arizona, car caravans came from American Indian Movement survival schools in Oakland and Pine Ridge, and airplanes brought Native delegations, white supporters, and scientists from around the world, all coordinated by the Albuquerque-based AIEC to protest uranium mining on Mount Taylor. Citing the deaths of uranium miners and rising cancer rates in surrounding communities, LaDuke called this "a question of genocide."

The Mount Taylor Alliance that emerged from this event included Native, Chicano, and white groups who shared the decolonizing and anti-capitalist orientation of the Third World delegations that took the stage in New York City three years later. They connected uranium, oil, and coal as part of the same system of global exploitation—it was Gulf Oil that wanted to cash in on the uranium beneath Mount Taylor. AIM leader John Trudell exhorted

"If you are going to fight the enemy through the anti-nuclear movement, let's fight them that way. . . . This is not just an anti-nuclear movement, this is a movement to free ourselves from the enemy." Such protests became increasingly common, as did their less visible counterpart, lawsuits by Native nations, downwinders, and uranium workers against the US government demanding compensation and blocking new mines.

Nuclear extraction and waste became central concerns for global pan-Indigenous organizing throughout the 1980s and '90s. The legal efforts of affected groups led to Congressional hearings and eventually the passage of the 1990 Radiation Exposure Compensation Act. Among other hard-won policy victories, in 2005 the Navajo Nation passed a moratorium on uranium mining long sought by Diné activists. Some Diné scientists, such as Perry H. Charley, founder of the Diné Environmental Institute, have become radiation experts training others in monitoring and remediation. The Western Shoshone, with Indigenous and white environmental groups, waged a long battle of attrition against nuclear waste storage at Yucca Mountain that sent the Department of Energy back to the drawing board—there is still no ten-thousand-year plan, no true wasteland that can swallow the detritus of last century's corrosive ambitions.

Historians see a profoundly ambivalent legacy for the antinuclear movement. It changed political common sense about what costs the public was willing to pay for power. Ken Butigan calls this an "elite coalition shift": by the early nineties, politicians themselves were driving arms control deals, and nuclear power was a nonstarter for utility companies. President George H. W. Bush signed a moratorium on all atomic weapons testing on October 3, 1992. That day, the writer Rebecca Solnit was at the Peace Camp for the Healing Global Wounds ceremony lead by the Western Shoshone National Council. Activists decided not to cross the white line into the arms of waiting security guards. "It didn't make sense to do the same things over again," she wrote, believing that the Herriman-esque loop was broken.

Yet, in making this optimistic point, she could not foresee that "subcritical" detonations would continue on Western Shoshone land, or that the fortunes of the uranium industry would fall and then rise again, with a renewed drive for mining across the Southwest in the 2010s that appealed to residents desperate for jobs. What should we make of the antinuclear movement, historian Paul Rubinson asks, if the stockpile, weapons labs, defense budget, and waste drums are all permanent fixtures of our future? Perhaps the only struggle that could even come close to success was against "the worst kind of bomb," but that singular focus gave tacit approval to all the "reasonable" bombs, not to mention the reasonable prisons and pipelines. What can this broadly-popular coalition with snippets of anti-capitalist and anti-imperialist politics deep in its DNA tell us about building power for today's climate movement, for decolonization, for abolition? Even Peace Camp denizens, shaking radioactive grit out of their sleeping bags, needed to claim the testing moratorium as a victory, in the hope of fighting again.

Perhaps the persistence of radiation serves as a sinister mirror for the necessary persistence of liberation struggles under changing names and evolving philosophies. If "only justice can stop a curse," then only those with the knowledge of injustice in their bodies can say when justice is done. It's not for the perpetrators to decide that they've made amends by offering money in place of land and life—or by building smarter bombs. When these flawed and desperately needed victories are thrown to hungry people in the desert, who have held together just barely, they can't let go of one another.

When people entered the nuclear complex, they became part of a culture that takes certain risks to be inevitable. A fixed truth of this world is that the technologies our society desires also put society at risk—as the slogan on the first Earth Day posters went, WE HAVE MET THE ENEMY, AND HE IS US. Yet that claim ignores how such desires are born and how their costs are distributed across the population. Sociologist Robert Bullard famously mapped this distribution in his 1991 book, *Dumping in Dixie*: toxic-waste sites in the Southeast had intentionally been placed in communities of color. If these sites really posed no danger, why did white communities refuse them? Further, would this wrong be corrected by dumping an equal or greater amount in white parts of town? Dina Gilio-Whitaker draws a contrast between equity, in which the environmental toll of corporate profits and imperial strength is redistributed, and justice, where all communities have the right to prevent and remediate harms—currently a privilege strongly associated with whiteness and wealth.

The notion endemic to mainstream environmentalism, that humanity at large is the enemy and individuals need to make enlightened choices, is hard to square with our overdetermined-risk regime. In 1953 the Civil Defense Administration premiered a film, *The House in the Middle*, which showed how a clean, well-maintained home survives a nuclear blast while its slovenly, irresponsible neighbors perish. Shot at the Nevada Test Site, it was an advertisement for buying new house paint.

If freedom has meant the ability of average white people to benefit from capital's acceleration, that horizon is limited by our own permeable bodies. Rational people *should not* love that they are free to be discarded when they become sick, disabled, damaged. Such arguments from self-interest fail because, as Cold War psychologists found when they scrutinized the concept, there is no such thing as rationality. The interests of any particular self are historical, social, and emotional.

Acoma Pueblo poet Simon Ortiz, reflecting on his experience working in the uranium mines, writes, "The American poor and the workers and white middleclass, who are probably the most ignorant of all US citizens, must understand how they, like Indian people, are forced to serve a national interest." The national interest gave white uranium miners somewhat safer jobs, somewhat better pay, and a conviction that they were not forced, but rather were exceptionally free—Du Bois's wages of whiteness that, today, persist in the assumption that the people who deserve clean food and water are the people who can afford to buy it. For Ortiz, fighting back means "standing again / within and among all things," beyond the illusion of choice and the fantasy of self-preservation.

Our energized age

In the 1957 joint congressional hearings on nuclear radiation, senators and representatives peppered Hardin B. Jones, the Berkeley professor of medical physics, with questions. They wanted to know if radiation decreased the life expectancy of people exposed—and if so, how much radiation and how many days or years? Jones went into the evidence from laboratory mice, calculating that one year in mouse time was equivalent to ten years in human time. His data came with caveats: countless variables affected life span that made radiation hard to isolate. Despite this uncertainty, Jones asserted that even low-level radiation caused harm. He doubted the threshold doctrine and favored a cumulative-exposure model: tentatively, he proposed that one roentgen of radiation equals five days of human life, two roentgens cost ten days, and so forth.

His aim in making this argument was not to throw peacetime nuclear enterprise into doubt. "The sum of evidence would lead to the conclusion that radiation probably does affect man's health subtly," Jones testified, "and—like money and time—it should be exchanged for equivalent advantages." Scientists needed accurate measurements so that they could ensure a worthwhile return on the human lives invested in the nuclear complex. "Advantages minus cost equals net gain," Jones asserted coolly. Under costs, he calculated that strontium 90 "may eventually cause a worldwide increase in leukemia, accounting for about two percent of all deaths," and human-made radiation would generally take about one year off the American life span. However, this was less than the cost of 470 days incurred by driving a car. These were simply the "mechanical mishaps we risk as a partial cost of the 'advantages' of our mechanized and energized age."

But risk and benefit are local. They inhere in our bodies, houses, and towns. Think about how much money a family will spend to save a child with leukemia, the home foreclosures and bankruptcies, how social media posts beg for your charity to buy back the days and years of sick people's lives. A threadbare self-help culture frames this as individual tragedy, refusing to be accountable but tithing with the uneasy knowledge that anyone could be next, and equally forsaken.

Hardin B. Jones was an interesting person to make the case for "advantages minus cost equals net gain," since he also had an unusually pessimistic attitude toward cancer treatment. As a medical expert, he promoted the idea that cancer therapies were ineffective and patients should be left alone, although his colleagues in oncology were developing an arsenal of new tools that eventually increased survival. One has to wonder if his fatalism about cancer bore any relation to his cost-benefit analysis of "our mechanized and energized age." It's important to pay the costs promptly, lest humanity's account fall into arrears.

Floy Agnes Naranjo Lee, over her career, developed a battery of techniques to quantify what radiation did to cells and organisms. She helped to chip away at the uncertainty that Jones complained of, the imprecisions in his balance sheet. But all the while that the AEC funded biology research, it also bought uranium from mines that it refused to regulate, set off bombs, and underwrote commercial nuclear power with no plan for waste disposal. At the highest levels, the calculation of "net gain" seemed strangely foreshortened, as though, like Jones's cancer patients, the future would just have to fend for itself.

In 1979, the same year that President Carter announced plans to produce the neutron bomb, Lee made her way back to Los Alamos to be near her family. Returning to the site where the nuclear age, and her life as a radiation biologist, began, she saw things that hadn't been visible in 1946. Namely, she noticed the long-term impact of Los Alamos National Laboratory on the Pueblo people, beyond the mistrust and discrimination of the war years. "At least it's made some of the Indians, I would say, more wealthy," she remarked of the lab's efforts to contract with Native-owned businesses. Nuclear industries are a central economic force in many towns across the Southwest. As sociologist Stephanie Malin observes, "The people and the communities that are most damaged . . . are often constrained by historical and economic circumstances" to support everything from uranium mining to waste disposal.

For instance, when authorities threatened to shut down a casino run by the Pojoaque Pueblo in the 1990s, the Pueblo's leaders seriously considered a Department of Energy offer of $10 million a year to bury nuclear waste on their land. "We don't want nuclear waste more than anybody else, but we know it's very lucrative," Governor Jacob Viarrial explained, even as the adjacent San Ildefonso Pueblo began detecting radioactive tritium from a LANL dump in its drinking water. Despite the region's reliance on the laboratory, the wealth of Los Alamos, where 12 percent of the population were millionaires in 2010, is mainly confined to white professionals. The town is surrounded by some of the poorest counties in America's third-poorest state.

"I think the worst effect," Lee said about the lab, "is the radiation that has caused leukemia. I have four relatives, two are my sister and my brother, died of leukemia. A cousin, two cousins have died of leukemia. My technician I had at Los Alamos in the seventies, she is dying of leukemia." This is the type of litany that the downwinders of Nevada and Utah recite on the evening news, but Lee was not an antinuclear citizen crusader; she was a lifelong member of the nuclear complex. Her intimate familiarity with the mathematics of risk and the physics of radiation did not lead her to dismiss these cases as coincidence. The deaths of her family and friends were not a matter of bad luck.

Yet, when cancer happened outside the carefully controlled conditions of the lab, she knew there was no hope of scientific certainty. "I think that the radiation has something to do with it. I have no way of proving that; it's just a speculation." Here, she spoke not as a trailblazer in the field of radiobiology, but as a member of a community engulfed in ambient risk. Her voice was one of a chorus. Cancers were widespread among employees of Los Alamos and in neighboring towns. Darleen Ortiz, the daughter of laboratory custodian Max Ortiz, remembered, "Every day when my father came home, we would run and jump all over him. Whatever he had on his clothes I'm sure we ended up getting it all over us." Families drank water from the streams, fished, hunted, and harvested plants; both of Ortiz's parents died of rare cancers. "Who knows," she wondered, "what is in our systems?" It becomes impossible to link causes and effects through this fog. Lee understood better than most why it was so hard, the exacting standards to which any claims would be held.

Workers at Los Alamos—Native, Hispanic, and white—"knew where we stood," said technician Phil Schofield. "At that time, production of weapons material was more important than human life." It was hard to know anything more specific than that because until the fall of the Soviet Union, activities at LANL were strictly classified and exempted from legal scrutiny. Even as the antinuclear movement swept the United States in the late 1970s, Los Alamos remained a loyal company town, with only a few small protests mounted by outsiders. The fall of the Berlin Wall opened the floodgates for struggles over Indigenous sovereignty, minority and workers' rights, and environmental justice.

Hispanic workers at LANL formed a roundtable in the early 1990s to push back against lax safety and mismanagement, which grew into the multiracial Concerned Citizens for LANL Employee Rights. The Native American Graves Protection and Repatriation Act of 1990 gave Pueblo governments the right to survey their sacred sites behind the LANL security fence. In 1994, people-of-color-led environmental groups won an amendment to the Clean Water and Clean Air Acts protecting "minority and low-income populations" from the disproportionate harms of pollution. This enabled widespread radiation sampling in Pueblo and Diné communities and forced Los Alamos into a government-to-government monitoring agreement with the neighboring Pueblos of Santa Clara, San Ildefonso, Cochiti, and Jemez. Projects such as the geothermal exploration that Frank Harlow had helped to model never left the computer screen; more and more LANL research would be done using computer simulations.

Workers and neighbors of Los Alamos were among the many groups that fought for the 1990 Radiation Exposure Compensation Act, a turning point in accountability for the secretive nuclear program. This victory was not based on a bulletproof correlation between specific amounts of radiation and specific cancers, but based on the political power of their shared demands. Nevertheless, in distributing "compassionate payments," the state again placed the burden of proof on victims, who often lacked the time and resources to reconstruct their radiation exposure over many years. There was little documentation from mines or remote ranches, and many had no access to doctors or lawyers. When asked in 2004 if people are getting through the process and getting compensation, Patricia George, of Nuclear Risk Management for Native Communities, replied, "Very few that I've helped."

Advocates describe a kind of nuclear austerity, waiting for people to give up or die in order to minimize public expense for the aftermath of the $5.5 trillion arms race. The collective risk that so many people bore unknowingly produced a highly individualized set of futures: some would get cancer, some would get compensation, if they were fortunate enough to have resources or advocates. Many would live in the eternal present of uncertainty, an increasingly common mode of life.

The environmental, racial, and economic violence of the nuclear complex wasn't the beginning of this story. The prologue to Los Alamos, the period of the "West cure," bohemian artists, tourist traps, and pottery collecting, created the Southwest in the American imagination as a wasteland and a place of buried treasure. Willa Cather's narrative of white arrivals strengthened by mingling their voices with the echoes of the Native past would help bomb makers enjoy Pueblo art without worrying about the fate of their cooks and maids. It allowed cultural appreciation to run on the same frictionless mental machinery as algorithms of death, metabolizing the ceremonial kiva into a space for nuclear fission experiments.

Native people throughout the region were also active in these processes, not only building and maintaining the infrastructures of Los Alamos itself, but creating art and seeking knowledge that negotiated their position as both insiders and outsiders on their own land. As Floy Agnes Naranjo Lee attested, one could invest a life's work in "the Hill," as the lab was often called, and still see clearly "what radiation does." Some artists today, such as Mallery Quetawki of Zuni Pueblo, communicate what radiation does and how to manage its presence; Quetawki creates paintings that help her audiences "conceptualize what is happening on the land and in their bodies" in terms of their distinctive traditions and knowledge systems.

In the midst of nuclear colonialism, imperfect alliances developed between groups in the Southwest who lived in the shadow of radiation. Their resistance connected them with the national and global antinuclear movement, which at its best came there to build power rather than extract it. It's important to underscore the work of Black, Indigenous, and other POC activists, from Smith's Necessary Bread group to the Mount Taylor Alliance and many more, who tried to direct antinuclear mass mobilization toward the systems of capitalism and imperialism that perpetuate racialized harm and extraction. The imperative for a particularly dangerous kind of power was stunted through unprecedented public action, though the systems that produced the bomb continued their work by other means.

There's nothing wrong with going somewhere new in search of meaning or connection, as the cartoonist George Herriman did. In *Krazy Kat*, the Diné patterns and pottery that proliferate across the landscape are a sort of testimony, a refusal to let the desert be a wasteland. Part of the attraction for Herriman was immersing himself in a different history from his own, seeking respite from an America that would turn on him in a second if it saw the word *colored* on his birth certificate.

At the same time, as a tourist in the Southwest, he used what he found there as material, fitting it into familiar comedy tropes. In a Christmas card for his friends Jean Harlow and Hal Rosson, Herriman drew a group of cartoon Indians as cupids shooting arrows at the couple, who allegedly fell in love on the Tucson, Arizona, set of the movie *Bombshell*. The figures are labeled with the names of the area's Native nations, which were not likely to mean much to the card's celebrity recipients. Though it alludes to histories of armed resistance, this caricature shows Herriman casually deploying the racist formulas of his era that he at other times confounded.

Displacement and transformation, deception and recognition mark the contours of Herriman's Southwest. The ever-shifting aliveness of his scenes suggest that this landscape can unmoor visitors from the linear time and space of capitalism, which was nevertheless encroaching on the region as he worked. A number of *Krazy Kat* strips are condemnations of wealth, prejudice, and hypocrisy, with the humble Krazy representing "the heart of the proletariat," for instance, when she adopts baby skunks spurned by Coconino's philanthropists at a charity ball. In a strip now perhaps overly freighted with biographical significance, the Stork reveals that Krazy was born in a washtub "in the cellar of the haunted house." While Krazy's animal neighbors pretend to royal lineage, Krazy fondly sings the story of her origins, "a tale which must never be told, and yet which everyone knows." Herriman—another Janus-faced figure—explored the secrets people keep from themselves, and the lies that sustain a stratified society, while carefully guarding his own origins. Still he indulged in a view, or a hope, that the land held a deeper truth that would outlast the passing shadows of that society.

Sentenced, as critic Eyal Amiran puts it, "to perform his invisibility," Herriman gestured at the "tale which must never be told"— the unspoken "common sense" of American life in its violent affections and denials. The transformation of the Southwest into a spiritual resource and a repository of risk is that kind of tale, with radiation as its invisbile vector. The transformation is only partial and incomplete; the US "Southwest" is imposed on multiple Indigenous worlds, each with continuous pasts and futures that refuse the apocalyptic timeline of nuclear logic. Even the settler claim to land and resources gives rise to strange mutations, forcing some to confront what Simon Ortiz calls the "destructive and uncompassionate and deceptive" nature of the economic order that enlists their desires.

TO BEAR AWAY
THE TREASURE

S tories of new resources such as oil, uranium, or the land of North America itself are often told as stories of finding buried treasure: a lucky individual strikes it rich through a combination of destiny, genius, and pluck. These resources were "only waiting for the necessities of man to unlock their doors and bear away the treasure," advised Iowa land agent Charles H. Kent. This desire is lodged deep in the American political unconscious; much official history is organized around its inevitable fulfillment. No wonder that it's difficult to see how fundamentally strange these treasures are. Their value was not obvious or inevitable, but emerged from the web of visions and dreams, violence and deception, identity and inheritance woven around them.

Digging for actual chests of gold and jewels caught on as a popular activity even before the Revolutionary War. Urban and rural communities from Maine to Virginia were periodically seized by a mania for treasure hunting. Normally skeptical and thrifty, farmers dropped their plows to tunnel for gold, inspired by rumors, newspaper headlines, and premonitory dreams. Men, women, and children reported visions of treasure in hillsides or swamps, setting off hunts that could last for months and bankrupt entire towns. Many believed that digging at midnight, under a full moon, worked best. Some put special faith in the predictions of Black and elderly women, whom they saw as more attuned to occult forces—knowledge normally shunned as demonic was sanctioned by the most pious when it might lead to fortune.

Benjamin Franklin complained in 1729 about the "Odd Humour of digging for money." In colonial Philadelphia, "you can hardly walk half a Mile out of Town on any Side, without observing several Pits dug with that Design." This odd humor was especially offensive to Franklin, who preached "Industry and Frugality" as America's core values—an easy enough line for someone who had never walked behind a plow. Elites like Franklin looked down upon the ignorant lower classes who aspired above their station, chiding them to get back to work. He blamed the treasure-hunting craze on magical thinking, an "easy Credulity of what they so earnestly wished might be true."

Yet Franklin failed to see that the origin of the lowly treasure hunter's wish lay in the origin of America, however unreasonable. These toilers only wanted what the rich had obtained by stealing vast territories from Indigenous people, monopolizing the world's commodities, and securing their gains with the blood of the poor. A treasure chest, whether the hoard of a lost civilization or the booty of pirates who preyed on transatlantic commerce, could magically fix the contradiction of unequal social arrangements within settler society. Farmers only wanted what their creditors had: money that grew more money. "All his life he pays interest," said one rural Massachusetts minister of his heavily mortgaged flock. Many wound up in debtors' prison; in the best case, "it is not til the close of his life that he gets free from debt."

Digging a fifty-foot hole was no easy undertaking; the point was, through sheer speed and force, to seize the very fountainhead of wealth. Franklin was right that there was "some peculiar Charm . . . something very bewitching" about the pursuit of treasure. He helped cast the spell himself with his fables of American opportunity and self-making. Throughout these pages, the hidden work of making the landscape bend to such contradictory fables has unfolded. The hardy settler in his log cabin received a government bounty for Indigenous scalps. Investors in the West demanded federal dams to make their arid lands profitable. Oil companies colluded to write the story of their industry as a divine benediction. Even uranium, perhaps the most dubious of prizes, took on its dazzling value entirely through the Atomic Energy Commission's mandate to pursue global military and economic dominance.

Perhaps Franklin scorned colonial Philadelphia's treasure hunters because they had gone rogue, digging up his streets rather than following the national interest to a useful form of extraction. Individuals often realized that their interests might diverge from those prescribed by elites, fueling populist uprisings as well as potholes. Their discontent was easily harnessed, however, to the promise of the frontier—whether in the form of land or the next big speculation. A humble farmer could have a chance at the same windfalls as a William Penn or a Lord Calvert, if he was willing to risk everything on the venture.

Those settlers who carried out the occupation of North America on behalf of Penn, Calvert, and the rest had reason to doubt that the land was a divine gift; gifts don't require bloodshed to collect. Even when it left them in hard circumstances, dominated by the wealthy of their own race, they believed in the rationale of racial superiority and the promise that their share of the bounty lay over the horizon—or below the ground. People of all races dream of treasure, of magical relief from worry, but Black and Brown people have systematically been denied any share of the real prosperity created with their land and labor. In twenty-first-century America, where a diverse populace is supposed to compete for resources on an equal playing field, this history of white hoarding makes equal opportunity a cruel joke. On this count, I think of the free Black woman named Dinah Prince, "called a witch and sorcerer," who led treasure hunters in York, Maine, in the 1820s. Even her dreams were a resource from which her white neighbors hoped to profit.

What Ben Franklin dismissed as the "peculiar Charm" of treasure hunting is more like a national enchantment. The idea of finding treasure through divine agency does important psychological work. It makes God the decider and nature the provider, erasing the Indigenous, Black, and poor people from whom land and labor were stolen. It also erases class oppression with the myth that anyone can rise in the world through faith and hard work. If God planted vast, hidden riches in North America for a few chosen people to exploit, then the pursuit of those riches was a sacred activity; the devastating consequences lay beyond human control. To survive capitalism and to keep capitalism alive, people had to make it spiritual. This was not a delusion imposed from the top down, but rather a coproduction that enlisted everyone from scrappy evangelical oil prospectors to titans such as John D. Rockefeller, who wreathed his obscene wealth in the sacred aura of "God's gold."

Throughout these pages, visionaries and swindlers have found inventive ways to transmute both physical matter and faith into value. They promoted themselves as scientific experts as well as moral authorities. Some, such as Schoolcraft, never earned the gratitude and renown they believed they were owed for tapping the "resource" of Indigenous traditions and molding them into a white inheritance.

Those who made it to the inner sanctum of power, such as the physicists Alvin Graves and Edward Teller, succeeded precisely because they so seamlessly fused fuel and ideology. Teller made nuclear weapons and energy inseparable from the triumph of capitalism over godless communism. The interlocking dependencies of science, economics, and religion formed the backbone of a promise more subtle and complex than the familiar account of Manifest Destiny. Even when the dire costs of their experiments became undeniable, it was hard for a faithful public to doubt them, and it certainly seems as if they never doubted themselves. These men were the prophets of eternal prosperity. We should think of them when today's billionaires trumpet plans for mining precious metals on Mars—another dream of buried treasure, the dream of a godsend that will save us from capitalism and save capitalism from itself.

Challenges to American empire are rejections of this deep-seated faith, but they must also conjure alternatives. What the story of spiritualized capitalism tells us is not that we need to strip away all enchantments and proceed on a rational basis. No purely rational world exists. Power is more than raw materials, and more than a logic game—it emerges from relations that shape our beliefs about why we act, what we seek, and who we are. The science fiction writer Octavia Butler makes this point in *Parable of the Sower*, where a new religion empowers communities of the poor and oppressed in a dystopian America run by Christian fundamentalists.

Perhaps only in science fiction could a single religion unite the world's dispossessed. Yet Butler's principle that "God is change" speaks to many people today working toward liberatory futures. Their belief weaves a loose kinship: a vision of collective power that is decentered and dispersed, restorative and redistributive. It connects Water Protectors resisting oil pipelines with drawn-out negotiations over dam relicensing; campaigns for public utilities with Indigenous-owned wind farms; and mass marches against world-destroying industries with the building of new Native earthworks. All of these are complicated far beyond my descriptions here, but all offer new possibilities for investing in relations and divesting from structures of whiteness and empire.

US empire and its tellings of history often suppress collective forms of life and struggle, making them unimaginable even as they persist. This book only lightly touched on how radical politics—movements of workers, people of color, queer people, poor people, pacifists and militants—have made the United States more survivable despite being policed and pushed to the margins. Comparing freedom struggles to a swarm of ants crossing a chasm, Upton Sinclair wrote, "They cling to each other's bodies, even in death; they make a bridge, and the rest go over." I believe in clinging to the dead in their particularity, their complicity and betrayals, as well as their heroism.

Beyond these gestures I wouldn't presume to a grand theory of power in the social or political sense, which many writers put forth more profoundly than I can. In a blunt and literal way, I am interested in the stories people tell about material and spiritual resources. I've dwelled perhaps too much on exploitation, and not enough on resistance, in an effort to deconstruct systems of power that now seem eternal and immovable. I worry about how dissent, in the flexible and opportunistic alchemy of neoliberal capitalism, can also be turned to a profitable resource. In tracing power's roots, I want to reinforce how deep our refusal must go.

The gravitational force of capitalism is not due to its beneficial or inevitable nature but reflects the totality of belief. When nuclear fallout began raining down upon white, middle-class Americans in the 1950s, just as the fires and floods of global warming threaten them today, it was difficult to locate the source of the danger because it had been positioned as the life of the nation—to cease nuclear testing, or to leave fossil fuels in the ground, would invite the collapse of the American project. With the growth of the secretive nuclear state, paranoia and conspiracy theories took root in response to the unconvincing reassurances of Alvin Graves and his colleagues. Beyond the seductions of paranoia rise more durable understandings of what has happened and why. From Spiritualists condemning the "ruinous prosperity" of resource extraction to Alice Walker's proclamation that "only justice can stop a curse," many have seen capitalism and nationalism, extraction and hegemony, as the true danger to "people and the land and their continuance."

In Leslie Marmon Silko's *Ceremony*, a Laguna Pueblo elder asks about the atomic bomb, "Why did they make a thing like that?" Some of the scientists building the bomb hesitated over the same question, but they already had a story in mind about blazing the path of progress—they even saw themselves as heirs of the Pueblo people, building nuclear kivas to commune with the invisible world. Silko's story is that the mining of uranium, the Trinity test, and the Cold War are converging lines of "witchery's final ceremonial sand painting." Nuclear scientists sometimes agreed that they were communing with dark forces: Oppenheimer called it sin, Atomic Energy Commission chairman Glenn Seaborg termed it "nuclear alchemy," and Teller openly admitted that the treasure might cost them their souls. They were hardly the first enterprising Americans to consider this possibility.

For treasure hunters in Ben Franklin's day, the perils of pursuit were vividly real: submerged in muddy pits in the middle of the night, they reported assaults by demons, spirits, and wraiths that sent sober men screaming into the hills. Those who fortified themselves with whiskey fared even worse. A cross or a magic circle gave only fleeting protection. Fear was rarely fatal, however. Treasure hunters played out the thief's terrors on a spectral stage.

The more educated and enlightened believed that the power of reason could banish ghosts, or better yet employ them in the borderland of folklore and literature. Popular writers like Washington Irving and Nathaniel Hawthorne seemed to enclose and metabolize the threat of haunted lands, to extract the pleasure from readers' guilty knowledge. We could think of fiction, lost-race theories, and more respectable mainstream sciences as composing a magic circle to bend reality, to alter the facts on the ground so that victims become perpetrators, and then insubstantial phantoms. This occult view, of course, would disgust Henry Schoolcraft, who paid his tribute to race science in plundered skulls, and scorned the "polytheistic theories and wild dogmas" of Native people. His own wild dogmas, appearing perfectly natural to him, went unremarked.

Just as treasure hunters were pursued by spirits, perhaps there were vengeful forces at work in Schoolcraft's life, even if he didn't believe in them. We might ask whether the victims of his ambition or that devilish ambition itself haunted him, taking the form, for instance, of the phantasmal Grave Creek stone. A similar curse gripped Jonathan Watson and all those possessed by a thirst for oil who roamed Petrolia in search of a big strike that never came. It's important to take seriously the power of the dead, and of the stories we tell about them, to make known the secret cruelties and obsessions that we inherit.

Ghost stories, as they're often told in the US, grant the illusive comfort of individual punishment. What guidance do they offer when, as sociologist Avery Gordon writes, "entire societies become haunted by terrible deeds that are systematically occurring and are simultaneously denied"? Suffering has a political infrastructure, the result of cursed imperatives rather than personal shortcomings. The power of this curse, like that of radiation, is invisible and easily ignored even when everyone knows its horror. Though Alvin Graves was narrowly saved from a lethal dose of radiation by his colleague's shadow, he conjured a world without shadows, where the light of atomic science would secure eternal wealth and dominance for America.

Leslie Marmon Silko's suggestion is that US empire is the creation of witchery, evil magic, within a Pueblo cosmos. Writing about the same mine-scarred landscape, Simon Ortiz argues that the Pueblo world and that of the United States are both inside and outside each other; he warns US citizens that the forces harming Native people of the Southwest "are the same forces which steal the human fabric of their own American communities and lives." As Ortiz sees it, neither can make it "beyond survival" without the other. The point is not that some poetic cataclysm would avenge the original theft of the land, as the white purveyors of Indian curses guiltily imagined in the nineteenth century. Cataclysms are increasingly routine, brought about by the powerful in the ordinary process of securing their advantages, and when they occur our society sacrifices the people it has historically deemed most expendable.

At each site in this book, settlers and prospectors, scientists and writers, gazed at signs of the Indigenous past and read them as abandoned ruins. They differed on whether these were the ruins of a lost white race, or of Native people who were due to vanish, but either story served to render the past into a resource. At each site, this work happened in tandem with the extraction of material power from the land, transmuting narrative into commodity, faith into profit. Generals who fought wars of Indigenous extermination saw in ceremonial earthworks the fallen battlements of a lost white race. But Indigenous people are still building earthworks in North America today.

The haunting prospect of ruin has not strayed far from its original function as a guilty justification for imperial conquest. It acts in the context of every successive crisis to instill what anthropologist Cameron Hu calls "vigilance toward continually renewed danger." While tracing how settler science and spiritual investments reshaped particular places, and how those places shaped US capitalist ideologies, I have also tried to unwork the erasures so embedded in histories of energy, landscape, and technology. To do so is to embrace the imperative that the structures of capitalist and settler colonial power actually be ruined. That, after all, is what the thread of anxious desire traced in this book so urgently defers. Myths of extinction push outside their frame the even more disturbing possibility: that the mutations of the country could turn people's minds to justice, and that they could seek it with each other. So many of our stories dance around the horror of a treasure that is cursed, and the fear of letting it go. The point is to see that not as ruin, but as life itself.

ACKNOWLEDGMENTS

The city of Baltimore, where I live, is part of the ancestral homelands of the Piscataway and Susquehannock peoples. Its vital urban Native community is documented in the 2021 Guide to Indigenous Baltimore created by Dr. Ashley Miner, Dr. Elizabeth Rule, and their collaborators. The city was a major port in the domestic slave trade and the first to introduce residential segregation laws in the Jim Crow era; the past is not past here, and attending to present-day struggles has helped me understand continuities throughout the eras and regions I write about.

This book moves across a lot of ground, and I could only begin to understand these places and histories with the help of many, many people. Most I only know through their writing, and they appear in the endnotes, a gallery of my gratitude for the work that scholars put into the world. I especially encourage readers to consult the work of Dina Gilio-Whitaker and the contributors to Nick Estes's *Standing with Standing Rock* for perspectives on Indigenous environmental justice. I don't consider myself on the level of the authors I've cited in terms of specialized knowledge or theoretical reach, but I hope they find it worthwhile to bring these stories and terrains into conversation, that the gestural connections I've made are openings.

Other people snaked the state highways with me and wondered at the troubling ease with which land and its histories are overwritten, caught up in the spell of infrastructure and the fissures where the spell breaks. Our ability to experience places is tied to power flows—oil pipelines, managed rivers, roads built for extractive industries. Yet traveling these paths with people who relentlessly question power relations has helped me to read the "planned promised land" against its grain. Graham Coreil-Allen, Alexa Richardson, Matt Weaver, Stephanie Barber, Isa Leal, Alishea Galvin, and Phil Rocco, along with many other friends, were and are crucial companions in this regard.

Conversations and correspondence with Kai Minosh Pyle, Patricia Reifel, Sid Jamieson, Charles Hall, Christopher F. Jones, Randy A. John, Ph.D., Shannon Epplett, Laurence Hauptman, David Webber, Joel Dunn, Hartman Deetz, and Darryl Hines are woven into this text and I'm grateful for the time they took to share their knowledge.

I received research advice and assistance from dedicated archivists and curators, including Susan Beates at the Drake Well Museum, Eric Hemenway of the Little Traverse Bay Bands of Odawa Indians, Diane Bird of the New Mexico Museum of Indian Arts and Culture, Rebecca Collinsworth of the Los Alamos Historical Society, Melanie LaBorwit of the New Mexico History Museum, Brice Obermayer of the Delaware Tribe Historic Preservation Office, Lemley Mullett of the West Virginia and Regional History Center, the Walther P. Reuther Library at Wayne State University, Rebecca Bowen of the Seneca Nation Archives, and John Tyler Moore at the National Security Research Center. The staff of the Johns Hopkins Library Services Center, Interlibrary Loan Services, and Special Collections aided in the gathering of countless sources, and Zach Christensen provided critical technical assistance with the manuscript.

Support from the Consortium for the History of Science, Technology, and Medicine and its director Babak Ashrafi allowed me to begin research for this project a long time ago, and Adrianna Link of the American Philosophical Society offered editorial guidance. In the extended process of writing and revising, I received invaluable feedback on the manuscript from Gustave Lester, Anna Christensen, Hartman Deetz, Mikita Brottman, Paul Jaskunas, John Barry, Dana Reijerkirk, Isa Leal, and Michael Hanes, as well as from Sally Howe, my extremely patient editor at Scribner.

I worry a lot, as many historians do, about what it means to write about the people of past generations. The dead can't know what their traces will mean in the future, whether they'll be met with sympathy, recognition, or judgment. Anything left behind can be misappropriated, but there's no other way to send a message. I've done my best to approach the dead with recognition, to see them within their worlds and the possible worlds they imagined, to think through how the pasts and futures of a long-ago moment live in our time.

In coming toward knowing a place where my relatives arrived as settlers only a century ago and busied themselves with reaching the middle class, I am grateful that my family, especially my grandma Angie, didn't let the contradictions of this society go unremarked. I began this book with an interest in the scientific and occult ways that settlers in the US tried to understand the landscape, recognizing in their desire for communion many of the problematic practices and ideas that adhere to historic places today. The challenge of tracing these longings and appropriations is clear, as I could simply be repeating them in a contemporary register. I've done my best to faithfully interpret the ideas of others and to understand how these voices reverberate across a changing landscape, sounding the worlds that have always been here and the worlds that are always possible.

NOTES

Mutations of the country

1 *hiding something more sinister:* See David E. Nye, *America as Second Creation: Technology and Narratives of New Beginnings* (Cambridge, MA: MIT Press, 2003).

2 *as simple as turning a key in a lock:* Charles H. Kent, *How to Achieve Success: A Manual for Young People* (New York: Christian Herald, 1897).

4 *but by white traders and missionaries:* Kai Pyle, "Ozaawindib, the Ojibwe Trans Woman the US Declared a Chief," *Activist History Review*, June 13, 2019.

4 *until her tears formed the lake that bore her name:* Philip P. Mason, *Schoolcraft's Expedition to Lake Itasca* (East Lansing, MI: MSU Press, 2012), xxiv; Mary Henderson Eastman, *The American Aboriginal Portfolio* (Philadelphia: Lippincott, Grambo, 1853), 16–17; Edward C. Gale, "The Legend of Lake Itasca," *Minnesota History*, September 1931, 233.

5 *they admitted that it "took" in the country's imagination:* Gale, "Legend of Lake Itasca," 219.

5 *when they dared to, described it with horror:* Pyle, "Ozaawindib." Pyle points out that it's important not to idealize Native nonbinary gender categories as though they anticipated today's queer critiques, and that Two-Spirit people experienced varying levels of acceptance and support in different Indigenous communities at different times.

6 *the Ojibwe named it for Ozaawindib:* Kai Pyle, "Ozaawindib (Late 1700s–?)," MNopedia (Minnesota Historical Society).

6 *wrote one missionary working in the region:* Quoted in Hart, "The Origin and Meaning," 228.

6 *today regard Itasca as a Dakota name:* Book files ca. 1817–57, n.d., Box 74, Papers of Henry Rowe Schoolcraft, Library of Congress; Pyle, "Ozaawindib" and personal correspondence; Theodore C. Blegen, "That Name Itasca," *Minnesota History*, June 1932, 171.

7 *his own park "swampy, muddy, and dirty":* Rich Heyman, "Locating the Mississippi: Landscape, Nature, and National Territoriality at the Mississippi Headwaters," *American Quarterly* 62, no. 2 (2010): 309.

7 *the single, iconic source of the mighty Mississippi:* Ibid.

8 *prosperity through nuclear development:* Doug Brugge, Timothy Benally, and

Esther Yazzie-Lewis, eds., *The Navajo People and Uranium Mining* (Albuquerque: University of New Mexico Press, 2007), 6.

10 *but of the living, and is the purpose of this history:* Eve Tuck and C. Ree, "A Glossary of Haunting," *Handbook of Autoethnography*, edited by Stacy Holman Jones, Tony E. Adams, and Carolyn Ellis (Walnut Creek, California: Left Coast Press, 2013), 642-651.

11 *"antiquity as a national and scientific space":* Berenika Byszewski, "Colonizing Chaco Canyon: Mapping Antiquity in the Territorial Southwest," *Formations of United States Colonialism*, edited by Alyosha Goldstein (North Carolina: Duke University Press, 2014), 59.

13 *accept the Indigenous origins of the country's ancient monuments:* Jason Colavito, *The Mound Builder Myth: Fake History and the Hunt for a "Lost White Race"* (Norman: University of Oklahoma Press, 2020).

The myth of the Mound Builders

21 *"easy, free, and plentiful" life in their solitary log cabins:* Timothy Flint, *The History and Geography of the Mississippi Valley* (Cincinnati: E. H. Flint and L. R. Lincoln, 1832), 130; Thomas Duncomb, *The British Emigrant's Advocate* (London: Lumpkin and Marshall, W. B. Johnson, 1837), 10.

21 *spared neither women, children, nor the aged:* J. H. Newton et al., *History of the Pan-handle: Being Historical Collections of the Counties of Ohio, Brooke, Marshall and Hancock, West Virginia* (Wheeling, WV: J. A. Caldwell, 1879), 61; *Official Bulletin of the National Society of the Sons of the American Revolution,* December 1913, 22; Roxanne Dunbar-Ortiz, *An Indigenous Peoples' History of the United States* (Boston: Beacon Press, 2014), 71–72.

22 *"economic base of the US wealth and power must be seen":* Butler quoted in Terry A. Barnhart, *American Antiquities: Revisiting the Origins of American Archaeology* (Lincoln and London: University of Nebraska Press, 2015), 95; Dunbar-Ortiz, *Indigenous Peoples' History,* 124.

22 *"in western Virginia is remarkable":* Philip W. Sturm, "Kinship Migration to Northwestern Virginia, 1785–1815: The Myth of the Southern Frontiersman" (PhD diss., West Virginia University, 2004), 222.

23 *his body, they said, was left unburied:* Ibid., 222–26; US Federal Census, 1840, Wood County, VA; Henry Robert Burke, "Tragedy on the Muskingum," https://www.wvgenweb.org/marshall/tomfam.htm. Burke, a local historian focused on Ohio and West Virginia's African American history, places this event in 1804, but Robert appears to have died in 1808. Burke states that he reconstructed this story from sparse sources; descendants of the Tomlinson family confirm the details of Robert's death based on their own public genealogical research, but Sturm was unable to find documentary confirmation in regional archives.

23 *as more than an obstruction to progress:* Ephraim George Squier, *Observa-*

tions on the Aboriginal Monuments of the Mississippi Valley . . . (Bartlett and Welford, 1847), 75.

23 *the "sublime imaginations" of onlookers:* "Mission to the Ottawa and Chippewa Indians," *Missionary Chronicle* 6 (November 1838): 348. This view was further established as science in Samuel Morton's notorious 1839 phrenological text, *Crania Americana*, which characterizes Indians as "averse to cultivation, and slow in acquiring knowledge; restless, resentful, and fond of war" (6).

24 *to investors they promised a share of the riches within:* Colavito, *Mound Builder Myth*, 228–29.

24 *exponential riches placed there by Providence:* Alan Taylor, "The Early Republic's Supernatural Economy: Treasure Seeking in the American Northeast, 1780–1830," *American Quarterly* 38, no. 1 (1986): 6–34.

24 *and often onward to Canada:* Sturm, "Kinship Migration to Northwestern Virginia," 239.

25 *interests was North America's pre-Indian lost race:* "Mammoth Mound at Grave Creek, Va.," *Southern Patriot*, July 24, 1839; Newton et al., *History of the Pan-handle*, 252; Colavito, *Mound Builder Myth*, 229.

26 *to open the mound to begin with:* Newton et al., *History of the Pan-handle*, 369.

27 *argument for Native land rights in the present day:* Sean P. Harvey, "'Must Not Their Languages Be Savage and Barbarous Like Them?': Philology, Indian Removal, and Race Science," *Journal of the Early Republic* 30, no. 4 (Winter 2010): 505–32; Colavito, *Mound Builder Myth*, 244–70.

27 *perversely insist that they are "the real Native Americans":* Colavito, *Mound Builder Myth*, 330–37.

28 *science, history, and artistic and spiritual relations with place:* Chadwick Allen, "Vital Earth/Vibrant Earthworks/Living Earthworks Vocabularies," in *Routledge Handbook of Critical Indigenous Studies*, ed. Brendan Hokowhitu et al. (Oxford and New York: Routledge, 2021), 270–72; LeAnne Howe and Jim Wilson, "Life in a 21st Century Mound City," in Robert Warrior, ed., *The World of Indigenous North America*, 2014).

28 *still playing out in court:* Christine Ballengee-Morris, "They came, they claimed, they named, and we blame: Art education in negotiation and conflict," *Studies in Art Education* (2010), 277; "The Beginning," Moundbuilders Country Club, https://www.moundbuilderscc.com/files/The%20 Beginning.pdf; Sarah Bahr, "A Push to Move the Golf Course Atop a Native American 'Stonehenge'" *New York Times* (April 12, 2021).

29 *policy of Indian removal:* Squier and Davis, *Ancient Monuments of the Mississippi Valley*, 306.

30 *Douglass roundly demolished in this 1854 speech:* Frederick Douglass, "The Claims of the Negro, Ethnologically Considered" (Rochester, NY: Lee, Mann, 1854). As Britt Rusert discusses in her book *Fugitive Science*, Douglass did not reject the principle that character and intelligence are inscribed in the human face; rather, he argued that these traits are not racial

but individual. He sought equal representation of African and African-descended people in scientific attempts to link physical with mental traits. On later Black engagement with race science, see Ayah Nuriddin, "The Black Politics of Eugenics," *Nursing Clio* (June 1, 2017), https://nursingclio .org/2017/06/01/the-black-politics-of-eugenics/.

30 *fantastical voyages of Egyptians or Israelites:* James M. Blaut, *The Colonizer's Model of the World* (New York: Guilford Press, 1993), 11–14; Ephraim George Squier, "Aboriginal Monuments of the State of New York," article 9 of the *Smithsonian Contributions to Knowledge*, vol. 2 (Washington, DC: Smithsonian Institution, 1851), 99.

31 *continuous history of Indigenous habitation:* Benjamin Smith Barton, *Observations on Some Parts of Natural History* (London: printed for the author, sold by C. Dilly, 1787), 65; Samuel G. Morton, *An Inquiry into the Distinctive Characteristics of the Aboriginal Race of America* (Philadelphia: J. Penington, 1844), 17–18.

32 *a potential clue to the mystery:* Timothy Flint, "Indian Mounds," *Western Monthly Review*, 1827.

34 *belief was heavily trafficked:* Cyrus F. Newcomb, *The Book of Algoonah: Being a Concise Account of the History of the Early People of the Continent of America, Known as Mound Builders* (Little and Becker, 1884); "Judge Cyrus F. Newcomb Passes Away," *Durango Wage Earner*, January 5, 1905; *Colorado Daily Chieftain*, June 16, 1875; *Better Way* 6, no. 7 (February 15, 1890): 4.

Henry Rowe Schoolcraft strikes gold

38 *did not know a word of their languages:* Richard G. Bremer, *Indian Agent and Wilderness Scholar: The Life of Henry Rowe Schoolcraft* (Mt. Pleasant, MI: Clarke Historical Library, Central Michigan University, 1987), 57.

39 *"the country by its former inhabitants":* James Burns, *Human Nature*, July 1, 1870, quoted in Joseph Osgood Barrett, *The Spiritual Pilgrim: A Biography of James M. Peebles* (Boston: Colby and Rich, 1878), 59.

40 *"fallen columns and our encrusted medals":* Henry Rowe Schoolcraft (HRS) to Jane Johnston Schoolcraft, January 26, 1838, Box 43, Henry Rowe Schoolcraft Papers, Library of Congress (LOC).

41 *the noble destiny that Indians never could:* HRS to Washington Irving, March 28, 1842, Box 18, Reel 9, LOC.

42 *did not support the case for Native savagery:* HRS to Baron von Lotte, September 1, 1842, Box 18, Reel 9, LOC. Louise Erdrich quoted in Susan Bernardin, "Alternate Origin Stories and Unexpected Archives: The Question of the Indigenous Literary," *Legacy* 34:1 (2017), 218. Schoolcraft was familiar with the writing and reading of birchbark scrolls by Ojibwe people,

which he termed "a rude notation for their war and medicine and sacred mystic songs."

43 *present-day Indians lacked such writing systems:* Thomas Townsend, "Grave Creek Mound," *Monthly Chronicle of Interesting and Useful Knowledge,* February 1, 1839; Colavito, *Mound Builder Myth,* 229–31; Rick Steelhammer, "170-Year-Old Mystery Solved; Grave Creek Stone Hoax Linked to Wheeling Doctor," *Charleston Gazette,* October 13, 2008.

44 *whose bones rested inside the mound:* Henry Rowe Schoolcraft, "Account of the Mound at Grave Creek Flats in Virginia," *Journal of the Royal Geographical Society of London,* 1842. This interpretation seems to precede the first archived correspondence between Schoolcraft and the Royal Geographical Society's secretary, J. E. Alexander, on January 8, 1842, for Schoolcraft's interpretation changed rapidly afterward and he attempted to recall his preliminary report from the RGS.

"As I am thinking . . . My land"

46 *had arrived in an Indian world and chose to adapt:* Historian Richard White first defined the "middle ground" in reference to the political and cultural intersections of this period in his influential book of that name. Richard White, *The Middle Ground: Indians, Empires, and Republics in the Great Lakes Region, 1650–1815* (Cambridge: Cambridge University Press, 1990).

46 *colonial governments, and Native leaders:* I follow Robert Dale Parker and Richard White in using the adjective métis for the complex cultural milieu of this time and place, not in reference to the Métis, a distinct self-defined Indigenous people.

47 *In English, she was Jane:* Biographical information is drawn from the introductory chapter to Jane Johnston Schoolcraft, *The Sound the Stars Make Rushing through the Sky: The Writings of Jane Johnston Schoolcraft,* ed. Robert Dale Parker (Philadelphia: University of Pennsylvania Press, 2007) and from Maureen Konkle, "Recovering Jane Schoolcraft's Cultural Activism in the Nineteenth Century," *The Oxford Handbook of Indigenous American Literature,* edited by James H. Cox and Daniel Heath Justice, (Oxford: Oxford University Press, 2014).

47 *less than two hundred in the bitter winters:* Population estimates drawn from Bremer, *Indian Agent,* 58; Schoolcraft, *Sound the Stars Make,* 18–19.

48 *according to a British commander:* Quoted in Janet Elizabeth Chute, *The Legacy of Shingwaukonse: A Century of Native Leadership* (Toronto: University of Toronto Press, 1998), 30.

49 *territories were his main source of material:* Schoolcraft, *Sound the Stars Make,* 16; Bernard C. Peters, "Indian-Grave Robbing at Sault Ste. Marie, 1826," *Michigan Historical Review* 23, no. 2 (Fall 1997): 49–80.

49 *Indian relations were a means to that end:* Bremer, *Indian Agent*, 58. As Peters's careful investigation reveals, both Pitcher and Schoolcraft sent the remains of Native people to Samuel Morton's skull collection. It seems that Schoolcraft did not do so until ten years after this 1826 incident. He receives credit for plate XXVIII in *Crania Americana*, labeled as the skull of a "Chippeway Indian." That he could do so while married to Jane and living in intimate proximity to her family and many other Ojibwe people reflects both his casual dehumanization of Native people and the macabre medico-scientific prestige of grave robbing, which targeted burial places of poor, Black, and Native communities. Peters, "Indian-Grave Robbing," 75–78; see Michael Sappol, *A Traffic of Dead Bodies: Anatomy and Embodied Social Identity in Nineteenth-Century America* (Princeton, NJ: Princeton University Press, 2004).

50 *"refined manners and education":* Henry Rowe Schoolcraft, *Personal Memoirs of a Residence of Thirty Years with the Indian Tribes on the American Frontiers* (Philadelphia: Lippincott, Grambo, 1851), 207.

50 *"Stranger am I to all delight":* Schoolcraft, *Sound the Stars Make*, 120.

53 *"that great virtue of a woman—quiescence":* Correspondence of September 12 and 25, 1829, ibid., 37–38.

54 *the omnivorous custom of the nineteenth-century press:* Virgil J. Vogel, "Place Names from Longfellow's 'Song of Hiawatha,'" *Names* 39, no 3 (September 1991).

55 *and to the Indian Bureau as science:* Georg Anton Lorenz Diefenbach to HRS, July 11, 1842, Box 18, Reel 9, LOC. For more on the active role of ethnography's "subjects," see Ned Blackhawk and Isaiah Lorado Wilner, eds., *Indigenous Visions: Rediscovering the World of Franz Boas* (New Haven: Yale University Press, 2018).

56 *"Ahh but I am sad":* Translation by Dennis Jones, Heidi Stark, and James Vukelich, in Schoolcraft, *Sound the Stars Make*, 143.

58 *"with a euro-American father, and as a poet":* Heid E. Erdrich, "'Name': Literary Ancestry as Presence," in *Centering Anishinaabeg Studies: Understanding the World through Stories*, ed. Jill Doerfler, Niigaanwewidam James Sinclair, and Heidi Kiiwetinepinesiik Stark (East Lansing: Michigan State University Press, 2013), 22. Dr. Shannon Epplett describes his performance and research in "The Dramaturgy of Erasure: Staging Jane Johnston Schoolcraft," (unpublished paper) and in a conference presentation of that name at the Mid-American Theater Conference, 2015 (https://www.you tube.com/watch?v=5460bmGJ_PY).

60 *had undeniable popular and scholarly appeal:* Henry Rowe Schoolcraft, "Brief Notices of a Runic Inscription Found in North America, Communicated by Henry R. Schoolcraft in Letters to Charles C. Rafn, Secretary," *Mémoires de la Société royale des antiquaires du Nord*, 1842, 119; *Incentives to the Study of the Ancient Period of American History: An Address, Delivered before the New-York Historical Society, at Its Forty-Second Anniversary, 17th November, 1846* (New York: Press of the Historical Society, 1847), 8; Henry

Rowe Schoolcraft, "Observations Respecting the Grave Creek Mound," *Transactions of the American Ethnological Society*, 1845, 367–420.

60 *desperate to put lost-race fantasies to rest:* Schoolcraft, "Observations Respecting the Grave Creek Mound," 367–420.

61 *called the* Walum Olum: Joanne Barker, "The Specters of Recognition," *Formations of United States Colonialism*, edited by Alyosha Goldstein (North Carolina: Duke University Press, 2014), 35-39.

61 *flexible, and adaptive to the demands of the moment:* Terry Barnhart, *Ephraim George Squier and the Development of American Anthropology* (Lincoln: University of Nebraska Press, 2005), 136–37.

61 *what can be taken with enough force:* Henry Rowe Schoolcraft, *Oneóta, Or, Characteristics of the Red Race of America* (Wiley and Putnam, 1845), 35. I count at least four republications of this anecdote and poem between 1845 and 1856. In some, Schoolcraft cites as his source a news story in the *Wheeling Times and Advertiser*, which does not exist in the paper's archive on the date he specifies; it's possible that he submitted the story and the paper declined it. He was a great recycler of material.

63 *for "us poor conquered whites":* Mary Howard Schoolcraft, *The Black Gauntlet: A Tale of Plantation Life in South Carolina* (Philadelphia: J. B. Lippincott, 1860); Jeremy Mumford, "Mixed-Race Identity in a Nineteenth-Century Family: The Schoolcrafts of Sault Ste. Marie, 1824–27," *Michigan Historical Review* 25, no. 1 (1999): 1–23; Jane Schoolcraft to Mary Howard Schoolcraft, August 10, 1867, HRS Papers, LOC. Mary Howard's pro-slavery novel was dedicated to Henry, and she brought an enslaved woman named Polly to be their servant in Washington. Henry assured Mary of his own pro-slavery beliefs. An abolitionist minister befriended the unpopular couple and tried to help Polly escape to freedom in the North—Mary discovered Polly's plan and sent her back to South Carolina. See Bremer, *Indian Agent*, 310.

64 *"to pursue all the elements of their own destruction":* Schoolcraft, *Personal Memoirs*, 109; Henry Rowe Schoolcraft, *Information Respecting the History, Condition and Prospects of the Indian Tribes of the United States* (Philadelphia: Lippincott, Grambo, 1853), 58.

Spirits released from human bondage

66 *"a hallmark of being an authentic American":* Darryl V. Caterine, "Heirs through Fear: Indian Curses, Accursed Indian Lands, and White Christian Sovereignty in America," *Nova Religio* 18, no. 1 (August 2014): 37–57.

67 *in the first of many escape attempts: Cincinnati Gazette*, January 22, 1867. Similar prison revolts were reported in 1868 and 1870.

67 *which hobbyists combed for Indigenous artifacts: Work & Hope*, "Souvenir of the West Virginia Penitentiary, Moundsville," 1929.

67 *river and the hills on either side:* Delf Norona, *Moundsville's Mammoth Mound*

(West Virginia Archeological Society, 1962); E. Thomas Hemmings, "The Core Drilling Project at Grave Creek Mound: Preliminary Results and Radiocarbon Date," *West Virginia Archeologist* 26 (1977), 59-68.

68   *wheels and yokes for the westward-rolling empire:* "Our Institutions," *Wheeling Register*, April 18, 1886; US Census Bureau, *Census Reports Eleventh Census: 1890*, vol. 3, no. 2 (Washington, DC: US Government Printing Office, 1895); US Census Bureau, *Thirteenth Census of the United States: Statistics for West Virginia* (Washington, DC: US Government Printing Office, 1910), 583. The total prison population of the United States remained relatively small, though steadily growing, until the 1980s, so this is not a claim that imprisonment literally replaced slavery. Black people were disproportionately imprisoned due to racist laws and law enforcement, especially in the South, which acted as a form of coercive social control affecting even those who were not locked up. This also amounted to a criminalization of poverty for people of all races.

68   *"One little slip and down you will come too":* Katy Ryan and Yvonne Hammond, "*Work & Hope* and the West Virginia State Penitentiary," *West Virginia History: A Journal of Regional Studies* 11, no. 1 (July 17, 2017): 34.

69   *in his memoir, "it was damnation":* Caleb Smith, *The Prison and the American Imagination* (New Haven, CT: Yale University Press, 2011), 36–38; Earl Ellicott Dudding, *The Trail of the Dead Years* (Huntington, WV: Prisoners Relief Society, 1932), 43.

70   *the guards put down inmate revolts:* "A Day in the West Virginia Penitentiary," *Cincinnati Gazette*, January 16, 1874; "Our Institutions," *Wheeling Register*, April 18, 1886.

71   *after Emancipation, John was still enslaved:* "A Protest from the Workingmen," *Wheeling Register*, April 1, 1878; Ryan and Hammond, "*Work & Hope*," 35.

72   *"form of eastern idolatry":* Henry Rowe Schoolcraft, *Historical and Statistical Information Respecting the History, Condition and Prospects of the Indian Tribes of the United States* (Lippincott, Grambo, 1851), 89; Henry Rowe Schoolcraft, *The Indian Tribes of the United States*, vol. 1 (Philadelphia: J. B. Lippincott, 1884), 216.

72   *not taxpayer funds, maintained the convicts:* Cahokia Mound Chapter, *Illinois History of the Daughters of the American Revolution* (Chrisman, IL, 1929), 217–18. The DAR had multiple mound-themed chapters, including in Moundsville.

73   *"I will set every one of you free!":* B. C. Warren, *Arsareth: A Tale of the Luray Caverns* (New York: A. Lovell, 1893), 208.

73   *at least one man was leased from a local jail:* Richard Veit, "A Case of Archaeological Amnesia: A Contextual Biography of Montroville Wilson Dickeson (1810–1882), Early American Archaeologist," *Archaeology of Eastern North America* 25 (1997): 105; Charles Peabody, "Notes on Negro Music," *Journal of American Folklore* 16, no. 62 (1903): 151.

74   *none of their dead were safe:* Jodi A. Byrd, *The Transit of Empire: Indige-*

nous Critiques of Colonialism (Minneapolis: University of Minnesota Press, 2011), 120–22; Tiya Miles and Sharon Patricia Holland, editors, *Crossing Waters, Crossing Worlds: The African Diaspora in Indian Country* (Durham: Duke University Press, 2006); Walter Rucker, "Grave Decorations," *The Greenwood Encyclopedia of African American Folklore*, ed. Anand Prahlad (Westport, CT: Greenwood Press, 2006), 543. These African-American burials were individual mounded grave sites, rather than large-scale earthworks, which were traditionally decorated with shells, broken pottery, or glass. I am grateful to Darryl Hines for pointing out this resonance and sharing his research with me.

76   *and in a much shorter time: Work & Hope,* 1929; Millard Fillmore Compton, *History of the Mound Builders* (Moundsville, WV: Marshall County Bank, 1923).

78   *and relief again, until you reach the gift shop:* Ryan and Hammond, *"Work & Hope,"* 35.

78   *"all the paranormal activity that happens there":* Sherri Brake, *The Haunted History of the West Virginia Penitentiary: Afterlife with No Parole* (Create-Space Independent Publishing Platform, 2011).

80   *mounds' layering of knowledge and expression:* Allen, "Vibrant Earth / Vital Earthworks"; Eric Gary Anderson, "Earthworks and Contemporary Indigenous American Literature: Foundations and Futures," *Native South* 9:1 (August 12, 2016): 1–26.

81   *"while looking at the mounds they built":* LeAnne Howe, "Embodied Tribalography: Mound Building, Ball Games, and Native Endurance in the Southeast," *Studies in American Indian Literatures* 26: 2 (2014): 76; Chadwick Allen, "Performing Serpent Mound: A Trans-Indigenous Meditation," *Theatre Journal* 67:3 (2015), 398-404.

The Pithole at the end of the world

85   *though origins are never as simple as they seem:* Edgar Wesley Owen, *Trek of the Oil Finders* (Tulsa, OK: American Association of Petroleum Geologists, 1975), 12.

86   *known for its particularly heedless debauchery:* Brian Black, *Petrolia: The Landscape of America's First Oil Boom* (Baltimore: Johns Hopkins University Press, 2000), 146, 152, 169.

88   *Quaker State, left in 1995:* Agis Salpukas, "Inside Oil City, Hope Runs Dry," *New York Times,* July 26, 1995.

88   *"is that the kids move away":* Gabriel Winant, *The Next Shift: The Fall of Industry and the Rise of Health Care in Rust Belt America* (Cambridge, MA: Harvard University Press, 2021), 20; Pennsylvania Department of Labor and Industry, "Venango County Profile," April 2021, https://www.work stats.dli.pa.gov/Documents/County%20Profiles/Venango%20County.pdf.

89 *to build a docile white middle class:* on the valuation of care work, see The Care Collective, *The Care Manifesto: The Politics of Interdependence* (New York: Verso, 2020).

89 *subsidy to businesses who can't attract their own workers:* Michael R. Strain, "A Jobs Agenda for the Right," *National Affairs,* Winter 2014.

90 *to shop at Dollar General:* Allana Akhtar, "A UBS Report Says Dollar General Pays Workers the Least among 25 Major Retailers," *Business Insider,* Oct 22, 2020.

91 *a brain of accumulated matter:* Eugene Thacker, *In the Dust of This Planet* (Winchester, UK, and Washington, DC: Zero Books, 2011); Jackie Orr, "Enchanting Catastrophe: Magical Subrealism and BP's Macondo," *Catalyst Journal,* September 8, 2015, https://doi.org/10.28968/cftt.v1i1.28813.

92 *as they would attempt to do in Petrolia:* Karen A. Selsor et al., "Late Prehistoric Petroleum Collection in Pennsylvania: Radiocarbon Evidence," *American Antiquity* 65, no. 4 (2000): 749–55; Judith E. Thomas et al., "Documentary, Archaeological, and Radiocarbon Evidence of Prehistoric and Protohistoric Petroleum Production in Pennsylvania," *Oil-Industry History* 3:1 (2002) 19-33.

92 *other Native groups over the expanding fur trade:* Kurt W. Carr et al., *The Archaeology of Native Americans in Pennsylvania* (Philadelphia: University of Pennsylvania Press, 2020), 481; Laurence M. Hauptman, *Coming Full Circle: The Seneca Nation of Indians, 1848–1934* (Norman: University of Oklahoma Press, 2019), xi.

93 *conjured more exotic scenarios:* Samuel John Mills Eaton, *Petroleum: A History of the Oil Region of Venango County, Pennsylvania* (J. P. Skelly, 1866), 55; Thomas et al., "Documentary, Archaeological, and Radiocarbon Evidence"; M. H. Deardorff, "Zeisberger's Allegheny River Indian Towns: 1767-1770," *Pennsylvania Archaeologist* 16:1 (1946), 12-14.

93 *started as a kind of local tourism stunt:* John J. McLaurin, *Sketches in Crude-Oil: Some Accidents and Incidents of the Petroleum Development in All Parts of the Globe* (Harrisburg, PA: J. J. McLaurin, 1896), 16–18; Susan J. Beates, email correspondence, August 23, 2020.

94 *arms for their British allies:* Michael Leroy Oberg, *Native America: A History* (Hoboken, NJ: John Wiley & Sons, 2018), 123–24.

95 *that became the gold standard in US warfare:* "From George Washington to Major General John Sullivan, 31 May 1779," *Papers of George Washington, Revolutionary War Series,* vol. 20, 8 April–31 May 1779, ed. Edward G. Lengel (Charlottesville: University of Virginia Press, 2010), 716–19; Rhiannon Koehler, "Hostile Nations: Quantifying the Destruction of the Sullivan-Clinton Genocide of 1779," *American Indian Quarterly* 42, no. 4 (2018): 427–53.

95 *keeping the peace after the US invasion:* Seneca Nation Culture and History, https://sni.org/culture/historic-seneca-leaders/.

96 *a map from white officials as proof of ownership:* Thomas Donaldson, *Extra Census Bulletin. Indians. The Six Nations of New York* . . . (Washington, DC: US Census Printing Office, 1892), 28; Thomas S. Abler, *Cornplanter: Chief Warrior of the Allegany Senecas* (Syracuse, NY: Syracuse University Press, 2007), 133; *Sga:nyodai:yoh* in Hauptman, *Coming Full Circle,* xiii.

96 *descendants continued to claim Oil City decades later:* Anthony Wallace, *Death and Rebirth of the Seneca* (New York: Knopf, 1969), 182; F. C. Johnson, ed., *The Historical Record of Wyoming Valley: A Compilation of Matters of Local History from the Columns of the* Wilkes-Barre Record (Wilkes-Barre, PA: Press of the Wilkes-Barre Record, 1897), 105.

96 *"variety of Fruit Trees . . . which were planted by the Indians":* William Temple Franklin and Robert Morris, *An Account of the Soil, Growing Timber, and Other Productions* . . . ([London: s.n.], 1791; Ann Arbor, MI: Text Creation Partnership, 2005), http://name.umdl.umich.edu/N17835.0001.001.

97 *requiring respect for the materials used:* George S. Snyderman, "The Case of Daniel P.: An Example of Seneca Healing," *Journal of the Washington Academy of Sciences* 39:7 (1949), 218; Wallace, *Death and Rebirth of the Seneca,* 186–87.

97 *start their own competing product lines:* Brooks McNamara, "The Indian Medicine Show," *Educational Theatre Journal* 23, no. 4 (1971): 438.

98 *work for him, at least according to later recollections:* Vernon C. Mulchansingh, "The Oil Industry in the Economy of Trinidad," *Caribbean Studies* 11, no. 1 (1971): 73–74; "Graphic Sketch of Col. Drake," *Scientific American,* November 27, 1869, 341; Paul Lucier, *Scientists and Swindlers: Consulting on Coal and Oil in America, 1820–1890* (Baltimore: Johns Hopkins University Press, 2008), 203–5.

99 *hit oil at seventy feet below the ground:* Black, *Petrolia,* 31–34, 204–5; Samuel John Mills Eaton, *Petroleum: A History of the Oil Region of Venango County, Pennsylvania: Its Resources, Mode of Development, and Value: Embracing a Discussion of Ancient Oil Operations* (Philadelphia: J. P. Skelly, 1866), 70. The claim that Drake borrowed money is contested by Lucier and others but widely repeated, for instance by Black.

99 *"to realms of wealth hitherto unknown":* Eaton, *Petroleum,* 69.

101 *petroleum for their great civilization from North America:* Pennsylvania Grade Crude Assn., "Who Dug Pennsylvania's 2000 Mysterious Oil Pits?" *Time,* April 22, 1940; "Oil Rush," *Popular Science,* August 1959, 84; Thomas Anderton, "Who Were the Oil Tycoons of Pre-Columbian Pennsylvania?," in *The Lost History of Ancient America,* ed. Frank Joseph (Wayne, NJ: Career Press, 2017).

101 *accounts of these rituals were likely white inventions:* J. T. Henry, *The Early and Later History of Petroleum,* 11.

102 *water that could have extinguished them had oil in it:* "Frightful Explosion of an Oil Well," *Sunbury (PA) Gazette,* May 11, 1861; Black, *Petrolia,* 89, 121, 154.

NOTES

Petrolia's spiritual awakening

105 *explaining it as "magnetic influence, or some other cause":* William Wright, *The Oil Regions of Pennsylvania* (New York: Harper and Brothers, 1865), 62.

105 *number of times they had missed entirely:* "Wizard Oil Finder," *Atchison (KS) Daily Globe*, December 29, 1897, 4.

106 *landscape of heaven and the pursuits of the afterlife:* Andrew Jackson Davis, *A Stellar Key to the Summer Land, Part I* (Boston: William White, 1867), 174.

107 *North America belonged to Indians:* "Oil Interested Indians before White Men Came," *Oil and Gas Journal*, April 2, 1920, 76.

108 *through "the counsels of his heavenly teachers":* James M. Peebles, *The Practical of Spiritualism: A Biographical Sketch of Abraham James* (Chicago: Horton and Leonard, 1868); "Oil Smeller Abroad: A Spiritual Prophecy Verified," *Milwaukee Journal Sentinel*, February 17, 1868; "Early Days in Oil Creek: Death of the Discoverer of the Pleasantville Oil Fields," *New York Times*, November 29, 1884, 3.

109 *with the land valued at up to $6,000 per acre:* Peebles, *Practical*, 66; Abraham James, "Card from Mr. James," *Banner of Light*, June 27, 1868, 8.

110 *"and there thrust his cane into the earth":* Peebles, *Practical*, 80.

110 *"political—while simultaneously drawing power from them":* Philip Joseph Deloria, *Playing Indian* (New Haven, CT: Yale University Press, 1998), 191.

110 *"exterminating war upon the Western tribes":* "Convention of Spiritualists," *Cleveland Plain Dealer*, September 7, 1867.

111 *managed as wards of the state:* Carla Fredericks and Jesse Heibel, "Standing Rock, the Sioux Treaties, and the Limits of the Supremacy Clause," *University of Colorado Law Review* 89, no. 2 (2018): 477–532; Oberg, *Native America: A History*, 199–202.

112 *"and going off alone into their country":* James M. Peebles, "Sumner and the Indians" *BoL*, January 26, 1867, 8; James M. Peebles, "Lo! The Poor Indian!," *BoL*, June 22, 1867, 8; Barrett, *Spiritual Pilgrim*, 173.

112 *agreed to address the gathered Spiritualists:* "Peter Wilson," Tribal Writers Digital Library, Sequoyah National Research Center, University of Arkansas at Little Rock, Collections and Archives Exhibits, https://ualrexhibits .org/tribalwriters/artifacts/Wilson_Introduction.html. Wilson's name was variously spelled *Waowawanaonk, Wau-wah-wa-na-onk,* or *De jih'-non-da-weh-hoh,* meaning "they hear his voice" or "the pacificator."

112 *that they had everything wrong:* Molly McGarry, *Ghosts of Futures Past: Spiritualism and the Cultural Politics of Nineteenth-Century America* (Berkeley: University of California Press, 2008), 92–93; James M. Peebles, "Dr. P. Wilson, the Indian," *BoL*, September 26, 1868, 8.

113 *brutal punishment in boarding schools:* Carole Goldberg, "A Native Vision of Justice," 111 *Michigan Law Review* 835 (2013): 842; Office of Indian Affairs, "Rules Governing the Court of Indian Offenses," March 30, 1883.

114 *perhaps Wilson demanded spiritual sovereignty:* These were deeply connected issues; Cherokee scholar Jace Weaver writes that Native American religious practices are "inexorably tied to the land." Jace Weaver, "Losing My Religion: Native American Religious Traditions and American Religious Freedom," in *Native American Religious Identity: Unforgotten Gods,* ed. Jace Weaver (Maryknoll, NY: Orbis Books, 1998), 219.

114 *"dirty, thieving, dissolute" Indians:* "Spiritualists and Indians," *Chicago Daily Tribune* (1872–1922), August 3, 1895.

115 *robbed the Seneca of all their land:* Laurence M. Hauptman, "Governor Blacksnake and the Seneca Indian Struggle to Save the Oil Spring Reservation," *Mid-America* 81, no. 1 (1999): 57.

115 *their land became a target for extraction:* William Edward Webb, *Buffalo Land: An Authentic Narrative of the Adventures and Misadventures of a Late Scientific and Sporting Party upon the Great Plains of the West . . .* (E. Hannaford, 1873), 384.

116 *financial need to lease land for drilling:* Hauptman, *Coming Full Circle,* 29.

116 *practically drooling over the prospect:* "Seneca Reservation Oil Leases," *Paint, Oil and Drug Review,* 1897, 33.

116 *drilling just outside their borders:* US Department of the Interior, "Oil Leases of the Seneca Indians: Letter from the Secretary of the Interior Transmitting in Response to Senate Resolutions of April 29, 1897, Report Relative to the Oil Leases of the Seneca Indians" (Washington, DC: US Government Printing Office, 1897), 4.

117 *happened to Seneca homes and crops:* P. C. Boyle, ed., *The Derrick's Hand-Book of Petroleum: A Complete Chronological and Statistical Review of Petroleum Developments from 1859 to 1898* (Oil City, PA: Derrick Publishing Company, 1898), 636.

117 *yielded a hundred barrels a day:* "Old Tonahauqua's Spirit," *Two Worlds* 144, no. 3 (August 15, 1890): 469.

117 *though Cayce had less luck than James:* Sidney D. Kirkpatrick, "Riches from the Earth" (self-pub.), www.integrativeenergyusa.com/cayce.

118 *gesturing at the heavenly kingdom:* James M. Peebles, "Spiritualism in Titusville, Pa.," *BoL,* January 26, 1867, 8.

118 *"illumine distant cities, and spiritually enlighten human minds":* Peebles, *Practical of Spiritualism,* 62.

118 *Union victory in the Civil War:* Darren Dochuk, *Anointed with Oil: How Christianity and Crude Made Modern America* (New York: Basic Books, 2019), 23.

119 *"which red men as well as white men were heirs":* Ibid., 33.

119 *geographically and metaphorically on the Union side:* Mark A. Lause, *Free Spirits: Spiritualism, Republicanism, and Radicalism in the Civil War Era* (Champaign: University of Illinois Press, 2016), 44; Jeremy Zallen, *American Lucifers: The Dark History of Artificial Light, 1750–1865* (Chapel Hill: University of North Carolina Press, 2019).

119 *"given to us in our day of national trial":* First Annual Report (New York: United States Petroleum Company, December 1, 1865), 4–5.

120 *"written in letters of blood":* Robert S. Cox, *Body and Soul: A Sympathetic History of American Spiritualism* (Charlottesville: University of Virginia Press, 2003), 182. John Patrick Deveney, *Paschal Beverly Randolph: A Nineteenth-Century Black American Spiritualist, Rosicrucian, and Sex Magician* (SUNY Press, 1997), 172; R. J. Ellis and Henry Louis Gates, "'Grievances at the Treatment She Received': Harriet E. Wilson's Spiritualist Career in Boston, 1868—1900," *American Literary History* 24, no. 2 (2012): 234–64.

120 *"the solution of the mighty problem of the nation's destiny":* Eaton, *Petroleum.*

121 *"the rich get richer" by preying on the increasingly miserable poor:* D. H. Hamilton, "Reconstruction," *Banner of Light*, February 4, 1865, 3.

121 *"gambling in all the natural products of the country":* Cora L. V. Richmond, *Abraham Lincoln* (Chicago: Church of the Soul, 1910), 6.

121 *peacefully "reconcile capital and labor":* Hamilton, "Reconstruction," 3.

122 *"mould society into a more beautiful character":* Peebles, *Practical of Spiritualism,* 73.

Ruinous prosperity

123 *sweeping from site to site at a stunning pace:* Black, *Petrolia.*

124 *it had too many new neighbors:* Boyle, *Derrick's Hand-Book*, 108.

125 *"loss rather than let you have it at that price!":* Cited in Henry, *Early and Later History of Petroleum*, 232.

126 *violence against Native Americans, Aboriginal Australians, and others:* Dunbar-Ortiz, *Indigenous Peoples' History.*

126 *basis of US authority over Indigenous lands:* Nick Estes, *Our History Is the Future*, (London and New York: Verso, 2019), 76.

127 *"a condition of bondage and serfdom":* Ida M. Tarbell, *The History of the Standard Oil Company* (New York: McClure, Phillips, 1904), 259.

127 *no church or monopoly to intervene:* Dochuk, *Anointed with Oil*, 47–49.

128 *spoke of his endeavors as "godlike":* Ron Chernow, *Titan: The Life of John D. Rockefeller, Sr.* (New York: Vintage, 2004), 153.

128 *"energy and perseverance" of the oil operators:* Samuel P. Irvin, *The Oil Bubble* (S. P. Irvin, 1868), 21.

129 *"according to the dictates of my conscience":* John T. Flynn, *God's Gold* (Rahway, NJ: Quinn and Boden, 1932), 401.

130 *in the name of small, independent producers:* B. M. Pietsch, "Lyman Stewart and Early Fundamentalism," *Church History* 82, no. 3 (September 2013): 623–24.

131 *come to dominate American Christianity:* Pew Research Center, "America's Changing Religious Landscape: The Changing Religious Composition of the U.S.," 2015, https://www.pewforum.org/2015/05/12/chapter-1-the

-changing-religious-composition-of-the-u-s/. Fundamentalism and evangelism are not identical; fundamentalists are a specific group urging return to strict, originalist interpretations of the Bible, while evangelism is a much broader description of "born-again" Christian groups that use charismatic preaching and individual revelations such as speaking in tongues. As movements, the two groups are connected by the economic and political structures established by Stewart and continued by later wealthy funders.

131 *the new political right that began in the 1950s:* Pietsch, "Lyman Stewart and Early Fundamentalism," 619–20; Dochuk, *Anointed with Oil*, 331.

133 *"than the passage of the most destructive engines of war":* "A Blessing and a Curse," *Major & Knapp Illustrated Monthly* (New York) 2, no. 4 (April 1, 1871): 2.

133 *"and all the things that are therein shall be burned up":* Henry Parry Liddon, *Sermons Preached before the University of Oxford: Chiefly during the Years 1863–1865* (Boston: E. P. Dutton, 1868), 49; "Petroleum, Old and New," *Merchants Magazine and Commercial Review* 47 (July 1862): 27.

134 *eventually lost everything drilling dry holes:* "A Pioneer Gone," *Titusville (PA) Herald*, August 24, 1959 (repr. from June 18, 1894), 5. Elizabeth (Libby) Lowe Watson divorced Jonathan in 1878, getting out in time to salvage a part of his fortune and purchase a fruit orchard in California. Spiritualist and reformist women of the era were fond of fruit orchards as a symbol of human labor's harmony with a benevolent nature, a sharp contrast to the ruthless extraction left behind in Petrolia. Watson enjoyed a happier fate than her former husband, leading the California Equal Suffrage Association as well as a Spiritualist church in San Francisco. See Ann Braude, *Radical Spirits: Spiritualism and Women's Rights in Nineteenth-Century America* (Bloomington: Indiana University Press, 2001).

135 *and papers reported that it gave 280 barrels in its early days:* "Discovery by the Spirit-Agency," *Golden Gate* 9, no. 18 (November 16 1889): 7.

God's gold

138 *every Protestant minister in the United States:* Quinn Slobodian, *Globalists: The End of Empire and the Birth of Neoliberalism* (Cambridge, MA: Harvard University Press, 2018), 18; Kim Phillips-Fein, *Invisible Hands: The Making of the Conservative Movement from the New Deal to Reagan* (New York: W. W. Norton, 2009).

139 *losing their humble savings to crooked schemes:* Edmund Morris, *Derrick and Drill, Or, An Insight into the Discovery, Development, and Present Condition and Future Prospects of Petroleum* (New York: J. Miller, 1865), 263.

139 *"and no one can tell whither":* Irvin, *Oil Bubble*, 35–38.

140 *shocks often also lost their minds:* Daniel Connelly, "Among the Bulls and the Bears," *Appleton's Journal* 10, no. 235 (September 20, 1873): 369–70.

141 *"there will soon be an advance in the price":* Peebles, *Practical of Spiritualism*, 48.

141 *opening Wall Street's first female-owned brokerage:* W. B. Northrop, "Mediumship as a Paying Business," *Annals of Psychic Science* 3, no. 6 (1906): 394; Amanda Frisken, *Victoria Woodhull's Sexual Revolution: Political Theater and the Popular Press in Nineteenth-Century America* (Philadelphia: University of Pennsylvania Press, 2012). Woodhull, after much slander and degradation by the popular press, reneged on her earlier writings about free love and women's rights, shifting to a much more conservative outlook after her presidential run was cut short by her arrest on trumped-up pornography charges. It should be noted that she was a eugenicist throughout her career, advocating varying degrees of reproductive limitations for people she viewed as "unfit." The politics of first-wave feminist eugenics don't map cleanly onto reproductive politics of the present day, as these feminists often claimed that women's full equality would bring about an end to the conditions that caused "degenerate" and unwanted offspring.

141 *"is, and always has been, a sort of maelstrom":* Connelly, "Among the Bulls and the Bears," 369.

Born in freedom

145 *global "mastery over land, sea, and air":* Gregory A. Waller, "The American Petroleum Institute Sponsored Motion Pictures in the Service of Public Relations," Marina Dahlquist and Patrick Vonderau, eds., *Petrocinema: Sponsored Film and the Oil Industry* (Bloomsbury Academic, 2021), 150.

146 *a century of unprecedented industrial power:* Elizabeth East, "Capitalist Organizing and Organizations: The Case of the American Petroleum Institute" (PhD diss., University of Tennessee, December 1, 2017), 124–30.

146 *"petroleum for the use of generations yet unborn":* Quoted in Dochuk, *Anointed with Oil*, 263.

146 *"treading on dangerous ground," warned one investor:* "Protests Made against Raising Fuel Oil Prices," *Boston Globe*, July 30, 1934; Roger Babson, "Warns against Price Boosts," *Arizona Republic*, September 6, 1937; Annelise Orleck, "'We Are That Mythical Thing Called the Public': Militant Housewives during the Great Depression," *Feminist Studies* 19, no. 1 (1993): 147–72.

147 *the "black and cruel demon" oil:* Upton Sinclair, *Oil!* (Pasadena, CA: published by the author, 1928), 146, 178, 526–27.

148 *"or to those who become its slaves":* Fritz Leiber, "The Black Gondolier," in *Over the Edge* (Sauk City, WI: Arkham House, 1964); republished in *The Black Gondolier and Other Stories* (New York: Open Road Media, 2014).

149 *oil as the lifeblood of a Christian, democratic nation:* East, "Capitalist Organizing"; "16,500 Dry Holes," *Life*, April 14, 1952, 109; Matthew T. Huber, *Lifeblood : Oil, Freedom, and the Forces of Capital* (Minneapolis: University of Minnesota Press, 2013).

149 *abundance was the master narrative of Cold War America:* "A.P.I. Public Relations Program Follows Decentralized Plan," *World Petroleum*, November 1947, 70–71; "Understand Rivalry," *Life*, September 29, 1947, 65.

150 *is a hidden origin of the world we have today:* Edward Teller, "Energy Patterns of the Future," in *Energy and Man: A Symposium* (New York: Appleton-Century-Crofts, 1960), 58; Benjamin Franta, "Early Oil Industry Knowledge of CO_2 and Global Warming," *Nature Climate Change* 8, no. 12 (December 2018): 1024–25, .

152 *a way of surviving and a treasured heritage:* Katelyn Ferral, "Inside the World of 'Small' Oil," *Allegheny Front*, November 13, 2015.

153 *bracing for a "mass abandonment":* Laura Legere and Anya Litvak, "Pennsylvania Faces New Wave of Abandoned Oil and Gas Wells," *U.S. News & World Report*, April 11, 2020, https://bit.ly/2xRZGhg.

153 *without worrying about where its profits went:* Christopher F. Jones, *Routes of Power: Energy and Modern America* (Cambridge, MA: Harvard University Press, 2016), 1–4.

154 *"covetous branch that thinks it's the tree":* Estes, *Our History Is the Future.*

154 *their land and knowledge back:* see Gina Gilio-Whitaker, *As Long as Grass Grows: The Indigenous Fight for Environmental Justice, from Colonization to Standing Rock* (Boston: Beacon Press, 2019).

155 *mutual good relations among these worlds:* Vanessa Watts, "Indigenous Place-Thought and Agency Amongst Humans and Non Humans (First Woman and Sky Woman Go On a European World Tour!)," *Decolonization: Indigeneity, Education & Society* 2, no. 1 (May 4, 2013).

155 *"transforms them into threats to our very existence":* Zoe Todd, "Fish, Kin and Hope: Tending to Water Violations in Amiskwaciwâskahikan and Treaty Six Territory," *Afterall: A Journal of Art, Context and Enquiry* 43 (March 2017): 102–7.

156 *"which said Nation might designate" as an apprentice:* Herrick, *Empire Oil*, 23.

156 *wells yielding a hundred barrels a day:* Randy A. John, *Who Is Andrew John?* (Allegany Territory of the Seneca Nation of Indians: RAJ Publications, 2021), 79–81; J. R. Jewell, US Indian Agent, "Report of New York Agency," in *Annual Report of the Commissioner of Indian Affairs to the Secretary of the Interior* (Washington, DC: US Government Printing Office, 1897), 207.

157 *prices to Fancher, Rockefeller, and their friends:* Hauptman, *Coming Full Circle*, 163–68.

157 *cabal had determined to simply take it from them anyway:* "Seneca Oil Co.," *United States Investor* 15, no. 24 (April 30, 1904): 25; Jewell, "Report of New York Agency," 203–10; Hauptman, *Coming Full Circle*, 163–68.

157 *The allotment bills failed:* John, *Who Is Andrew John?*, 84–96; Hauptman, *Coming Full Circle*, 163–68; David Freeman Hawke, *John D.: The Founding Father of the Rockefellers* (New York: Harper and Row, 1980), 135.

158 *leaving economic devastation in its wake:* Abrahm Lustgarten, "Navajo Generating Station Powers and Paralyzes the Western U.S.," ProPublica,

NOTES

June 16, 2015; Andrew Curley, "Taa' hwo' aji' t'eego: Sovereignty, Live-lihood, and Challenging Coal in the Navajo Nation" (PhD diss., Cornell University, 2016); Gilio-Whitaker, *As Long as Grass Grows*. Gilio-Whitaker discusses other examples of the dilemmas faced by Indigenous groups engaged in energy development.

158 *Corwin and Watt's film: Denying Access: NoDAPL to NoNAPL*, directed by Jason Corwin and Tami Watt (Seneca Media and Communications Center, 2020); Jason Corwin, interview with the author, July 2020.

160 *name is also one of claiming power:* Anthony Giacobbe, "Seneca Nation Final Report: Installation of a 1.5 MW Wind Turbine," Office of Scientific and Technical Information, Department of Energy, September 21, 2017, https://www.osti.gov/servlets/purl/1393481; Jason Corwin, interview with author.

160 *those hundreds of millions of acres:* Estes, *Our History Is the Future*. The United States signed on to the resolution in 2010, with the understanding that it is nonbinding, and little action has been taken on its recommendations. Dunbar-Ortiz traces a longer history of pan-Indigenous movements back to the Shawnee leader Tecumseh's strategy of unifying Native peoples from the Great Lakes to the Gulf of Mexico in the early nineteenth century (*Indigenous Peoples' History*, 84–86).

160 *"colonial economic modalities and mediums of exchange":* Andrew Curley, "Beyond Environmentalism: #NoDAPL as Assertion of Tribal Sovereignty," and Michelle L. Cook, "Striking at the Heart of Capital," both in *Standing with Standing Rock: Voices from the #NoDAPL Movement*, ed. Nick Estes and Jaskiran Dhillon (Minneapolis: University of Minnesota Press, 2019).

161 *against the logics of wealth extraction and white supremacy:* Martin Luther King Jr., *Where Do We Go from Here: Chaos or Community?* (New York: Harper and Rowe, 1967), 166; Martin Luther King Jr., *Why We Can't Wait* (1963; repr., New York: Penguin, 2000), 109–11.

162 *kinship as a "diplomatic strategy" can be a powerful thing:* Kim TallBear, "The US-Dakota War and Failed Settler Kinship," *Anthropology News* 57, no. 9 (September 2016); all quotations from TallBear except for Un Mundo Donde Quepan Muchos Mundos, a slogan of the Indigenous Mexican Zapatista movement.

163 *"perfect, than we ever dared to dream":* William Denton and Elizabeth M. Foote Denton, *The Soul of Things: Or, Psychometric Researches and Discoveries*, vol. 2 (Wellesley, MA: Mrs. EMF Denton, 1873), 3.

Assets from the rock

171 *"curious research and elaborate investigation":* DeWitt Clinton, "The Iroquois: Address Delivered before the New-York Historical Society, Dec. 6, 1811,"

318

in *The Life and Writings of DeWitt Clinton*, ed. William W. Campbell (New York: Baker and Scribner, 1849), 266.

171   *would one day arrest the water's descent:* Susan Q. Stranahan, *Susquehanna: River of Dreams* (Baltimore: Johns Hopkins University Press, 1993), 40–44.

173   *"likely can never be tested in any meaningful way":* Jay F. Custer, "A Postcolonial Perspective," in *Middle Atlantic Prehistory: Foundations and Practice*, ed. Heather A. Wholey and Carole L. Nash (Lanham, MD: Rowman and Littlefield, 2018), 344.

174   *obscured the complex pathways of Native survival:* Jean M. O'Brien, *Firsting and Lasting: Writing Indians Out of Existence in New England* (Minneapolis: University of Minnesota Press, 2010), xiii–xxiv; Lee Francis 4, Weshoyot Alvitre, and Will Fenton, *Ghost River: The Fall and Rise of the Conestoga* (Library Company of Philadelphia (2019), https://ghostriver.org/.

175   *annual consumption of a midsize city at the time:* Nicholas B. Wainwright, *History of the Philadelphia Electric Company, 1881–1961* (Philadelphia: Philadelphia Electric Company, 1961), 169; Jones, *Routes of Power*, 188. Jones uses the example of prosperous Lancaster, Pennsylvania, in 1917.

175   *unnecessary this amenity seemed to ordinary people:* Edison filed his light bulb patent in 1880; in 1912, 15.9 percent of dwellings had electric service. *Historical Statistics of the United States, Colonial Times to 1970* (1975), pt. 2, 827.

176   *took a lot of money and effort:* Walter R. Moulton, "A Model 'House Electric' in Baltimore," *Electrical Review* 68, no. 17 (April 22, 1916).

176   *"Domestic refrigeration is here to stay!":* Wainwright, *History of the Philadelphia Electric Company*, 196.

179   *"on the ground helpless under its knees":* "Pinchot Asks Help of Congressmen," *New York Times*, July 20, 1925.

179   *was a socialist scourge:* Naomi Oreskes, "The Fact of Uncertainty, the Uncertainty of Facts and the Cultural Resonance of Doubt," *Philosophical Transactions of the Royal Society A: Mathematical, Physical and Engineering Sciences* 373, no. 2055 (November 28, 2015): 2014.0455.

179   *couldn't take on debt without raising taxes:* Albert C. Ritchie, "Conowingo Reviewed," *Baltimore Sun*, November 4, 1926, 15.

The deluge

181   *"brightest promise lay in American engineering":* Joan Didion, "At the Dam," *The White Album* (New York: Farrar, Straus, and Giroux, 1990),199.

185   *only extended back about eight thousand years:* "The Antiquity of Man in America," *Scientific Monthly* 24, no. 5 (May 1927): 477–79; Edwin N. Wilmsen, "An Outline of Early Man Studies in the United States," *American Antiquity* 31, no. 2, pt. 1 (October 1965): 178–79.

185   *with few changes until the violent relocations of the modern era:* Richard J.

Dent Jr., "The Idea of the Past," in *Chesapeake Prehistory: Old Traditions, New Directions* (Springer Science and Business Media, 2007), 23–69.

185 *sold the human remains to collectors:* Stephenson and Ferguson, 1963, iv; Lisa Kraus and Jason Shellenhamer, "The Man Who Stole the Past: The Yinger Assault on the Hughes Site," February 1, 2019, Natural History Society of Maryland.

188 *"somewhat sorry and depressing":* William B. Marye, "Petroglyphs near Bald Friar," in *A Report of the Susquehanna River Expedition Sponsored in 1916 by the Museum of the American Indian Heye Foundation*, pt. III, ed. W. K. Moorehead (Andover, MA: Andover Press, 1938), 98.

190 *folklorist Lewis Spence, author of* Atlantis in America*:* Charles E. Orser, *Race and Practice in Archaeological Interpretation* (Philadelphia: University of Pennsylvania Press, 2004), 66–69.

190 *eleven thousand and possibly as far as a hundred thousand years:* Pre-Clovis sites (prior to 11,000 BCE) are an ongoing source of heated controversy; Kehoe simply states, "This is a research puzzle that continues to challenge archaeologists." Alice Beck Kehoe, *North America before the European Invasions* (New York: Routledge, 2017), 9–19. Paulette F.C. Steeves makes the case that a hundred-thousand-year horizon accords with Indigenous histories and should be acknowledged as part of decolonizing archaeology. Steeves, *The Indigenous Paleolithic of the Western Hemisphere* (Lincoln: University of Nebraska Press, 2021).

190 *thousands of years older than previous estimates:* Charlie Hall, interview; Paulette F.C. Steeves, *The Indigenous Paleolithic of the Western Hemisphere* (Lincoln: University of Nebraska Press, 2021).

191 *"the likenesses among men are far greater than their differences":* UNESCO, "The Race Question," *UNESCO and Its Programme* 3, no. 31 (Paris: UNESCO, 1950).

192 *relations that underpinned their existence as nations:* Estes, *Our History Is the Future*; Sebastián Gil-Riaño, "Re-locating Antiracist Science: The 1950 UNESCO Statement on Race and Economic Development in the Global South," *British Journal for the History of Science* 51, no. 2 (2018): 281–303.

192 *"we may need to agree to disagree":* Kim TallBear, "Decolonizing (≠ Reconciling): Science, Technology, and Indigenous Relations," MacLennan Lecture in the History of Science, University of King's College, 2020, https://www.youtube.com/watch?v=1-yVjSQ5ZPc&t=4550s.

193 *knowledge woven into the history of the place:* Sonya Atalay, "Diba Jimooyung—Telling Our Story: Colonization and Decolonization of Archaeological Practice from an Anishinaabe Perspective," in *Handbook of Postcolonial Archaeology*, ed. Jane Lydon and Uzma Z. Rizvi (London and New York: Routledge, 2016); Sonya Atalay, "Engaging Archaeology: Positivism, Objectivity, and Rigor in Activist Archeology," in *Transforming Archaeology: Activist Practices and Prospects*, ed. Sonya Atalay et al. (New York: Routledge, 2014).

Lake Perfidy

195 *"happen to have been found on Indian land":* Thomas King, *The Inconvenient Indian* (Minneapolis: University of Minnesota Press, 2012), 232.

195 *"a destroyer of nations":* Nick Estes, *Our History Is the Future* (New York: Verso, 2020), 181.

195 *landlords, speculators, and industrial-scale agriculture:* David P. Billington, Donald C. Jackson, and Martin V. Melosi, *The History of Large Federal Dams: Planning, Design, and Construction in the Era of Big Dams* (Denver, CO: US Department of the Interior, Bureau of Reclamation, 2005), 450–51; Donald Worster, *Rivers of Empire: Water, Aridity, and the Growth of the American West* (New York: Pantheon Books, 1985), 170–74; Edward Gillette, "Reclamation from the Viewpoint of the Settler," *Irrigation Age* 31, no. 8 (June 1916): 119–20.

197 *"henceforth doomed to slow decay":* US Congress, *Congressional Record* 35, no 2 (Washington, DC: US Government Printing Office, 1902), 1383–84.

197 *pulled from the endless ranks of the unemployed:* Jane Griffith, "Hoover Dam: Land, Labor, and Settler Colonial Cultural Production," *Cultural Studies ↔ Critical Methodologies* 17, no. 1 (February 1, 2017): 30–40.

198 *burned through the once-fertile soil of the Midwestern prairies:* Richard Lowitt, *The New Deal and the West* (Bloomington: Indiana University Press, 1984), 152.

199 *Manifest Destiny was quickly expanding its global scope:* US Department of the Interior, Bureau of Reclamation, "Grand Coulee Dam Statistics and Facts," https://www.usbr.gov/pn/grandcoulee/pubs/factsheet.pdf; Tom Steury, "Water to the Promised Land," *Washington State Magazine*, Fall 2013. The Columbia Basin Project left about one-third of its planned service area, over three hundred thousand acres, without water and reliant on deep aquifer wells; as of 2021, bond sales and state money have funded an expansion of the system to an additional eighty-five hundred acres.

199 *dammed, except for the Yellowstone:* David Ekbladh, "'Mr. TVA': Grass-Roots Development, David Lilienthal, and the Rise and Fall of the Tennessee Valley Authority as a Symbol for U.S. Overseas Development, 1933–1973," *Diplomatic History* 26, no. 3 (2002): 335–74; Marc Reisner, *Cadillac Desert* (Viking, 1986), 320; Richard White, *"It's Your Misfortune and None of My Own," A New History of the American West* (Norman, OK: University of Oklahoma Press, 1991), 402; Bruce Babbitt, "Dams Must Be Looked at Critically, with Eye toward Environment," *Wisconsin State Journal*, November 29, 1998, 3B; Patrick McCully, *Silenced Rivers: The Ecology and Politics of Large Dams* (London and Atlantic Highlands, NJ: Zed Books, 1996), 6.

201 *Seneca Nation newsletter describes it:* Paul C. Rosier, "'Modern America Desperately Needs to Listen': The Emerging Indian in an Age of Environ-

mental Crisis," *Journal of American History* 100, no. 3 (December 2013): 716-17; Laurence M. Hauptman, *In the Shadow of Kinzua: The Seneca Nation of Indians since World War II* (Syracuse, NY: Syracuse University Press, 2014), 74–75; Seneca-Iroquois National Museum and Dana Reijerkerk, Reclaiming Ohi:yo': Restoring the Altered Landscape of the Beautiful River (2018): https://scalar.usc.edu/works/ohiyo/index.

201 *Indian Self-Determination and Education Assistance Act:* Hauptman, *In the Shadow of Kinzua*, 32.

202 *build their own hydropower station:* Michael A. Kremer, "AIMing for the Dam in 1971: The Indian Occupation of the Winter Dam," McIntyre Library, University of Wisconsin–Eau Claire, 2007.

203 *"catastrophe in any other way than by expediting it":* Varsha Venkatasubramanian, "Dammed and Damned," *Current Affairs*, June 2020; Andreas Malm, *How to Blow Up a Pipeline* (New York: Verso, 2021).

203 *buried treasure to a thing cultivated in common:* Anodyne Lindstrom and Sara Hoff, "Investor-Owned Utilities Served 72% of U.S. Electricity Customers in 2017," US Energy Information Administration, 2019; James Bruggers, "A Legacy of the New Deal, Electric Cooperatives Struggle to Democratize and Make a Green Transition," *Inside Climate News*, February 28, 2021.

204 *"peace, cooperation, and justice":* Estes, *Our History Is the Future*, 3; Red Nation, "10 Point Program," https://therednation.org/10-point-program/; Red Nation, "Principles of Unity," https://therednation.org/about/.

Rock flows

206 *anxiety of civilizational succession:* Fred Rasmussen, "Raymond Thompson, 71, Brigadier General, Writer," *Baltimore Sun*, December 13, 1997.

210 *"maintain any trapping function":* James S. Pew et al., Petition for Rehearing of FERC's Order Issuing New License, April 19, 2021, 3.

211 *"insane at even the thought of a dam":* Nye, *America as Second Creation*, 254–58; McFee, *Encounters with the Archdruid*, 159.

211 *taxpayers should also get the dam:* Sebastien Malo, "Enviros sue FERC over re-licensing of Exelon's Conowingo dam," *Reuters*, June 18, 2021; David A. Berry, *Maryland's Lower Susquehanna River Valley: Where the River Meets the Bay* (Charleston, SC: Arcadia Publishing, 2009), 253.

211 *responsibility for the waterway:* Chief Irving Powless Jr., "Motion to Intervene of the Onondaga Nation," Onondaga Nation, December 13, 2013.

212 *"not the important part, I don't think":* Sid Jamieson, interview, January 22, 2021.

213 *Jamieson remarked at the opening of the exhibit:* Quoted in Lutz, "Petroglyphs Find a Home."

NOTES

A tale which must never be told

218 *his colleagues to call him "the Greek":* Eyal Amiran, "George Herriman's Black Sentence: The Legibility of Race in 'Krazy Kat,'" *Mosaic: An Interdisciplinary Critical Journal* 33, no. 3 (2000), 62–64; Michael Tisserand, *Krazy: George Herriman, a Life in Black and White* (New York: HarperCollins, 2018).

219 *both a cat joke and a reference to slave spirituals:* Chris Ware argues for this interpretation, that *Krazy* is racially coded, in "To Walk in Beauty," *New York Review*, January 29, 2017, though other comics scholars disagree or feel the racial dynamics of the strip are more unstable and multivalent.

219 *"and blown away by the wind":* Eric Gary Anderson, *American Indian Literature and the Southwest: Contexts and Dispositions* (Austin: University of Texas Press, 1999), 169–74, 183.

219 *projecting their own expectations about gender roles:* Gabrielle Bellot, "The Gender Fluidity of Krazy Kat," *New Yorker*, January 19, 2017. I don't use the singular pronoun *they* for Krazy because Herriman didn't use it, and the lack of a widely accepted nonbinary gender category in the US mainstream is part of the structure of the strip's humor. Comics artist Matthew New points out the "eye of the beholder" mutability of Krazy's pronouns in a blog post, "Shifting Backgrounds: Identity in *Krazy Kat*," April 2018, http://mathew-new.squarespace.com/new-blog-4/2018/3/24/fluid-sands -identity-in-krazy-kat.

220 *Native peoples whose worlds were invaded:* Joseph R. Aguilar, "Asserting Sovereignty: An Indigenous Archaeology of the Pueblo Revolt Period at Tunyo, San Ildefonso Pueblo, New Mexico," PhD Dissertation (Philadelphia: University of Pennsylvania, 2019), 14.

221 *often on display in the Southwest:* Philip J. Deloria, *Indians in Unexpected Places* (Lawrence: University Press of Kansas, 2004), 233–35.

221 *control over that land:* James T. Dennison, "Scratches Under the Surface of Mesa Verde," *Mesa Verde Notes* 4:2 (1933); J. Walter Fewkes, "Ancient Remains in Colorado," *Scientific American* (May 23, 1920): 609; Krista Langlois, "Indigenous knowledge helps untangle the mystery of Mesa Verde," *High Country News*, Oct. 2, 2017.

222 *"the primitive manner of their ancestors":* Anthony Shelton, "The Imaginary Southwest: Commodity Disavowal," in *Les cultures à l'œuvre: Rencontres en art*, ed. Michèle Coquet, Brigitte Derlon, and Monique Jeudy-Ballini (Paris: Éditions de la MSH, 2005), 76–80; Michelle McGeough, "Indigenous Curatorial Practices and Methodologies," *Wicazo Sa Review* 27, no. 1 (2012): 15; "Notes on Current Art: Indian Paintings in the Exhibition of the Independents," *New York Times*, March 14, 1920.

222 *or imitations purchased from catalogs:* Elizabeth Hutchinson, *The Indian Craze: Primitivism, Modernism, and Transculturation in American Art, 1890–1915* (Durham, NC: Duke University Press, 2009).

323

222 *living on the land were outlawed:* Marian Naranjo interviewed by Austin Fisher, "Ceremony in the Atomic Age," *Rio Grande Sun,* July 27, 2019.

223 *detonated over the Southwest between 1945 and 1962:* Joseph Masco, *The Nuclear Borderlands: The Manhattan Project in Post–Cold War New Mexico* (Princeton, NJ: Princeton University Press, 2006), 18.

223 *contaminates homes, water, livestock, and sacred sites:* see Gabrielle Hecht, *Being Nuclear: Africans and the Global Uranium Trade* (Cambridge: MIT Press, 2014).

227 *customs of a supposedly vanishing past:* Randall C. Davis, "'The Path toward Civilization': Sociocultural Evolution and the Delight Makers," *American Literary Realism, 1870–1910* 27, no. 2 (1995): 37–52.

227 *imbued with "real" Indigenous meaning:* Tessie Naranjo, "Social Change and Pottery Making at Santa Clara Pueblo" (PhD diss., University of New Mexico, 1992); Dwight P. Lanmon and Francis Harlow, "The Pottery of Acoma Pueblo (c. 1840–Present)," *American Indian Art Magazine* (2012).

228 *to promote their preferred styles:* Shelton, "The Imaginary Southwest," 75–97.

228 *version of a productive activity:* Richard O. Clemmer, "The Leisure Class versus the Tourists: The Hidden Struggle in the Collecting of Pueblo Pottery at the Turn of the Twentieth Century," *History & Anthropology* 19, no. 3 (September 2008): 187–207.

228 *decorative perfection of museums:* Tessie Naranjo, "Pottery Making in a Changing World," *Expedition Magazine*, 1994; Naranjo, "Social Change and Pottery-Making."

230 *oil, and other mineral treasures to white prospectors:* The Diné histories in this and the preceding paragraph are drawn from Traci Brynne Voyles, *Wastelanding: Legacies of Uranium Mining in Navajo Country* (Minneapolis: University of Minnesota Press, 2015).

230 *Washington, where the bill was struck down:* Donald L. Fixico, *The Invasion of Indian Country in the Twentieth Century: American Capitalism and Tribal Natural Resources* (Niwot: University Press of Colorado, 1998), 63–70; Dunbar-Ortiz, *Indigenous People's History*, 171.

231 *really is dangerously polluted:* Voyles, *Wastelanding*, 9-10

232 *scientists and soldiers to Los Alamos:* This and subsequent quotes from Church cited in Shelley Armitage, "Shared and Shifting Land(Scapes): Making Memoir and Personal Ecology in the Pajarito Journals of Peggy Pond Church," *Frontiers: A Journal of Women Studies* 27, no. 3 (2006): 111–39.

233 *imagined Indigenous timelessness:* Jon Hunner, *Inventing Los Alamos: The Growth of an Atomic Community* (Norman: University of Oklahoma Press, 2007), 30; Peter B. Hales, *Atomic Spaces: Living on the Manhattan Project* (Urbana: University of Illinois Press, 1997), 208.

233 *"and I love to watch her":* Hales, *Atomic Spaces*, 207–8.

NOTES

Collecting Los Alamos

235 *a bursting dam, or the detonation of a nuclear bomb:* Francis H. Harlow, *Adventures in Physics and Pueblo Pottery* (Santa Fe: Museum of New Mexico Press, 2016). Further dates, life events, and quotations from Harlow are drawn from this memoir unless otherwise noted.

236 *rained down upon nearby inhabited islands:* Thomas Kunkle and Byron Ristvet, "Castle Bravo: Fifty Years of Legend and Lore: A Guide to Off-Site Radiation Exposures" (Kirtland AFB, New Mexico: Defense Threat Reduction Agency, 2013), 52.

237 *helicopters for "American Indian tribes and chiefs":* Katie Lange, "Why Army Helicopters Have Native American Names," Inside DOD, November 29, 2019, https://www.defense.gov/Explore/Inside-DOD/Blog/article/2052989/why-army-helicopters-have-native-american-names/.

237 *today—if they can get in:* Alfonso Ortiz, *The Tewa World: Space, Time, Being, and Becoming in a Pueblo Society* (Chicago: University of Chicago Press, 1971); Masco, *Nuclear Borderlands*, 119–22.

238 *together under the name Pueblos:* Dunbar-Ortiz, *Indigenous People's History*, 125; Samuel Duwe, *Tewa Worlds: An Archaeological History of Being and Becoming in the Pueblo Southwest* (Tucson: University of Arizona Press, 2020).

238 *bringing back forbidden traditions:* Eric A. Powell, "The First American Revolution," *Archaeology* (March/April 2017); "Seven Generations of Red Power in New Mexico," Albuquerque Museum, Cultural Services Department, City of Albuquerque, curated by Nick Estes and Rebecca Prinster.

238 *and negotiated a surrender:* Aguilar, "Asserting Sovereignty," 88.

241 *"We had families, we had to pay bills":* Peter Malmgren and Kay Matthews, *Los Alamos Revisited: A Workers' History* (Wink Books, 2017), 149.

241 *stopped a Los Alamos project in its tracks:* Masco, *Nuclear Borderlands*, 114, 134–35.

242 *"forever held by our children":* Centers for Disease Control and Prevention, "LAHDRA: Los Alamos Historical Document Retrieval and Assessment Project," 2010, https://wwwn.cdc.gov/LAHDRA/.

"And the other face was terrible"

243 *besides that it was bad:* All quotes from Floy Agnes Naranjo Lee, unless otherwise indicated, are drawn from her 2017 oral history interview with Cindy Kelly of the Atomic Heritage Foundation, at which she was accompanied by her daughter, Patricia Reifel (https://www.manhattanproject voices.org/oral-histories/floy-agnes-lees-interview). Career and life events are drawn from this interview, other cited sources, and personal correspondence with Patricia Reifel. Lee passed away in 2018.

243 *scientific censorship persisted long after that:* Janet Farrell Brodie, "Radiation

Secrecy and Censorship after Hiroshima and Nagasaki," *Journal of Social History* 48, no. 4 (2015): 842–64.

245 *and that heart disease ran in the family:* Alex Wellerstein, "The Demon Core," *New Yorker*, May 21, 2016; Philip L. Fradkin, *Fallout: An American Nuclear Tragedy* (1989; repr., Boulder, CO: Johnson Books, 2004), 90–91. It should be noted that the first fatal radiation incident at Los Alamos had occurred exactly nine months earlier, on August 21, 1945, when physicist Harry Daghlian Jr. conducted a criticality experiment with the same plutonium core, dubbed the "demon core" after it also killed Slotin. In her oral history interview, Lee did not mention knowledge of the Daghlian incident; laboratory officials told the press that Daghlian died from "burns in an industrial accident," making no mention of radiation in a continuation of wartime censorship.

245 *military investment in a new superweapon:* Edward Teller, *The Legacy of Hiroshima* (Garden City, NY: Doubleday, 1962), 22.

245 *as President Truman put it, "all those kids":* Truman quoted in the diary of Henry A. Wallace, 10 August 1945, Wallace Papers, University of Iowa, quoted in Michael J. Hogan, ed., *Hiroshima in History and Memory* (Cambridge: Cambridge University Press, 1996), 73.

245 *"fiddling with politics will save our souls":* "Edward Teller's Reply to Szilard's Request, July 4, 1945," https://www.atomicarchive.com/resources/documents/manhattan-project/teller-petition-response.html.

246 *that the damage can be contained:* This imagery drawn from Aziz Rana, who traces how the ideal of white freedom has been constituted by racial and economic subjugation throughout US history. Aziz Rana, *The Two Faces of American Freedom* (Cambridge, MA: Harvard University Press, 2010).

247 *"hitherto inaccessible intellectual and moral energies":* Walter Lippmann, "International Control of Atomic Energy," in *One World or None*, ed. Dexter Masters and Katharine Way (New York: McGraw-Hill, 1946), 180.

248 *"proud to be a trailblazer":* Patricia Reifel, email correspondence, January 24, 2021.

248 *nearby parents to shape school policies:* John R. Gram and Theodore Jojola, *Education at the Edge of Empire: Negotiating Pueblo Identity in New Mexico's Indian Boarding Schools* (Seattle: University of Washington Press, 2015).

249 *reconquest that persisted until 2018:* Jennifer Marley, "A Brief History of Indian Market," *The Red Nation*, August 21, 2021; Paula Gunn Allen, "The Autobiography of a Confluence," in *I Tell You Now: Autobiographical Essays by Native American Writers*, ed. Arnold Krupat and Brian Swann (Lincoln: University of Nebraska Press, 1987), 145, 153.

250 *willing to volunteer for wartime medical research:* Advisory Committee on Human Radiation Experiments, "Chapter 5: The Manhattan District Experiments," *DOE Openness: Human Radiation Experiments* (Washington, DC, 1995); Barton C. Hacker, *The Dragon's Tail: Radiation Safety in the*

Manhattan Project, 1942–1946 (Berkeley: University of California Press, 1987), 63–64.

250 *would the leukocyte count tell the tale:* Hacker, *Dragon's Tail*, 29, 51.

251 *two "perfectly normal children":* *The Nature of Radioactive Fallout and Its Effects on Man: Hearings before the Special Subcommittee on Radiation of the Joint Committee on Atomic Energy . . .* , 85th Cong., 1st sess. (Washington, DC: Government Printing Office, 1957), 103–4.

251 *"concocted in the minds of weak malingerers":* Quoted in Stewart Udall, *The Myths of August: A Personal Exploration of Our Tragic Cold War Affair with the Atom* (New Brunswick: Rutgers University Press, 1994), 243.

251 *though the land remained radioactive for decades:* Zohl De Ishtar, "Poisoned Lives, Contaminated Lands: Marshall Islanders Are Paying a High Price for the United States Nuclear Arsenal," *Seattle Journal for Social Justice* 2, no.1(2003), 288–91.

252 *"received less radiation than they actually did":* *Nature of Radioactive Fallout*, 103; Fradkin, *Fallout*, 90.

252 *"precipitated" by radiation damage:* Louis H. Hempelmann, Clarence C. Lushbaugh, and George L. Voelz, "What Has Happened to the Survivors of the Los Alamos Nuclear Accidents?," Conference for Radiation Accident Preparedness, Oak Ridge, TN, October 19–20, 1979, https://www.orau.org/ptp/pdf/accidentsurvivorslanl.pdf.

253 *national identities would fade away:* James B. LaGrand, *Indian Metropolis: Native Americans in Chicago, 1945–75* (Urbana: University of Illinois Press, 2002), 113.

253 *"involvement with research was nearly all-consuming":* Patricia Reifel, email correspondence, January 27, 2021.

254 *hiking with Al Graves and his wife, Elizabeth:* Hugh Gusterson, *People of the Bomb: Portraits of America's Nuclear Complex* (Minneapolis: University of Minnesota Press, 2004); Lee, Atomic Heritage Foundation interview.

254 *"poor housekeeping" of radioactive materials:* Sam Roe and Jeremy Manier, "The Bomb's Chicago Fallout," *Chicago Tribune*, Feb. 2, 2001.

254 *"let alone count—blood cells under the microscope":* Austin Brues, "Those Early Days as We Remember Them (Part I)—Met Lab and Argonne's Early History," https://www.ne.anl.gov/About/early-history-of-argonne/1/.

254 *desert was a barren and disposable wasteland:* "Clyde P. Stroud," Biographical Questionnaire for New Mexicans in the Armed Forces, War Records Library, Museum of New Mexico, Historical Society of New Mexico; Clyde P. Stroud, "A Survey of the Insects of White Sands National Monument, Tularosa Basin, New Mexico," *American Midland Naturalist* 44, no. 3 (November 1950): 659–77.

255 *low-intensity neutrons to lab animals:* C. R. Fellhauer, G. A. Garlock, and F. R. Clark, "Decontamination and Dismantlement of the JANUS Reactor," Argonne National Laboratory Decontamination and Decommissioning Program, 1997, 3.

255 *could not be named when it struck among the ranks:* Robert Sokal, "A Sketch

of My Scientific Autobiography," *Human Biology* 84, no. 5 (October 2012): 495; "Administration and Editorial," in Austin M. Brues, ed., *Argonne National Laboratory Division of Biological and Medical Research Quarterly Report*, August, September, and October 1952, 5.

255 *American Association for Cancer Research in 1954:* AACR, "In Memoriam," https://www.aacr.org/professionals/membership/in-memoriam/stroud -lee-agnes-obituary/.

256 *"glassware and care for the lab mice and rats":* Reifel, email correspondence, January 24, 2021.

257 *"Indians to go on after a bachelor's":* Roger L. Geiger explains that "subsidized graduate study was the rule across American higher education," covering more than 80 percent of PhD students during the 1960s. Geiger, *American Higher Education since World War II: A History* (Princeton, NJ: Princeton University Press, 2019), 112–15.

257 *abnormal chromosomes from tissue samples:* "Clinical Laboratory Automation," *Computer* (September/October, 1971): 25-26; A. M. Brues, et al., "Computer analysis of chromosomes of the Chinese hamster," *Argonne National Laboratory Reports* (1968): 31–32.

258 *resign as the chair of chemistry at Caltech:* Derek A. Davenport, "Letters to F. J. Allen: An Informal Portrait of Linus Pauling," *Journal of Chemical Education* 73, no. 1 (January 1996): 21.

258 *"breakthrough in atomic-power development":* "The Clean Bomb," *Time*, July 8, 1957.

259 *"I think the public ought to know":* "Oral History of Dr. John W. Gofman, M.D., Ph.D., Interviewed by Loretta Hefner and Karoline Gourley, December 20, 1994," US Department of Energy, Office of Human Radiation Experiments, June 1995, https://ehss.energy.gov/ohre/roadmap /histories/0457/0457toc.html#Attitudes.

259 *never adjusted to solve this problem:* Pennsylvania insurance commissioner Herbert S. Denenberg quoted in Falk, *Global Fission*, 63.

259 *a pattern that would repeat across the country:* Gordon E. Dean, *Report on the Atom: What You Should Know about the Atomic Energy Program of the United States* (New York: Knopf, 1953), 68; Arjun Makhijani, Stephen I. Schwartz, and William J. Weida, "Nuclear Waste Management and Environmental Remediation," in *Atomic Audit: The Costs and Consequences of U.S. Nuclear Weapons since 1940*, ed. Stephen I. Schwartz (Washington, DC: Brookings Institution Press, 1998), 356; Thomas Raymond Wellock, *Critical Masses: Opposition to Nuclear Power in California, 1958–1978* (Madison: University of Wisconsin Press, 1998).

260 *how much risk, and for whom, is a political question:* Hacker, *Dragon's Tail*, 156–58; Barton C. Hacker, *Elements of Controversy: The Atomic Energy Commission and Radiation Safety in Nuclear Weapons Testing, 1947–1974* (Berkeley: University of California Press, 1994), 227.

262 *within an atomized universe of risk:* Jessie Wright-Mendoza, "How Insur-

ance Companies Used Bad Science to Discriminate," *JSTOR Daily*, September 17, 2018, https://daily.jstor.org/how-insurance-companies -used-bad-science-to-discriminate/; Mary L. Heen, "Ending Jim Crow Life Insurance Rates," *Northwestern Journal of Law & Social Policy* 4, no. 2 (2009); Megan J. Wolff, "The Myth of the Actuary: Life Insurance and Frederick L. Hoffman's Race Traits and Tendencies of the American Negro," *Public Health Reports* 121, no. 1 (January–February 2006): 84–91.

262 *most people are not free to choose:* Anne Warhover, "Zip Code Overrides DNA Code When It Comes to a Healthy Community," *Health Affairs*, January 30, 2014; Mark R. Cullen, Clint Cummins, and Victor R. Fuchs, "Geographic and Racial Variation in Premature Mortality in the U.S.: Analyzing the Disparities," *PLOS*, 2012,.

262 *to injured workers or their families:* Hacker, *Dragon's Tail*, 62.

263 *"part in decisions about world affairs":* Quoted in Paul Rubinson, *Rethinking the American Antinuclear Movement* (London: Taylor and Francis, 2018), 28.

263 *"give it back to the Indians":* Henry W. Newson, "Memorandum to Norris Bradbury, December 17, 1945, Possible Difficulties in Naval Tests, Los Alamos, New Mexico: Los Alamos National Laboratory," DOE/CIC 120851, quoted in Jonathan Weisgall, *Operation Crossroads: The Atomic Tests at Bikini Atoll* (Annapolis, MD: Naval Institute Press, 1994); Masco, *Nuclear Borderlands*, 161.

263 *bulwark against nuclear dread:* Joseph Masco, "Engineering the Future as Nuclear Ruin," *Imperial Debris: On Ruins and Ruination*, edited by Ann Laura Stoler (Durham: Duke University Press, 2013), 252–54; Jacqueline Foertsch, *Reckoning Day: Race, Place, and the Atom Bomb in Postwar America* (Nashville: Vanderbilt University Press, 2013), 2–3; "Fallout and Disarmament: A Debate between Linus Pauling and Edward Teller," *Daedalus* 87, no. 2 (1958): 147–63; Ralph E. Lapp, *The New Priesthood: The Scientific Elite and the Uses of Power* (New York: Harper and Row, 1965), 36.

264 *"They're going to fight to preserve the empire":* Nature of Radioactive Fallout, 1121; Hacker, *Elements of Controversy*, 277–78.

264 *"is the peace based on force":* Vincent J. Intondi, *African Americans against the Bomb: Nuclear Weapons, Colonialism, and the Black Freedom Movement* (Stanford, CA: Stanford University Press, 2015), 11–14.

"Only justice can stop a curse"

266 *deaths of 4,390 horses, cows, and sheep:* Anne Tucker, *Crimes and Splendors: The Desert Cantos of Richard Misrach* (New York: Little, Brown, 1996), 98. Photographer Richard Misrach's "Desert Cantos" series includes disturbing images taken in the 1980s of Nevada animal-dumping sites.

266 *had their best interests at heart:* Voyles, *Wastelanding*, 156; Masco, *Nuclear*

Borderlands, 42; Terrence R. Fehner and F. G. Gosling, *Atmospheric Nuclear Weapons Testing, 1951–1963* (US Department of Energy, 2006).

267   *protest camp outside the Nevada Test Site:* Rebecca Solnit, *Savage Dreams: A Journey into the Hidden Wars of the American West* (San Francisco: Sierra Club Books, 1994), 118.

267   *"non-cooperation, whatever is required":* Intondi, *African Americans against the Bomb*, 42–49.

268   *the formation of modern environmentalism:* Ammon Hennacy, *The Book of Ammon: The Autobiography of a Unique American Rebel* (self-pub., 1965), 299, 41, 80–83, 94; Brian D. Haley, "Ammon Hennacy and the Hopi Traditionalist Movement: Roots of the Counterculture's Favorite Indians," *Journal of the Southwest* 58, no. 1 (2016): 135–88. While the US counterculture heavily romanticized Native people, Paul Rosier emphasizes that some Native leaders and intellectuals in the 1950s and 60s actively promoted their own claims as "the first environmentalists," shaping and mobilizing the environmental movement as an ally.

269   *if he didn't secure a test ban:* Paul Rubinson, "'Crucified on a Cross of Atoms': Scientists, Politics, and the Test Ban Treaty," *Diplomatic History* 35, no. 2 (April 2011): 302; Fehner and Gosling, *Atmospheric Nuclear Weapons Testing*, 157; Rubinson, *Rethinking the American Antinuclear Movement*, 43–44, 76; Lawrence S. Wittner, "The Power of Protest," *Bulletin of the Atomic Scientists* 60, no. 4 (July 2004): 20–26.

269   *meltdown at the Three Mile Island plant in Pennsylvania:* J. Samuel Walker, *Three Mile Island: A Nuclear Crisis in Historical Perspective* (Berkeley: University of California Press, 2004), 6–10.

269   *"leaving machines and buildings undamaged":* *U.S. News & World Report*, cited in Sherri L. Wasserman, *The Neutron Bomb Controversy: A Study in Alliance Politics* (Westport, CT: Praeger, 1983), 22.

269   *cutting $140 billion from social programs:* Intondi, *African Americans against the Bomb*, 93.

270   *"homophobic, male-dominated, and class-bound":* Barbara Smith, "Feminist Writers Confront the Nuclear Abyss," in *Exposing Nuclear Phallacies*, ed. Diana E. H. Russell (New York: Pergamon Press, 1989).

271   *to speak about racial and economic justice:* Intondi, *African Americans against the Bomb*, 100–105.

271   *uneasy common ground in nuclear apocalypse:* Ronald Reagan, "Address before a Joint Session of the Congress on the State of the Union," January 25, 1984, USCB American Presidency Project, www.presidency.ucsb.edu/ws?pid=40205.

273   *which derisive legend one consults:* Lewis Nordyke, "They're Finding Fortune in the Hills," *Saturday Evening Post*, August 23, 1952, 80; Voyles, *Wastelanding*, 87-89, 91–94.

273   *the AEC chose to study them:* Ibid., 55–88.

273   *economies and female-headed households:* Ibid., 124–32.

275   *"I got another calling in my life":* Interview with Rosemary Lynch, June 8,

2004, Las Vegas, Nevada, conducted by Suzanne Becker, Nevada Test Site Oral History Project, University of Nevada, Las Vegas.

275 *God had tested the faithful since biblical times:* Ken Butigan, *Pilgrimage through a Burning World: Spiritual Practice and Nonviolent Protest at the Nevada Test Site* (Albany: SUNY Press, 2012).

276 *at age thirty-seven:* Joe Sanchez, "The Western Shoshone: Following Earth Mother's Instructions," *Race, Poverty & the Environment* 3, no. 3 (1992): 10–19; J. A. Fishel, "United States Called to Task on Indigenous Rights: The Western Shoshone Struggle and Success at the International Level," *American Indian Law Review* 31, no. 2 (2006): 625–28; Interview with Patricia George and Virginia Sanchez, September 11, 2004, Ely, Nevada, conducted by Mary Palevsky, Nevada Test Site Oral History Project, University of Nevada, Las Vegas; Becky Lemon, "Bellecourt Seeks Election Year Alternatives," *Native Nevadan*, April 1988, 5; "Seven Generations of Red Power in New Mexico," Albuquerque Museum.

276 *"a question of genocide":* "Short Notes," *Akwesasne Notes*, October 1, 1980; Winona LaDuke, "Conference at Mount Taylor," *Akwesasne Notes*, May 31, 1979; Voyles, *Wastelanding*, 177–81.

277 *"free ourselves from the enemy":* Tom Barry, "Land Rights, Not Uranium Mines," *Akwesasne Notes*, July 1, 1979

277 *in monitoring and remediation:* Perry H. Charley, personal correspondence, April 2019.

279 *"forced to serve a national interest":* Simon Ortiz, "Fight Back: Uranium Mining in the Grants Mineral Belt," *Race, Poverty & the Environment* 5, no. 3/4 (1995): 361.

Our energized age

281 *"our mechanized and energized age":* The 1957–58 testimony of Jones and other experts was later echoed in the mad rationality of strategist Herman Kahn's *On Thermonuclear War*, a notorious 1960 study that meticulously calculated the death, environmental devastation, and generational burden of disease resulting from various conflict scenarios.

283 *uranium mining to waste disposal:* Stephanie A. Malin, *The Price of Nuclear Power: Uranium Communities and Environmental Justice* (New Brunswick, NJ: Rutgers University Press, 2015).

283 *America's third-poorest state:* Viarrial public testimony quoted in Masco, *Nuclear Borderlands*, 155; Claire Provost, "Atomic City, USA: How Once-Secret Los Alamos Became a Millionaire's Enclave," *Guardian*, November 1, 2016; Trip Jennings, "Census: Los Alamos Wealthiest County in the West," *Santa Fe New Mexican*, April 12, 2011.

284 *"what is in our systems":* Malmgren and Matthews, *Los Alamos Revisited*, 136–39.

284 *"more important than human life"*: Ibid., 153.

284 *San Ildefonso, Cochiti, and Jemez:* Masco, *Nuclear Borderlands,* 114.

285 *increasingly common mode of life:* Interview with George and Sanchez; US Senate, *Hearing of the Committee on Health, Education, Labor, and Pensions, One Hundred Tenth Congress,* printed for the use of the Committee on Health, Education, Labor, and Pensions, October 23, 2007.

286 *distinctive traditions and knowledge systems:* Mallery Quetawki, "Indigenous Ways of Knowing and Art as Scientific Translation for Native American Communities Affected by Abandoned Uranium Mines," *Sustain* 40 (2019) 35.

286 *Arizona, set of the movie* Bombshell: Craig Yoe, ed., Krazy Kat *& the Art of George Herriman: A Celebration* (New York: Abrams ComicArts, 2011), 43, 106–7.

287 *violent affections and denials:* Amiran, "George Herriman's Black Sentence," 57.

287 *"which must never be told, and yet which everyone knows":* Krazy Kat, *Los Angeles Examiner,* May 5, 1918, February 11, 1917.

287 *"destructive and uncompassionate and deceptive":* Ortiz, *Woven Stone,* 361.

To bear away the treasure

290 *"easy Credulity of what they so earnestly wished might be true":* Benjamin Franklin, *The Writings of Benjamin Franklin, Volume II: 1722–1750,* ed. Albert Henry Smith (New York: Macmillan, 1905), 130–31.

290 *"close of his life that he gets free from debt":* "Rev. John Todd's Address Delivered before the Agricultural Society at Northampton," *New England Farmer and Gardener's Journal* 14, no. 21 (December 2, 1835): 162.

291 *white neighbors hoped to profit:* George Alexander Emery, *Ancient City of Gorgeana and Modern Town of York, Maine* (York, ME: Courant Steam Job Print, 1894), 196–202.

293 *today working toward liberatory futures:* adrienne maree brown and Walidah Imarisha, eds., *Octavia's Brood: Science Fiction Stories from Social Justice Movements* (Oakland: AK Press, 2015).

294 *danger to "people and the land and their continuance":* Ortiz, "Fight Back," 15.

294 *"final ceremonial sand painting":* Leslie Marmon Silko, *Ceremony* (New York: Penguin, 1986), 246–47; Leslie Marmon Silko, *Yellow Woman and a Beauty of the Spirit* (New York: Simon and Schuster, 1996), 44.

296 *"toward continually renewed danger":* Cameron Hu, "'A Jungle That Is Continually Encroaching': The Time of Disaster Management," *Environment and Planning D: Society and Space* 36, no. 1 (February 2018), 96.

Image Credits

147 University of Southern California Libraries and the California Historical Society.

150 Library of Congress.

151 Library of Congress.

170 John Wesley Powell, *Tenth Annual Report of the Bureau of Ethnology to the Secretary of the Smithsonian Institution* (Washington, DC: Government Printing Office, 1893).

178 Wouter Cool, 1936.

182 *Grandest Century in the World's History* (Philadelphia: National Publishing, 1900), Wikimedia Commons.

182 Ron Shawley, Wikimedia Commons.

196 Udo J. Keppler, "The Dummy Homesteader, or the Winning of the West," *Puck*, November 24, 1909, Library of Congress.

206 *Baltimore Sun*, March 26, 1950. Permission from Baltimore Sun Media. All rights reserved.

207 *Baltimore Sun*, September 21, 1960. Permission from Baltimore Sun Media. All rights reserved.

209 Paul Hutchins for the *Baltimore Sun*, July 19, 1973. Permission from Baltimore Sun Media. All rights reserved.

218 From *Krazy Kat & the Art of George Herriman* by Craig Yoe. Compilation copyright © 2011 Craig Yoe. Art courtesy of Chriss Wrenn. Used by permission of Abrams Comic Arts, an imprint of Abrams, New York. All rights reserved.

226 © 1935 King Features Syndicate Inc.

229 Photo by Burton Frasher. Courtesy of Frashers Fotos Collection/HJG and the Pomona Public Library, Pomona, California.

234 National Security Research Center.

240 Adam Martinez, Los Alamos History Museum.

244 Los Alamos National Laboratory, Paul Mullin Papers, New York Public Library.

252 © 1937 King Features Syndicate Inc.

256 National Security Research Center.

261 © 1944 King Features Syndicate Inc.

268 Library of Congress.

274 © King Features Syndicate Inc.

INDEX

mounds. *See also* earthworks;
   Grave Creek Mound
   contemporary Native literature
     on meaning of, 80–81
   lost-race theory on, 1, 11, 13, 16,
     25, 27, 28–34, 100
   Native preservation of history of,
     27–28
   Native relationship with place
     and, 28
   popular literature on meaning
     of, 31–34
   slave labor in excavation of, 72–74
Mount Taylor, uranium mining
   protests at, 272, 276–77
Mount Taylor Alliance, 276–77,
   286
*Muzzeniegun, The, or Literary
   Voyager* (Henry and Jane
   Schoolcraft), 50–52, 53

Naranjo, Marian, 222, 242
Naranjo, Santiago, 230
Naranjo, Tessie, 227, 228, 239
National Electric Light
   Association (NELA), 179
national identity
   folklore and, 40–41
   ruins related to feelings of, 20
Native activists. *See* activists
Native arts
   demands of white marketplace
     on, 222–23, 225
   popular fascination with, 222
Native culture
   preservation of history in spoken
     and written tradition in,
     27–28
   relationship with place in, 28
   stone inscriptions in, 42

Native nations. *See specific nations*
Native people
   antinuclear movement and,
     271–72, 275–77
   as archaeologists, 28, 194
   dam construction on land of,
     195–204
   European renaming of places of,
     171–72
   oil pipeline protests by, 153–54,
     158–59, 160
   as original Southwest occupants,
     220, 221
   race science research using skulls
     of, 48–49, 306
   racial hierarchies in spirit world
     and, 106–7
   relationships between Black
     communities and, 74
   sovereignty struggles of, 112,
     114, 153–54, 159, 199–200,
     202, 211
   uranium mining jobs and, 273,
     276, 278, 279
   uranium mining protests by, 8,
     265, 272–74, 276–77
   use of term, 10
   white artists' portrayal of, 222
   white supremacist racial
     hierarchies on abilities of,
     28–31
Navajo Nation (Diné), 219, 240
   antinuclear movement and, 276,
     277
   artists' engagement with culture
     of, 220–21
   cartoonist Herriman's portrayal
     of, 219–20, 286
   coal-burning power plant and,
     158

About the Author

Alicia Puglionesi is a writer and historian. She earned a PhD in the history of science, medicine, and technology from Johns Hopkins University in 2015 and has taught at Johns Hopkins and MICA. Her first book, *Common Phantoms: An American History of Psychic Science*, explores how the practices of seances, clairvoyance, and telepathy both questioned and reinscribed social boundaries. She lives in Baltimore.